I have tried to recreate events,  my memories of them. For reaso... safet... ... their anonymity I have changed the ...mes of individuals, aside from my own. I may also have omitted ... identifying characteristics and details such as physical properties, occupations and places of residence.

The Vicious Hunter

Oh, vicious hunter!

I was a beautiful flying bird,

Sprang from one tree of hope into another,

In search for the garden of peace, love, wisdom and prosperity,

You burned my nest,

And spread your poisonous seed for me,

Then trapped me and tore my fragile wings out,

You then set fire to my furs and decorated me with your hideous words,

Today, you have brought me into my own world,

To frighten my own kind from me into your trap!

Oh, vicious hunter,

Neither my flesh nor my kind's,

Can fill the stomach of your greed!

Laiq Sediqi

The Vicious Hunter
Laiq Sediqi

ISBN: 978-0-9926417-0-2

Printed in the United Kingdom

Book Cover Design by Gary Nip

Book Design Copyright © 2013 (Laiq Sediqi)

First Paperback Edition: 2013

This book is dedicated to Mother and Dada.

Thank you for your protection, help and guidance in this journey of life.

Contents

Introduction

I have lived my entire life in ruins and breathed the clouds of bombs, rockets, missiles, bullets and many other hideous weapons that ignorant scientists and technologists have discovered. I have lived with a dizzy head, thirst, hunger and a shrunken stomach. Death has followed me like a tail and I have been running from it since the day I was born. My ears have heard nothing more than the ugly sounds of war.

The land where I was born is the dreamland of empires. No language has yet been invented that could adequately portray the pain, suffering and humiliation that this nation went through. When one hears the name of the land where I was born, the first things that come into one's mind are: war, bloodshed, violence, oppression, inequality, suffering, poverty, disease... This poor, wounded and oppressed land is Afghanistan.

Afghanistan has geostrategic importance and it drags these savage empires towards itself. It is a land-locked country and is located in the central part of Asia surrounded by strong nations such as China, Russia, India, Pakistan and Iran. This ideal geographic location has become the root cause of all misery and pain suffered by Afghans.

Afghanistan is an extremely poor country where people are forced sell their children to survive. Yet the Afghan nation has become the subject of the savage empires' endless aggressions. Jawahrlal Nehru, the first prime minister of India, said,

> 'It is the habit of every aggressor nation to claim that it is acting on the defensive.'

From faraway lands cruel empires come disguising their true goals, trying to subjugate and shackle these helpless human beings in the chains of imperialism, in the name of self-defence. Over the last three decades poverty-stricken Afghans' houses and villages have become a perpetual battlefield for modern warfare, with its main victims being the civilians. Countless men, women and children have been slaughtered in this ferocious and endless war. The basic infrastructure of the country has been completely shattered. Afghanistan has become an ugly theatre for injustice and oppression. Speaking out against injustice in this insane world where everywhere brutes rule, is a dangerous thing to do. However not speaking out against the crimes that are being carried out is the equivalent of taking part. One reason brutal men carry on their brutalities around the world with impunity is that there are very few righteous men who dare to stand and speak out against their injustices. Though this book is a tale of a little boy growing up in the ferocious warzones and struggling for survival, the aim is to portray the suffering of a helpless nation and to speak out against the greatest injustice and crimes against humanity that has taken place in Afghanistan during the last over thirty years.

My Grandfather and the Angry River

My grandfather lived in Khugyani, which is one of twenty-two districts of Nangarhar Province in Afghanistan. Nangarhar is situated in the eastern part of Afghanistan and is also one of the warmest provinces. In Khugyani almost all inhabitants are from the Pashtun ethnic group, which is the largest in Afghanistan. The Afghan nation is an agricultural nation and consists of multiple ethnic groups such as Pashtun, Tajick, Hazara, Uzbek, Turkman, Baluch, Pasha-e and Nurestani. Most ethnic groups have their own unique culture and language. There has always been friction amongst these ethnic groups, reaching its peak in the last four decades. Ethnic groups murdered each other in the most barbaric fashions in the 1990s.

The Pashtun ethnicity is divided into many tribes, like a tree with different branches – some large and some small. There have always been brutal hostilities between the tribes in Afghanistan and the tribal people killed and fought each other regularly.

My grandfather was a peasant in Khugyani. He had a very simple existence. He had seven sons, three daughters and a tormented wife whose basic human rights were taken away from her by old traditions and in the name of God.

Women were kept indoors like prisoners for their entire lives, not only in Khugyani but in most parts of Afghanistan. They almost had no rights to their own lives. They were owned by men, used as breeding machines, and men would decide their fate. They could not even choose their own husband. Afghan women lived in these conditions for centuries. Old traditions and customs gave a false sense of superiority to the men and inferiority to the women.

There were three older brothers and one sister before my father was born and more followed. People as a whole in Afghanistan prefer to have sons rather than daughters for a variety of reasons. My grandfather was very proud of his seven sons. His older sons worked side-by-side with him in the field to earn bread for the family. My grandfather had nothing in his life but a small piece of land beside an angry river. Each year, once, twice or even three times the river broke its banks causing floods, consuming his land and crops as well as those of others. Each year my unfortunate grandfather watched the cruel river take his land piece by piece. He was confused and did not know what to do to stop it. It seems like nature does not like poor people, just as rich people don't. The river kept eating his land year after year until he was left with only a small patch that could not feed his family. He had to do something before his family starved to death.

Afghanistan was a feudal country. Khans and Maliks were the ones who grasped most of the land in Khugyani as they have done throughout Afghanistan. So my grandfather decided to send his sons to work for one of these powerful landlords in return for enough food so that they could sustain life. My grandfather continued to work on his own piece of land until the river swallowed it completely and he became a landless peasant. A peasant without land is like a fish without water. My grandfather then joined his sons and farmed for someone else in return for bread. He did not wish for more than that. He loved nothing more than spending time with his children and his wife. My grandfather's life was surrounded by misery and hardship, but misery and hardship could not stop joy and happiness from reaching his family. He enjoyed a peaceful life, away from the hostilities.

My father was always under a great deal of pressure when he was just a little child and thought that his parents did not care for him. At the age of eight his job was to go to the farm in the morning and work with his elder brothers, and after lunch he took the cattle to the forest where they grazed. He would also collect grass and bring it home so they would have enough to eat until the following afternoon. Sometimes, when he didn't do his job properly, Habib Kaka, his eldest brother, and my grandfather would beat him. This work was tough for a boy of his age. When he came back from the forest in the evenings he was exhausted. He did not have the energy to go and eat his dinner, so he went straight to bed and slept until the next morning, when he was again woken up early to go back to the farm. My father couldn't complain to anyone about his job. One day when he did complain to my grandfather, his father tore at his hair and asked, 'If you don't do it, then who else will?' At such a young age, my father was already tired of his life. He had a friend named Zulmay, but my father called him Zulmay Kaka (Uncle Zulmay). It is considered extremely rude to call older people by their first names in Afghanistan where a great deal of respect is paid to elders. Younger people must address them as Uncle, Aunty, Grandfather or Grandmother, etc.

Zulmay Kaka was one of a handful of people in the entire district of Khugyani who could read and write. Those who could read and write were very much respected in their communities; Afghans by nature pay a great deal of respect to men of knowledge. My father got to know Zulmay Kaka while he took the cattle to the forest. Zulmay Kaka took his own cattle, too, and always carried a book with him. My father would sit with him on a boulder beside the river as the sun was setting, the breeze picked up and the air cooled down. He listened to Zulmay Kaka whilst he read the book aloud to him. My father was amazed by this 'sorcery', but would sometimes think that he was making it up. It was not conceivable to him that the lifeless pages of a book could hold such stories. To try to catch him out my father would ask him to repeat the words on the page to see if he could tell the story word for word in the same way. Zulmay Kaka explained to him that books are man's best friends as they talk to you when you are lonely. He was a compassionate person.

Sometimes my father complained to him about his hard work and his miserable life. Zulmay Kaka would comfort him and declare that the only way to have a peaceful and prosperous life was to study and gain knowledge. My father often asked, 'How can I gain this knowledge?'But there was no school anywhere near my father's village at the time.

One day the village leaders and elders gathered and decided to open a school in the village for their children. In the rural areas of Afghanistan only elders can make such decisions. They all came to an agreement to open the school and the community members were to pay for the teachers' wages, but not in money, since money was not the local currency used. A bartering system was prevalent in rural areas of Afghanistan. It was difficult to find men with the knowledge of reading and writing, but after some months the teachers were found and the school was opened.

Zulmay Kaka informed my father of the school, and my father did not delay for a second. He took the cattle home earlier than usual and ran towards the field to get approval from his father. My father raised my grandfather's heart with this news; he wanted to send all his sons, but this would mean no one could work in the farm to provide food for the family. My two eldest uncles were too old for school. They were like my grandfather's hands and legs, without them his family would starve. They really were the backbone of the family. So he decided to allow my father and Merza Kaka to attend school. Merza Kaka was three years older than my father.

Grandfather sent them to school in the hope that one day his children would bring fortune to the family by gaining knowledge. Merza Kaka had the same aspirations as my father. He too knew that the only way to have a prosperous life was to study. Although Merza Kaka was good in school, he was very ill tempered and would become angry over the smallest of matters. Both he and my father were competitive in their studies, staying awake until late at night to cram and try to achieve the highest scores. My father loved school. It didn't have a physical building, so the students had to sit under the shade of trees to seek refuge from the midday burning heat. The teachers were harsh, as most teachers are in Afghanistan. Each teacher would carry a fresh tree branch to punish the students with. The students found strikes from these branches much more painful than any of the teachers' slapping or kicking.

My younger aunts, Zarmina Amma and Shukrya Amma (Amma means aunt), who were five and six years old at the time, used to beg their older brothers to tell them about school and take them along each morning. Merza Kaka and Father refused, as girls were not allowed to go to school. Another reason was that it was shameful for the boys to have their sisters seen in public with them by their male friends.

For my grandfather the education of Merza Kaka and Father was absolutely vital. He even liberated my father from his farming responsibilities. The only responsibility Father had was to take the cattle to the jungle in the afternoons. He would take his books along and study there. Zulmay Kaka was a great asset to him. He would help him with his lessons as well as encourage him in his studies. Zulmay Kaka reminded him that the only way to be rid of suffering was to gain knowledge. My father would sit beside the angry river that swallowed their land and his mind focused onto the pages of the book while his cattle fed themselves. Sometimes, while Father disappeared into his book, the cattle went deep into the forest or even miles away into other people's fields, damaging their crops. He then had to go after them, walking through marshlands. Some peasants whose crops had been damaged would beat my father for not keeping an eye on the animals. Despite these difficulties, he continued on with his education.

My poor grandfather and father, alongside all the people who lived in Khugyani, were utterly unaware of what was happening in the rest of the world. People were unaware in Khugyani that there was a destructive storm drifting towards Afghanistan. This storm was the coming of the predatory empires of the Soviet Union and the United States.

World War II with all of its horrors and destruction gave birth to the Afghan nation's torment; it gave birth to my tormenters. As most imperialistic powers perished in World War II, alongside the tens of millions of innocent human beings, the two new empires took their place. They divided Europe amongst themselves and were trying to divide Asia, Africa and Latin America, too. They were going country after country, dividing nations in half. The Soviet Union presented its ugly weapons into the hands of a helpless people to fight for *their* own interests and the USA similarly gave its own horrible weapons to fight for *their* own interests, too. By the end of the 1960s they had torn several nations apart, notably Korea and Vietnam. These two empires were on their way to Afghanistan too. They were like wildfire, shattering each country into which they went.

In the midst of the Cold War the urban young generation of Afghanistan was deeply dissatisfied with their society and wanted to bring about fundamental changes. Violent, old and superstitious traditions and ways of life were no longer tolerable for them. They wanted to do away with a way of life that took the very basic rights from the women and stopped progress in their country. Most of them were influenced by communism and believed that they could build a progressive society. There was also another group of Afghans who had been influenced by the Muslim brotherhood's Islamic ideology and they wanted to impose that ideology upon Afghans. Kabul University was the place where ideologies influenced students.

The year of 1978 was the last of my father's schooling. It also coincided with almost the end of President Mohammed Daoud Khan's regime. Daoud Khan was a cousin of Zahir Shah, Afghanistan's monarch, and in 1973, he toppled the monarchy in a bloodless coup d'état with the help of the communists. Daoud Khan declared himself as the first president of Afghanistan and attempted to bring about some fundamental changes in the economy, military, education and constitution of Afghanistan. By the end of Daoud Khan's regime, Merza Kaka and my father were mature boys. For Grandfather it was difficult to keep his sons away from the family, village and tribal hostilities. One day a group of military recruiters from the central government came to the school to choose the most intellectual students for the Military Academy in Kabul, the capital of Afghanistan. My father had only heard wonderful tales about Kabul throughout his life. There was so much progress in Kabul that those who visited from rural areas had difficulty in explaining everything they had seen to others back in the village. This was because rural dwellers knew nothing about industries, telephones, telegrams, electricity, buses, aeroplanes, TV, cinemas, tarmac roads, Western-style buildings and so forth. There was no science or technology in the whole of Khugyani; people still lived in the pre-industrial era.

MY GRANDFATHER AND THE ANGRY RIVER

Kabul was a fantasy place for people who lived in the pastoral areas. This was especially true for the younger people who would sit for hours talking about Kabul and its beauty. To them it was a place where boys and girls studied together in schools and universities, and where gorgeous women walked in the streets of the city with bare heads and without the need for men to accompany them. Women were not allowed to leave their houses unless fully-covered and escorted by a man. This was the one opportunity my father had to be rid of his miserable life and go to the beautiful city, but others also wanted to go. It was believed that this would lead to a life of prosperity, and would bring great honour to the families of those who worked for the central government during Daoud Khan's reign.

Everybody had to pass an exam before they could go to Kabul. After the exam only a handful of students were successful in gaining their rightful places with the elites, and amongst them were my father and Merza Kaka. When Father received the news, he was so excited. Grandfather was extremely pleased and was so proud. The night before they left for Kabul, the sheer joy prevented my father from sleeping. He stayed awake all night long and dreamed of Kabul. Grandmother cried all night long as she thought about losing her sons. Early in the morning, she packed their things as she cried. Merza Kaka and Father had to walk for many miles to get to the bus, as there was no road to connect the village to the main road. There was a river that separated the village from the rest of the neighbourhood and my grandparents escorted them.

My poor uncle and father walked for miles before finally reaching the bus. All the way my grandmother cried in spite of her husband telling her many times to stop. She cried even more when they said their final goodbyes. Although Grandfather tried not to show his emotions to his sons, he too burst into tears at their final farewell. Merza Kaka and Father went to Kabul with hearts filled with hope for a better and brighter future. But they would have had a far more peaceful life had they remained in their village.

After my uncle and father left, some terrible events took place in their family. One day Anwar Kaka, my second eldest uncle, climbed up a tall tree to chop firewood for cooking when he slumped to the ground and seriously damaged his brain as well as breaking his legs and arms. There was no hospital in the village and they were very far away from the capital of Nangarhar Province, Jalalabad, where people would have access to healthcare. People had a strong faith in Mullahs and witch-doctors, not only in Khugyani but also all over Afghanistan. They still do. Grandfather took my uncle to the Mullah who read a few verses and said he would be fine in the next few days. His treatment did not work at all. Anwar Kaka was in agonising pain and screamed all the time. Grandfather took him back to the Mullah a few times afterwards and each time he would give wheat or other crops in exchange for his treatment. The Mullah did his best but his treatment did not work. Anwar Kaka's health deteriorated daily.

My grandparents were very worried about their hard working son, as well as his wife and children. Grandfather knew that if he took his son to the hospital in Jalalabad he might recover. However it was not possible for a needy peasant man like my grandfather to take his son to Jalalabad Hospital. Money was not the only problem. There was no vehicle in the whole district. In fact, few people knew what vehicles were. Some had heard about them but had never seen them. When a vehicle arrived people would rush out of their houses to see it.

After a while, my uncle became mentally ill from the injury to his brain. It was later understood to be epilepsy, but people did not know what epilepsy was. They believed in genies. When my uncle's condition didn't improve, the Mullah said that he had walked over a genie's child and killed it, therefore the genies wanted to take revenge. The genies entered Anwar Kaka's body every evening. When his body began convulsing, people would put a shoe in his mouth and beat him until they thought they had beaten the genie out. This was widely practised throughout Afghanistan and most still do in rural areas. My poor uncle had to suffer dreadfully because of the strong superstitions of the poor peasants. As time elapsed Anwar Kaka's illness worsened and his family failed to expel the genies from his body. He was in excruciating pain until he eventually died, leaving behind his little children and a young wife.

My grandfather married off his eldest daughter to a man who lived far away from their village. A father in a rural area attempts to marry off his daughter within the confines of his village so as to keep a close eye on her and regularly visit her. However, my grandfather married his very young daughter into a distant relative's family who lived tens of miles away. Visiting their daughter was not a simple task. Arranged marriages often do not work well for some people and this was the case for my poor aunt. There was very little, if any, love in her husband's heart for her. Her husband and his mother regularly beat her for no reason. She had several children in quick succession before she was diagnosed with cancer. My aunt then spent her life in a man-made cage until she eventually escaped and left her children behind in this world of suffering.

As my father got into the bus he was amazed as it was the first time in his life that he had seen one. This was also the case for most of the other boys, who were later to become his comrades.

As they set off towards Kabul, my father gazed at the high mountains that surrounded them as they passed through the changing terrain. Geography books and school teachers say that Afghanistan is a mountainous country, but my father did not believe them because he had never seen any mountainous areas beyond the hill behind their compound. High mountains and beautifully wild rivers accompanied him all the way to Kabul.

The bus stopped at Mahi-par, on the outskirts of Kabul and very famous for its dam and tasty fish restaurants. Merza Kaka and Father bought fish with the money that my grandfather had given them to spend on food. They sat beside the wild river and ate.

The bus arrived in Kabul at midnight. My father finally saw his dream place: Kabul by night. The beauty of Kabul dazzled him. The night was so bright, everywhere lit up by electric bulbs. Back in Khugyani, his family did not have a single lamp to light. He was massively impressed with what Kabul offered him at first sight. Later on in life, when my siblings and I surrounded my father during the dark nights of poverty, he would tell us that Kabul at night time was as 'bright as crystals in the sunshine'. As the bus travelled through the city everyone was astonished by the high modern concrete buildings, tarmac roads, cars, buses, and the fine looking inhabitants who wandered the streets without anyone troubling them late at night.

As he entered Kabul Military Academy he started his new life, a life that was so different from the one he had always known. His life now was based on regulations: regulations for talking, walking, sleeping, eating and so forth. They received training from professional Afghan National Army mentors. Life was much better for my father there. Both Merza Kaka and Father worked hard in their lessons. Once, my father didn't go on time to his class, he was punished by the discipliners who gave him very hard slaps on both cheeks. They were not ordinary slaps, they were known as *Sli-Askari*, (military slaps). They are very well known all over Afghanistan. My father never broke any rules from then on.

A month elapsed but still my uncle and my father had not seen the city of Kabul in its entirety. One Friday they decided to go into the city centre itself, as Friday is the only day of rest for people in Afghanistan. When they reached the city, they were speechless when they saw the crowds of people, so many shops and modern buildings, smelt aromas from the restaurants. Afghan and Hindi music played in restaurants and shops. In the village the crowds were made up of men. Here, it was both men and women. Apart from his mother, sisters and close relatives, my father had never seen any other women. Women in Kabul walked without men escorting them. This was completely prohibited in Khugyani. A woman could not even step out of the door without her husband, brother or father's permission. A woman had to be escorted in any circumstances, but in Kabul my father noticed that some women were even driving electric trolley-buses. Some did not bother to cover their heads and you could even see their legs from the knees down! This was extremely exciting for the two of them. Boys and girls walked in the streets holding hands without people even bothering to take notice of them.

Kabul was a city that burst with happiness, joy and harmony. It was crammed with talented artists, comedians and actors who entertained people through TV, radio, theatre and cinema. Incredible concerts and performances were held day and night. Hippies came from the western world and wandered about smoking cannabis. It seemed that the broken ship of Afghans had finally reached the shore. It seemed like the prison of the old customs and traditions had begun to fall apart and Afghan women were about to be free.

Merza Kaka and my father decided to go to the cinema on the recommendation of their comrades. This was the first time in their lives they had been to the cinema or watched a Bollywood film. Inside they found men and women sitting side-by-side watching the movie. There was a lot of violence and some romantic scenes and when the film finished, my father assumed that everything he had watched in the movie was real. On leaving the cinema they ate in a restaurant, ordering delicious kebabs and listening to the Hindi music.

Daoud Khan, the first president of Afghanistan, had brought about some great economic, political, educational and social reforms to the country. Women swiftly broke away from the old traditions and customs in the cities.

As author Rodric Braithwaite observes in his book *AFGANTSY*:

> 'By the 1970s Afghanistan had many of the rudiments of a modern state. It was reasonably secure and you could travel and picnic and see the sights with comparatively little risk.'

However, these reforms were a great threat for the social and religious elites in the country, because they would take away their power and authority. Soon religious extremists defied the reforms, and most of them moved to Pakistan. With the help of the Pakistani government they frequently conspired against Afghanistan's government. In 1975, Islamic extremists, backed by the Pakistan government, attempted to overthrow President Daoud Khan, but they failed and fled again. The Pakistan government held onto them to use the in future against Afghanistan. The Pakistani government could not afford to have two strong neighbours, India and Afghanistan; having territorial disputes with both.

From the early nineteenth century until the early twentieth century, there was an intense strategic rivalry between the British and Russian Tsar empires for the domination of Central Asia. This rivalry over the domination of Central Asia was known as 'the Great Game'. The British Empire feared that if the Tsar's empire were to dominate Afghanistan it would pose a great threat to India – the backbone of the British Empire. For that reason the British Empire used every means to stop the Tsar's empire from dominating Afghanistan. For over a hundred years Afghans suffered tremendously at the hands of both empires, particularly the British. They invaded Afghanistan many times and annexed large parts of the country into their empires again and again.

In 1893, the British Empire and the Emir, or King of Afghanistan, signed a treaty called 'Durand Line'. In this treaty the British sectioned off a large part of Afghanistan and annexed it into their empire, now Pakistan. This treaty did not only extend more Afghan land into the British Empire, but it also divided the ethnic Pashtun in half. In general, Afghans didn't recognise the treaty from the very outset. Thus, the British Empire sowed the seed of hostility between Afghans and Pakistanis. And so long as the Kashmir and Durand line despustes are not resolved, Pakistan will continue to treat Afghanistan as its enemy and do whatever it can to destroy and destabilise it, just like it has been doing for the last almost four decades.

Afghanistan was about to be entangled in a new 'Great Game'. The only dissimilarity between the old and the new Great Game was that the British Empire was substituted by the US. They coveted Afghanistan and nothing could stop them. Afghanistan was as defenceless against the Soviet Union and the US as a tree against an axe. There was nothing the helpless Afghans could do to ward-off these two hungry predators.

A friendly Afghanistan was extremely crucial for the Soviet Union from the outset of the Cold War because they shared a long border. The Soviet Union had enormous influence over Afghanistan and was Afghanistan's largest trading partner, aid donor and military supplier. But for decades the United States was striving to draw Afghanistan in its own block. In 1953 John Foster Dulles, the American Secretary of State, came up with the idea of a 'Northern Tier' of Muslim states in the Middle East, including Afghanistan, which would act as a barrier to Soviet communism. He tried but failed to get Afghanistan to join the Baghdad Pact.[1]

Nikita Krushchev, the first Party Secretary of the Soviet Union, visited Kabul in 1955 and concluded that the Americans were doing all they could to draw Afghanistan into the American camp, because they intended to set up a military base there.[2] During the Daoud Khan's regime the US government was striving to reduce the Soviet influence over Afghanistan through its greatest ally in the region, the tyrant Shah of Iran. As author and historian Willian Blum points out in his book *Killing Hope*:

> 'For decades Washington and the Shah of Iran tried to pressure and bribe Afghanistan in order to roll back Russian influence in the country. During the Daoud regime Iran, encouraged by the United States, sought to replace the Soviet Union as Kabul's biggest donor with a $2 billion economic aid agreement. They also urged Afghanistan to join the Regional Co-operation for Development, which consisted of Iran, Pakistan and Turkey. At the same time, Iran's infamous secret police, SAVAK, was busy fingering suspected communist sympathisers in the Afghan government and military.'[3]

The Coming of the Savage Empires

In 1978, Daoud Khan was overthrown in a coup d'état by the People's Democratic Party of Afghanistan (PDPA) and was butchered alongside his family. Some say that the Soviet Union helped the PDPA during the military coup but it's not proven yet. This was the beginning of an endless war, which would take the lives of more than a million helpless men, oppressed women and hungry, unclothed children. It was the dawn of a war that would annihilate most of the basic infrastructure of Afghanistan. This was the shadow of a war that would force six million Afghans to abandon their houses and live in the refugee camps of Pakistan and Iran. From here on the government of the United States began to sponsor religious fanatics to fight and undermine the Soviet-backed communist government in Afghanistan. What a terrible era for Afghans.

It was just a coup d'état, but the communists liked to call it a revolution. Anyone who tried to oppose communism and their harsh policies were labelled 'counter-revolutionary', 'bandits' and 'terrorists'. Communism would never work in a country like Afghanistan, because the Afghan nation was extremely backward with a highly complex social structure. The leaders of two communist factions, Khalq and Parcham, were highly incompetent and lacked experience in leadership with most of their policies antagonising the rural population. They were also highly antagonistic with one another. They hated each other as much as they hated those who opposed communism and their policies. Nevertheless, they began their ambitious reforms to draw Afghanistan from the middle to the modern age.

The PDPA took land from influential rich people by force and redistributed it to the poor and landless. They opposed the cruel practice of arranged marriages, which had been practised in Afghanistan for centuries, and announced it to be illegal. They put uneducated women into literacy schools. They encouraged women to get jobs and work alongside men. They built many schools and clinics in the rural parts of Afghanistan. Tribal and religious leaders were not given roles in society or the government. Without a doubt they brought about very good reforms, but Afghans were far from being ripe for such changes. In May 1979, the British political scientist Fred Halliday observed that 'probably more has changed in the countryside over the last year than in the two centuries since the state was established'.[4]

Had the reforms of the communist government succeeded in Afghanistan, Afghan lives would have changed completely, in particular women's lives as they had been oppressed for so long. A 1986 US Army manual on Afghanistan discussing the decrees and the influence of the government concerning women cited the following changes:

- provisions of complete freedom of choice of marriage partner, and fixation of the minimum [marriage age] at 16 for women
- abolished forced marriages
- bring [women] out of seclusion, and initiate social programs
- extensive literacy programs, especially for women
- putting girls and boys in the same classroom
- concerned with changing gender roles and giving women a more active role in politics[5]

These changes by the PDPA shook the entire nation, in particular the social and religious elites. Landlords were most disturbed by the arrival of communism. The PDPA went into each province taking land from the landlords and giving it to the landless. The landless were happy and landlords glared at them. The women's issue was a very serious one, which turned almost the entire population of men against them. Religious sensitivities were not taken into consideration. Afghans were extremely religious and conservative. The new president of the communist government of Afghanistan, Nor Mohammed Taraki, assumed that he would be able to empty the mosques in a year. It seems the Afghan communists had very little knowledge of the very people they ruled. Many of their reforms were in contrary to the social and religious values of the Afghan nation. People denounced the reforms and upheaval began in some parts of the country; the most terrible began in the Herat Province when local people, alongside army soldiers, stormed the government offices slaughtering communist authority figures alongside their Soviet advisers. In retaliation the government later crushed them pitilessly, resulting in thousands of people being massacred. Instability was growing all over Afghanistan.

Iran, Pakistan and the United States were supporting the anti-government movements. The US Central Intelligence Agency (CIA) was broadcasting radio propaganda from Pakistan into Afghanistan to stir people up. The communist government in Afghanistan had no one to ask for help apart from the Soviet Union. They begged them to send troops into Afghansitan, to crush the anti-government movements, but the Soviet Union repeatedly refused. Indeed some Soviet leaders predicted what would happen if they did send their troops into Afghanistan.

On 20 March 1979 the Soviet Premier, Alexei N. Kosygin, told Nor Mohammed Taraki:

> 'The deployment of our forces in the territory of Afghanistan would immediately awaken international community and would invite sharply unfavourable multipronged consequences. This, in effect, would be a conflict not only with imperialist countries, but also with one's own people. Our mutual enemies are just waiting for the moment when the Soviet forces appear on the Afghan territory. This would give them the excuse to deploy on Afghan territory military formation hostile to you. I would again like to underline that the question of deploying our forces has been examined by us from every direction; we carefully studied all aspects of this action and came to the conclusion that if our troops were

interduced, the satuation in your country would not only not improve, but would worsen.'[6]

So many social and religious men who opposed communism were secretly murdered all over the country by the communist government, particularly when Afizullah Amin grasped power. Anyone who stood in their way was either ruthlessly killed or sent to the brutal dungeons and jails. They had transformed *Pul-e Charkhi* prison into a slaughterhouse. Large crowds of people were murdered there. They killed people en masse and buried them in mass graves, with some of them being unearthed only recently. They even murdered their own communists. From 1978 until the Soviet invasion of Afghanistan in 1979, tens of thousands of Afghans were executed by the Afghan communist government. The communist leaders thought they could silence people with terror and brutality, just as Joseph Stalin had.

By the end of 1970s, the United States government came to realise that Islamic fundamentalists were a perfect tool to be used against the spread of communism in the Islamic world. Hence it began to support them, and Afghanistan is a spectacular example of it. Large numbers of social and religious men fled the country to Pakistan where they were used to undermine the communist government in Afghanistan. The CIA began the largest secret operation in its brutal history in Afghanistan long before the Soviet invasion. It was called 'Operation Cyclone'. The CIA was funding and arming religious fundamentalists and Afghan dissenters to de-stabilise the regime in Afghanistan. The Soviet Union was very aware of the United States' secret movements in their own backyard, and they were very frightened that the US might install an anti-Soviet regime in Afghanistan if they were to succeed to topple the communist government. Yuri Andropov, the head of the KGB, wrote that the 'CIA's operation in Afghanistan is all part of a wider US plan to create a new Ottoman Empire, which will include the southern regions of the Soviet Union. Andropov warned of US missile bases and a plot with Iran and Pakistan to push into Central Asia.[7]

Gulbudin Hekmatyar, who is now considered a terrorist by the US government, was amongst the people that the US government funded with billions of US dollars back in the 1980s. Gulbudin Hekmatyar was a religious extremist in the 1970s who threw acid in the faces of women who didn't cover them with Hijab in Kabul University. Some of the CIA and US state department officials called him 'scary', 'vicious', 'a fascist definite dictatorship material'.[8] Gulbudin Hekmatyar will be remembered as one of the most ruthless people in the history of Afghanistan. The crimes he committed against the people are unspeakable. For years Kabul citizens lived beneath his rockets and missiles. Thousands of Afghans were slaughtered by this man's faction during the Mujahidin's factional war in 1992-1996. But he had been empowered by the United States government with billions of US taxpayers' money. There were other religious extremist as ruthless as Gulbudin Hekmatyar who have been funded by the US government during the Afghan-Soviet war. Maulvi Jalaluding Haqani, who now runs the Haqani Terrorist Network, alongside all other top commanders of the Taliban, was trained and funded by the US government. Today the US uses the plight of Afghan women as an excuse to disguise the ugly face of its domination of Afghanistan, while it was they who turned the lives of Afghan women into hell by putting their fate in the hands of the murderous religious fundamentalists.

The United States government repeatedly stated that they only helped the Mujahidin after the Soviet invasion of Afghanistan, but the reality was that they started funding the religious fundamentalists long before. Had the United States not helped them beforehand, the Mujahidin could not have defeated a well-disciplined Afghan Army equipped with modern Soviet weapons.

Zbigniew Brzezinski was the National Security Adviser for President Jimmy Carter's administration and was heavily involved in empowering religious fundamentalists and inducing the Soviet Union in Afghanistan. In 1998 Brzezinski had given the following interview regarding the covert war of the United States in Afghanistan:

Question: *The former Director of the CIA, Robert Gates, stated in his memoirs that the American intelligence services began to aid the Mujahidin six months before the Soviet intervention. In this period you were the National Security Adviser to President Carter. You therefore played a key role in this affair, is this correct?*

Brzezinski: *Yes. According to the official version of history, CIA aid to the Mujahidin began during the 1980s, that is to say, after the Soviet army invading Afghanistan on 24 December 1979. But the reality, closely guarded until now, is completely otherwise; indeed, it was 3 July 1979 that President Carter signed the first directive for secret aid to the opponents of the pro-Soviet regime in Kabul. And that very day I wrote a note to the president in which I explained to him in my opinion this aid was going to induce a Soviet military intervention.*

Question: *Despite this risk, you were an advocate of this covert action, but perhaps you yourself desired this Soviet entry into war and looked for a way to provoke it?*

Brzezinski: *It wasn't quite like that. We didn't push the Russians to intervene, but we knowingly increased the possibility that they would.*

Question: *When the Soviets justified their intervention by asserting that they intended to fight against secret US involvement in Afghanistan, nobody believed them. However, there was an element of truth in this. You don't regret any of this today?*

Brzezinski: *Regret what? That secret operation was an excellent idea. It had the effect of drawing the Russians into Afghan-Trap and you want me to regret it? The day that the Soviets officially crossed the border I wrote to President Carter, "We now have the opportunity of giving to the USSR its Vietnam War." Indeed for ten years Moscow had to carry on a war that was unsustainable for the regime, a conflict that brought about demoralisation and finally the breakup of the Soviet Empire.*

Question: *And neither do you regret having supported Islamic fundamentalism, which has given arms and advice to future terrorists?*

Brzezinski: *What is more important in world history? The Taliban or the collapse of the Soviet empire? Some agitated Muslims or the liberation of Central Europe and the end of the Cold War?*

Question: *"Some agitated Muslims"? But, it has been said and repeated: Islamic fundamentalism represents a world menace today...*

Brzezinski: *Nonsense! It is said that the west has a global policy in regard to Islam. That is stupid: there isn't a global Islam, look at Islam in a rational manner, without demagoguery or emotionalism, it is the leading religion of the world with 1.5 billion followers. But what is there in common among fundamentalist Saudi Arabia, moderate Morocco, militaristic Pakistan, pro-western Egypt or secularist Central Asia? Nothing more than what united the Christian countries...* [9]

When the Soviet Union invaded Afghanistan, the US government claimed that the Soviet Union had a 'Grand Strategy' to control the oil resources of the Persian Gulf and to reach the warm waters of the Indian Ocean. But today there is ample evidence that proves the Soviet Union had no grand strategy at all.

In 1979 Nor Muhammad Taraki, the president of the communist government, was killed by his deputy prime minister, Hafizullah Amin, and Amin seized power. Amin studied in the United States of America and many people at that time were convinced that he was a CIA agent. Even the US ambassader to Afghanistan was doubtful of Amin's connection with the CIA. In early 1979, he had asked his CIA station chief whether it was true that Amin was a CIA agent, but the CIA denied having any links with him. Author Rodric Braithwaite observed in his book *Afghantsy*:

> 'Some of his opponents accused him of having had links with the CIA while he was studying in New York. He replied that he was short of money at the time and that he had merely been stringing the CIA along.'

The Soviet leaders' relations with Amin became sour from the day he assassinated Nor Muhammad Taraki, a loyal puppet of the Soviet Union as well as a good friend of Leonid Brezhnev, the leader of the Soviet Union, who had promised to protect him. Amin's policies were extremely harsh and antagonised people all over Afghanistan. He imprisoned and shot countless people during the short time he was in power. William Blum points out in his book, *Killing Hope*:

> 'It can be said that Amin, by his ruthlessness, was doing just what an American agent would be expected to do: discrediting the People's Democratic Party, the party's reforms, the idea of socialism or communism, and the Soviet Union, all associated in one package.'

In late 1979, instability increased in Afghanistan, insurgents were getting stronger and defeating the government forces in rural Afghanistan and controlling large parts of it.

From the outset of the Cold War, the Soviet Union worked really hard to have a friendly government in Afghanistan, a country they shared a thousand-mile border with. They could not afford to have a hostile neighbour. Amin's harsh policies and his distrust by the Soviet Union, the fragility of the communist government of Afghanistan, the US secret activity in Afghanistan, and the Islamic revolution in Iran made the Soviet Union invade. On 24

December 1979, Soviet military paratroopers entered Kabul and shot Amin dead, seizing key locations and installing their new puppet Babrak Karmal as the head of the Afghan government. The fundamental mistake the Soviet Union made was sending their troops into Afghanistan on this date. They were ignorant of the fact that the US had set a trap for them. The US successfully caught the Soviets in its Afghan-Trap. But, the hypocritical politicians in the United States of America cunningly condemned the Soviet invasion of Afghanistan.

Afghans naturally despised watching conceited invaders marching into their villages, fields, cities and country. The day the invaders sent their troops into Afghanistan their defeat was enshrined in destiny. The further their troops marched into the country, the more enemies they made for themselves. Nevertheless, the US now trapped the Soviet Union in Afghanistan. At first things were going well for the Soviet Union. Soviet troops were guarding key areas and they trained Afghan security forces and let the Afghan Army fight the insurgents. The Soviet Union considered the insurgents would be defeated in a few months and then they would pull out of Afghanistan quickly. But they were slowly getting bogged down in a disastrous war. There is only one thing that makes matters worse for the invaders in Afghanistan and that is the harming and terrorising of civilians. The Soviet Union began to kill civilians during their war with the Mujahidin. By killing one Afghan, whether he was civilian or Mujahid, they had forced ten, twenty or perhaps many more Afghans to take up weapons and fight against them in order to take revenge. Day after day the Soviet troops' brutality was increasing. If one bullet was fired from a village at them, they then used various weapons at their disposal and destroyed the village and killed large numbers of people. The Soviet troops were well known for their brutality and plundering. They plundered anything they found useful in people's houses. Their aircrafts and fighter helicopters bombed people and villages indiscriminately. Little hungry children, tormented women and men were terrified of the sound. They attempted to subjugate Afghans through their barbarism and through instilling terror in the population.

In the beginning the CIA, MI6, the Saudis, French intelligence, ISI, etc, did not want the war against the Soviet in Afghanistan to be a fierce and quick one. They wanted to make the Soviets bleed steadily in their Afghan-Trap. But it was the helpless Afghans who suffered the most. It was their houses and villages that were ravaged. The war became more brutal each day and forced hundreds of thousands to desert their homes and head towards refugee camps each year, where the CIA, the ISI and others would place guns in their hands and send them back to their deaths. On one side the Soviet military massacred Afghans and on the other the CIA pushed them in front of the Soviet guns, tanks and aircrafts. Frank Anderson, the chief of the CIA's Afghan Task Force, stated, 'it's entirely true that this was a war that was fought with our goals but with their [Afghan] blood.'[10]

The CIA, the ISI and the Saudi monarchy encouraged Arab and other Islamic extremists to come into Afghanistan and fight for the United States and make its enemy, the Soviet Empire, bleed. As Professor of Economics, Michel Chossudovsky, points out:

> 'With the active encouragement of the CIA and Pakistan's ISI (Inter Services Intelligence), who wanted to turn the Afghan Jihad into a global war waged by all Muslim states against the Soviet Union, some 35,000 Muslim radicals from forty Islamic countries joined Afghanistan's fight between 1982 and 1992. Tens of thousands more came to study in Pakistani madrasahs. Eventually more than 100,000 foreign Muslim radicals were directly influenced by the Afghan Jihad.'[11]

Amongst these extremists was Osama Bin Laden. Back then when he was fighting for the United States he was a 'Freedom Fighter'. Today the United States elite scream to the world that they are the victims of Islamic terrorism, but in the 1980s they empowered them. Ronald Reagan, the president of the United States, invited the Afghan hardliners into the White House, where he stated that 'they are the moral equivalent of America's founding fathers'.

Very little opium was grown in the remote parts of Afghanistan before the arrival of the CIA in the Afghan-Pakistani borderland. But not long after their arrival poppy cultivation increased. Many people blamed the CIA for the opium trade in Afghanistan. The Soviet Union accused the CIA of running the opium business in Afghanistan to fund the Mujahidin factions. Almost all of the Mujahidin leaders who worked closely with the CIA and the Pakistani ISI were involved in drug trafficking. Gulbudin Hekmatyar, the leader of Hizb-e Isalmi Mujahidin faction, was the most powerful drug trafficker. From Pakistan convoys of CIA weapons entering Afghanistan, and from Afghanistan convoys of opium were sent to Pakistan. In 1995, Charles Cogan the former director of the CIA's operation in Afghanistan stated:

> 'Our mission was to do as much damage to the Soviets. We didn't really have the resources or the time to devote to the investigation of the drug trade. I don't think we need to apologise for this. Every situation has its fallout. There was fallout in terms of drugs, yes, but the main ojective was accomplished. The Soviets left Afghanistan.'[12]

A relative of my mother was living in a village close to a Soviet checkpoint, and four of her sons were working in Pakistan. They would send money to their families back in the village, once sending wristwatches for their wives. One day a group of Soviet troops came to search the village. As they entered their house they noticed the watches on the women's wrists. Soviet soldiers tried to take them, but one woman thought the soldiers were trying to rape her daughters-in-law. She struck at them with a shovel and hit one soldier. The Soviet soldiers locked all of them in a room and threw grenades in, killing twenty people: fourteen children, five women and an old man. Only one child survived from that family. When the brothers in Pakistan found out, they came back to Afghanistan to grieve for their families. Then they joined the Mujahidin to take their revenge but were subsequently killed during an air strike.

Soldiers are usually young and uninformed; they are taken into the schools of hatred and taught war, brutality and destruction, and then given weapons. Usually when the occupation force face resistance and suffer casualities in the occupied country, they often retaliate by massacring civilians. As the war escalated in all parts of Afghanistan, many Soviet soldiers considered everyone as their foe and murdered men, women and children in cold blood. A Soviet soldier later explained in an interview what he did to Afghans.

> 'There was no such a thing as a peaceful population, they were all guerrilla fighters. I remember how I rounded up women, children, and poured kerosene over them and then set fire to it. A young soldier killed an Afghan to just test his gun or was curious to see how a human's insides look or to see inside a smashed head.'[13]

Soviets soldiers burned Afghans alive. They rounded up defenceless Afghans in their hundreds and shot them dead in their villages. They drove their vehicles and tanks over poor Afghans; their aircraft obliterated humans, animals and villages. Livelihoods were destroyed with their lethal bombs, rockets and bullets. They kidnapped, raped and dishonoured Afghan women. They bombed wedding gatherings, just like the US and NATO occupation forces had done many times. They shot Afghans before first checking whether they were civilians or not. There was no difference between the suffering of the Afghans and the Jewish people of Europe and other Eastern Europeans during World War II. There was no difference between the Nazis and the Soviet troops. They too treated Afghans as sub-humans. They ravaged fields and crops, resulting in mass starvation. They planted mines in villages, on farms and wherever Afghans walked. They manufactured mines in the shape of children's toys. Adolf Hitler did not build weapons specifically for children, but the Soviet leaders did. Countless Afghan children picked up the toys that would blow them to pieces or amputate their legs, arms and hands or blind their eyes. They would be mutilated for the rest of their lives. Only men with power can do this. Power turns man into beast.

Today, Afghanistan is one of the most heavily mine-concentrated countries in the world. It has been estimated that the Soviet Union had sowed some ten million mines all over the land. In the last forty years countless innocent men, women and, in particular, children are killed and maimed by the very same mines that the Soviet military sowed. Many hungry peasants abandoned their agricultural lands, fearing the mines. The Soviet Union's slogan was 'Land for the peasant and food for the hungry', but they had taken both from the hungry Afghan peasants. The Mujahidin factions also carried out barbaric atrocities against the captured Soviet troops, often dismembering them.

The Afghan government sent my father to Paktia Province in the eastern part of Afghanistan once he graduated from military academy, and Merza Kaka remained in Kabul. My father was in the logistical department and his job was comparatively safe compared with others. Countless Afghan Army soldiers were sent to their deaths by those who were their brothers before the arrival of the two predatory empires. In a matter of years, the entire population was torn apart by the Soviets and the US. Both armed the entire population to shed each other's blood for their own goals. Afghans on both sides thought they were fighting for the freedom of their country. They were unaware that they were being used by the two superpowers. Merza Kaka and my father left their remote village in the hope of a brighter future; instead they were entangled in a vicious war.

The Saudi monarchy, the United States and the Pakistani government built and funded vast numbers of *Madrasas* (religious schools) on the Pakistani-Afghan border, which has radicalised hundreds of thousands of young Afghans ever since, most of the Taliban fighters derived from these madrasas. According to the journalist and writer Ahmad Rashid:

> 'In 1971 there were only 900 Madrasas in Pakistan, but by the end of the Zia era in 1988 there were 8,000 madrasas, and 25,000 unregistered ones, educating half a million students.'

According to the former president of Pakistan, Pervez Musharraf:

> 'Taliban were the heroes in those days. People from Madrasas were given military training, armed and sent across by us, by the United States, by everyone.'[14]

The United States government spent millions of dollars on a textbook project for unfortunate children of Afghanistan. These school textbooks were designed to radicalise the hungry Afghans. The director of the center for Afghanistan studies at the University of Nebraska Thomas E. Goutierre was the man behind this evil project and, surprisingly, called himself a friend of Afghans. The textbooks were filled with pictures of guns and bullets and weapons and taught Afghan children about *Jihad* (holy war), Mujahidin (holy warriors) and *Shahid* (martyr) and so on.[15] [16]

Today, those children who studied those textbooks fight the United States troops and are bombed in the name of terrorism. These textbooks were taught in the schools in Pakistan and Afghanistan. How can anyone commit such evil against innocent children? What wrongdoing have Afghan children committed that they were so severely being punished for? The only offence they had committed was to be born in Afghanistan, dreamland of the empires. How would mothers and fathers feel if someone else did such an appalling deed to their children in America? I am certain those who manufactured mines in the shape of children's toys and who designed textbooks to radicalise hungry children in Afghanistan were sick and unhappy humans, be they Americans or Russians. Behind their idealistic worlds they have veiled their barbaric deeds.

How the media is corrupted and how easily the governments deceive their nations is remarkable. The media told Soviets their sons were not even fighting in Afghanistan. The media said that their sons were helping Afghans to build schools, hospitals and roads. In reality they were doing the opposite, destroying Afghan villages, farms, schools and hospitals and killing children in their mothers' arms. Americans did not know what their government was doing in Afghanistan. They did not know that their government was pushing hundreds of thousands of poor Afghans to their deaths. They did not know that their government was empowering religious extremists and subsequently handing them the fate of Afghans.

The US was as brutal as the Soviet Union. The CIA provided explosives, and trained the Mujahidin to destroy the basic infrastructure in Afghanistan. CIA Afghan Task Force analyst Michael Scheuer stated that the CIA ordered Mujahidin to destroy 'things like dams, power pylons, powerlines, power generation plants, infrastracture targets, bridges that kind of things.' [17]

This was the way the US wanted the Soviet Union to bleed; radicalising Afghan children, empowering religious fundamentalists, destroying Afghanistan's basic infrastructure and prolonging war. The infrastructures that they ordered their ignorant proxies to destroy were built by Afghans and they belonged to Afghanistan. Afghanistan was not only the victim of the Soviet Union; she was as much the victim of the US.

From the early 1980s the Soviet Empire begged the US to compromise with them to end the war in Afghanistan. But the US was not willing to let them escape its 'Afghan-Trap'. Allowing the Soviet Union to get out of Afghanistan was the last thing the United States government wanted. They wanted to make the Soviets bleed, in Brzezinski's words, 'for as much and for as long as possible.' The US and its allies kept increasing their aid to the Mujahidin year after year to damage the Soviet military and economy so badly that it would never again recover.

The CIA gave much of the aid to the most extremist factions, such as Gulbudin Hekmatyar's, because extremist factions fought the Soviet Army fervently. As journalist and writer Ahmad Rashid points out in his book *Taliban*, 'Thanks to the CIA-ISI arms pipeline, the engine of Jihad was the radical Islamic parties.' The extremists were opposed to schools and education, too, considering schools to be the centre of communism. They burned down hundreds across Afghanistan and teachers were killed in large numbers.

However, whatever the US was doing to make the Soviets bleed was not enough and did not cripple the Soviet military operation in Afghanistan. They knew the only way to cripple the Soviet military was to destroy their air force. The Soviet Air Force was the backbone of its military operations in Afghanistan and they devastated the United State's proxy Mujahidin as well as helpless Afghans and their livelihoods.

In 1986 the United States decided to give Stinger missiles to the Mujahidin. The CIA trained the Mujahidin in Pakistan on how to use them. In the first few months of using these missiles, the Mujahidin regularly shot down Soviet or Afghan government aircraft. The Stinger missile broke the backbone of the Soviet military in Afghanistan. It also massively demoralised Soviet troops.

I Have Been Ejected out of the Glory of Nonexistence

My father sent all of his salary back to Merza Kaka every month, as he was not sure whether he would survive the ferocious battle. My uncle bought a piece of land in Kabul for both of them. One day Merza Kaka called my father to come Kabul but didn't tell him why. Father obtained permission for leave and then found out that Merza Kaka was to get married. A distant relative of the family who lived in Kabul had found a good family who had a young daughter, Simaa Khala (Khala means maternal aunt). When Simaa Khala was a child, her father took all the money from their home to buy land, but he disappeared with the money and was never seen again. Her second eldest brother joined the army in order to feed the family but was blown up by a landmine and killed. Simaa Khala herself was educated; she could read and write from a very early age and wanted to become a teacher. Her mother agreed to marry her daughter to Merza Kaka, so their marriage was arranged. Merza Kaka and my father agreed to give half of the land that they had bought to Simaa Khala's family as a dowry. In Afghan tradition the groom's family has to pay money or property to the bride's family as well as buy jewellery for the bride and cover most of the costs of the proposal and wedding ceremonies. Most people sell their land or borrow money from others to get married. After they are married, they spend the rest of their lives paying back the vast amount of money that they borrowed. Some have to work hard when they are young to make that money, and by the time they make the money they are old. Merza Kaka and my father both paid for the cost of the wedding.

According to Pashtun tradition, men and women cannot celebrate ceremonies together in the same room, with the exception of a few close relatives of the bride and groom. During the wedding they sent my father to the women's room to inform the bride's sister that the food was ready. My father saw Simaa Khala's younger sister, she captivated my father at first sight. He kept this to himself and went back to Gardaiz when the celebration was over. After some months, my father finally told Merza Kaka that he wanted to get married to the younger sister of Simaa Khala whom he had seen at the wedding. At first Merza Kaka said it was not possible. 'We can't both get married into the same family.' But Father insisted. So Merza Kaka and my father ended up marrying two sisters. Father took my mother to Gardaiz after their marriage.

Later on my mother's eldest brother, at the age of forty-five, married a thirteen-year-old girl called Farzana. She had dark hair, green eyes and very pale skin. She was possibly the prettiest woman I had ever seen in my life. Farzana did not agree to get married. She was studying in school and was so advanced in her lessons that even her teacher would assign her to help other students with their studies. She wanted to carry on her education. However, her parents feared the war and lawlessness and forced her into marriage with a highly inappropriate man. My mother told me that Farzana screamed that she did not want to marry this old man. She was a very young and pretty girl and my maternal uncle was old, tall, big and unappealing. People who attended the wedding were shocked to see Farzana and her husband standing together.

A year passed and my father and mother were happy. The marriage seemed to work for them, but the relationship between Simaa Khala and Merza Kaka was shaky from the very start. Merza Kaka would beat Simaa Khala now and then for petty issues.

Father was very busy with work and sometimes worked at night. My mother spent nights alone at home and when she heard explosions far away she worried about the people who had been killed. However, my mother gave birth to my oldest brother, Tariq. Poor Tariq was born in a world where there would be nothing but cruelty, bloodshed, suffering and misery. He would not have the same life as an American or Russian child because Soviet and American leaders deprived him of his basic human rights. My mother said that Tariq did not know how to cry for a very long time until he picked it up from other children around him. Tariq was no bother to my mother at night – unlike me – he was very quiet. Simultaneously, Simaa Khala gave birth to her first child, Akmal. Merza Kaka and my father were extremely happy that their wives both gave birth to sons.

When Mikhail Gorbachev became the leader of the Soviet Union in 1985, he repeatedly asked the United States for a compromise to end the war in Afghanistan, which Gorbachev called 'the bleeding wound'. In 1988, the governments of Afghanistan, Pakistan, the Soviet Union and America signed the 'Geneva Accords'. Amongst other things, the Soviet Union agreed to end the occupation of Afghanistan and pull out its troops by 1989, and both the Soviet Union and America promised they would stop supplying weapons to their proxies in Afghanistan. The Geneva Accords changed nothing and both superpowers continued sending mountains of weapons into Afghanistan. The United States wanted to bleed the Soviet Union in their Afghan-Trap and take their Vietnam revenge. Not only did the US not end the war in Afghanistan, they made it fiercer. The US and Saudis increased their funding of Mujahidin. The Pakistani government also filled its pockets with the US taxpayers' money. Pakistan was a great ally of the United States government during the Afghan-Soviet war. However, wolf and sheep can never become friends. Today ordinary Pakistanis are paying with their lives for the stupidity of their government.

By mid 1985, there were innumerable factions of the Mujahidin in all parts of Afghanistan who fought the Soviet troops as well as each other. The Soviet military were still in Afghanistan, but the Mujahidin factions had already started killing one another for the power. Pashtun, Tajik, Hazara and Uzbek factions hated one another as much as they hated the Soviet troops. All their leaders were waiting impatiently to seize power for themselves once the Soviet troops were forced out of Afghanistan. In 1990, the *Los Angeles Times* said that the Mujahidin 'have in recent weeks killed more of their own than the enemy'.[18]

One night in 1988 I opened my eyes for the first time in the dreamland of the vicious empires. I was born into a world filled with appalling wars, cruelties, hostilities, exploitations, superstitions, ignorance, intolerance, misunderstandings, pain, man-made divisions and boundaries, nationalities, dangerous ideologies, poverty, greed, inequality, and all the rest of it. I was born into a world that had become ugly and dangerous and chaotic. Man destroys this marvellous world alongside all these innumerable beautiful species that live in it. Men are neither at peace with themselves nor with other species and nature.

In the very same night that I opened my eyes, Soviet troops began to leave Afghanistan. My mother said that on the night I was born the Soviet helicopters flew very low and scared her. The war was over my innocent mother thought, and she could start a new peaceful and harmonious life with her husband and children. She was ignorant of the fact that it was the morning of another endless war of brutality, hardship and misery.

In 1989 the Soviet military completed its final withdrawal from Afghanistan. They had gone. But what they left behind were the memories and tales of their occupation. Today Afghanistan is filled with stories of Soviet barbarisms and cruelties. They maimed one third of the population. They reduced to ruins most of the houses, mosques, villages and cities. They forced six million Afghans out of their country and displaced millions of others inside Afghanistan. Millions suffered humiliation and had miserable lives in Pakistani refugee camps under the burning sun. Innumerable others were abused and humiliated in the streets of Iran by the Iranian government and police. The majority of them are illegal and are not allowed to have their own houses or able to send their children to university.

After ten years of war it appeared like a gigantic monster stamping over Afghanistan and crushing everything. There was not a single house, school, hospital or city left intact apart from Kabul, which was about to be crushed by the rockets and missiles of the United States' Mujahidin. Humans, animals and all things were devastated. Nobody knows exactly how many they killed. Undoubtedly, it was beyond a million Afghan men, women and children who had been crushed to death. Afghanistan smelled of blood, flesh and fire. It was crammed with graves and cemeteries and mines. Everywhere homes, villages, fields, gardens, valleys and deserts were nothing but human graves.

Now that the Soviet Union had withdrawn, the war was between the Afghanistan central government, which was still backed by the Soviet Union, and the Mujahidin, who still received a huge amount of weapons and money from the United States and its allies. The president of the Afghan government, Dr Nijibullah, encouraged by the Soviet Union, repeatedly pleaded with the Mujahidin factions to come and form a coalition government with him or hold an election and let Afghans decide on who they wanted as their leader. But the United States wanted its proxy Mujahidin factions to go for victory. The CIA, ISI, Saudi monarchy and the Mujahidin hoped they would be able to crush the Soviet-backed communist government in Kabul in a matter of months, but it took them another three years to topple it and with it took the lives of tens of thousands of Afghans. The Soviet Union sent sophisticated mobile missiles called scuds to the Afghan government. Scud missiles were similar to that of the German V-2s, which were used to hit London and other European cities during World War II. The size of the missile was roughly eleven metres or perhaps longer and was filled with chemical explosives that could flatten any Afghan village in the blink of an eye. It moved as fast as the speed of sound. At first scud missiles proved themselves to be very effective; especially when Mujahidin conducted a massive assault on Nangarhar Province, which was designed by the ISI. Scud missiles devastated the Mujahidin. They killed large numbers of them and gave a new hope to the fragile central government. Later, the Mujahidin understood how to protect themselves from this new destructive weapon. They operated in small numbers and scud missiles were no longer useful.

My parents decided to name me Laiq, it means intelligent. However, everyone in school and the village called me the opposite (Tanbal) unintelligent, for that is what I was. My father sent my mother with her two children back to Kabul, as it was no longer safe for us to be there. Merza Kaka was living in another part of Kabul with his wife and family. By now they also had two children, but their second child was a daughter. Merza Kaka was not as happy this time as he was when his wife gave birth to a son.

My father had built a small mud house with a bedroom, small kitchen and a small bathroom with a lavatory for us to live in. He also brought a little grey puppy for Tariq. We called him Palang (Tiger) as he looked like a tiger. When Palang came into our lives, Tariq spent most of his time playing and looking after him. He bathed Palang every day, and gave him his own food. Sometimes he insisted on bringing Palang into his bed at night to sleep with him, but Mother never allowed him to. In 1990, we had another baby brother called Arif. My father was very happy that he had three sons.

Throughout the Soviet and Mujahidin war, Kabul, the capital of Afghanistan, was not totally ravaged. The Mujahidin, however, hit Kabul with rockets and missiles. They were firing rockets from remote parts of Kabul to harm the Soviets and the government, but they mainly killed civilians. However, once the Soviets had left, now the war encircled Kabul and Mujahidin rockets regularly hit innocent civilians' houses. Mujahidin rockets were a nightmare for the entire Kabul population who lived in constant fear. Our mother was anxious all the time. No one knew when a rocket would crush their house. In the fierce winter of the same year, people in Kabul were faced with a serious shortage of food and fuel. Many died of starvation and the cold, most of whom were children who were too weak to survive. When the CIA ordered the Mujahidin to destroy infrastructures, they did. They destroyed almost all of the power stations and soon most people had no power.

At last, in 1991, the Soviet Union went to pieces and the United States remained the only superpower on the face of the earth. The invasion of Afghanistan was not the only reason for the fall of the Soviet Union, but certainly the Soviet-Afghan war was one of the many reasons for the breakup. The Cold War had ended but had devastated helpless human beings in the Third World. So many democratically elected leaders had been replaced with dictators. So many dangerous factions like that of the Mujahidin had been empowered in Asia, Africa and Latin America, and large numbers of people had been killed.

The end of the Soviet Union meant the end of Afghanistan's communist regime. The communist government at last collapsed in 1992 and the savage Mujahidin factions stormed the capital of Kabul, from mountains, valleys and rural areas in their tens of thousands, armed to the teeth with heavy US-supplied weapons. The world observed that the United States unexpectedly abandoned shattered Afghanistan and oppressed Afghans for these murderous extremist factions that it empowered. Why did the United States government, which regards itself as the champion of democracy, freedom, human rights and women's rights, unexpectedly abandon the Afghan nation to such malicious factions who were the enemy of all those things? Why did the United States abandon Afghan women to these extremist and misogynistic factions who denied women their basic rights? Why did the United States abandon Afghans to be tormented by the cruel Pakistani and Saudi governments?

After the collapse of the Soviet Union and the end of the Cold War, the United States and other western elites were faced with another big menace and that was economic power shift: a shift from the West to the East. Power shift rarely happens in world history and the last time was at the beginning of the twentieth century, when power shifted from Europe to North America. The East was asleep for several hundred years and now it has awoke. The giant, Asia, has been unshackled after two World Wars from Western imperialism and is rising at an unprecedented speed, and attempting to catch up with the western world economically, scientifically, technologically, militarily and politically. The only way the US and its Western allies can maintain their supremecy over the world is to dominate the world's natural resources, in particular oil, as well as geostrategically vital parts of the world, to threaten and to prevent these rising nations from forming alliances with each other. The economies of these rising nations are heavily dependent on oil and energy, and US elites are aware of this fact. In the name of 'War on

Terror' they have disguised their real aim, which is control of natural resources and geostrategically crucial parts of the world.

The economic rising of the East adds to the strategic importance of Afghanistan for the United States. Afghanistan is located in a key part of Eurasia and domination of Eurasia is crucial for the empire of the United States to remain the sole superpower in the twenty-first century. The United States and its allies never abandoned Afghanistan after the fall of the communist regime in 1992. They were there and were secretly working to pave the way for the domination of Afghanistan.

Some argue that if the United States wanted to dominate Afghanistan it would have done so after the fall of the communist regime. It is a very ludicrous argument. The United States and other western powers would have established a puppet government in Afghanistan in 1992, rather than nine years later in 2001, if they could, but they could not. For one big reason: the very religious fundamentalist factions that the United States and its western and non-western allies empowered were extremely anti-American and anti-western. But, smart elites of the United States and the western powers played the Islamic extremist card in the domination of Afghanistan. The corrupt governments of Pakistan and Saudi Arabia and their intelligence services were there to do the dirty business of the United States and other western powers in Afghanistan. The Saudi monarchy and the Pakistani government played a major role in paving the ground for the occupation of Afghanistan by the United States and its allies.

In 1992 I was four years old and extremely mischievous and bothered my mother day and night. I loved fire and liked to set light to things. The weather in Kabul is very hot in the summer and extremely cold in the winter, therefore my mother did not want us to go outside, especially in the afternoons. When everyone fell asleep in the afternoons, I would take the matchbox and set fire to dry shrubs, old clothes and plastics. Several times I burned my brothers' and mother's clothes, and for that I was severely punished. We had to frequently buy matches and the closest shop was two miles away from our house. Mother was tired of punishing me all the time. Her slaps and pinches did not work because I was used to them. She twisted my ears with her hands and lifted me from the ground. I always wanted her attention and would cry so loud that it perturbed everyone. My mother would say, 'I never asked God to give me a son like you.' She sometimes prayed to God to take me from her.

I had a pet chicken; I called it Telaa-e (Golden) as it was golden in colour. Wherever I went I took her with me. I liked Palang our cute dog, too. I used to put Palang and Telaa-e against each other to fight. Tariq did not like that and sometimes he would beat me. He used to tell me that it was cruel and God would put me in hell, but I was too young to know what hell was. Sometimes he would go and sit in the backyard for hours so that he could hide Palang from me. Mother tried a few times to take Telaa-e from me and put her with the other chickens, but she failed.

It was winter and the earth was covered with snow. We had a small fuel-stove that kept us warm. One afternoon, Mother turned it on and told us all to sleep. She stayed awake until I fell asleep, because she knew that if I didn't sleep I may set fire to something. I detested sleeping in the afternoons. I closed my eyes and pretended that I was asleep until she fell asleep too. Mother usually concealed the matchbox from me and I had to look for it. After a search I found the matchbox. I went out and attempted to light things, but nothing could catch fire in the snow.

I came back into the room and lit a match and threw it in the stove fuel-canister. I did not know that fuel is extremely flammable. I saw yellow flames instantly burst out of the canister. I was frightened and took my chicken from the corner of the room and ran out into the yard. I heard a big bang and saw a huge flame burst out of the window, then I heard my brothers' and mother's cries. I too began to cry, outside in the snow, for I was terrified. Luckily, Mother managed to escape through the second window alongside my brothers before they were burned. The neighbours heard the explosion and our cries, so they immediately came to check on us. The room was on fire, so the villagers rushed to douse the flames. Some used buckets, some pots and some plates filled with snow and water. In a few minutes they had put the fire out. But all our clothes were burned. Outside was very cold and nobody could bear to stay there any longer. Mother took everyone back into the room and the neighbours left. Mother took the matchbox and grasped me tight. I did not know what sort of punishment she would give me. She stood over my left hand and lit a match and stuck it into the back of my right hand. The pain was unbearable, I screamed a lot. This time the neighbours did not come. They knew my mother was punishing me. She lit one match after another and put them into the back of my hands until the last match was gone. As soon as she released me, I ran outside and buried my hands in the snow. Mother came out, sat in the snow and cried with me. Later she took me back inside and put toothpaste over my wounds, she believed the toothpaste would keep the wounds cool. Mother tried all forms of punishment, but none of them stopped me from playing with fire until one day when she mentioned demons to me. She said if I did not stop setting fire to things she would hand me over to the demons. I asked her to tell me about the demons. 'They have long sharp teeth and nails covered in human blood. They have long filthy hair and are always looking for mischievous children to eat.'

Mother utterly terrorised me when she told me those tales about the demons and for the first time managed to bring me under control. She used to tell one tale in the afternoon and one at night for months. She made up a tale called Balaa-e Chaasht (Afternoon Demon). The tale was about a little boy who did not sleep in the afternoons and one afternoon the demons took him away and ate him. After hearing that story, I did not dare to walk out of the room alone. For many days and nights I envisioned the Afternoon Demon. I didn't dare go to the toilet or walk outside in the dark. I was so terrified I sometimes dreamed of demons and sometimes I screamed in my sleep. I was no longer that little fearless boy.

During the last semi-peaceful days of Kabul my mother gave birth again. Father called an elderly nurse to help. My brothers, Father and I sat outside the room and Father asked us to pray to have another brother. We did pray,

41

but it did not work. Mother gave birth to our first little sister. Although Father was slightly disappointed, it seemed that he did not mind too much having a daughter.

The Mujahidin rockets that hit Kabul were increasing and killed tens of Afghans on a daily basis. Dr. Najibullah, Afghanistan's president, decided to peacefully hand over power to the Mujahidin in 1992 as he knew that after the fall of Soviet Union he would no longer be able to fight against the US and their allies. The United States and its allies rooted out communism from Afghanistan and replaced it with the Islamic fundamentalism and unleashed their barbaric Mujahidin factions to massacre, obliterate, rape, torture, loot, and taking Afghans back to the Stone Age.

On 25 April 1992 all Mujahidin factions, except Hizb-e Islami of Gulbudin Hekmatyar, gathered in Peshawar, Pakistan to share the power amongst themselves. They agreed to establish an Islamic state in Afghanistan. They selected Sebghatullah Mujadidi as president of the Islamic State of Afghanistan for two months, and for another four months by Burhanudin Rabani, and then elections would be held. Gulbudin Hekmatyar had been chosen as the prime minister of the new Islamic State, but he and his master, Pakistan, were dissatisfied with the amount of power he would receive. Gulbudin Hekmatyar ordered his faction to seize Kabul. But before they reached the capital, other factions had already seized key areas. Tens of thousands of armed groups poured from all corners of Afghanistan into Kabul and plundered whatever they found useful. The harassment of the Afghan nation began by the US's proxy. And the US sat and watched silently.

The Afghan nation had already been torn asunder. Now every ethnic group had its own faction and attempted to grasp the ugly throne of power in Kabul. The Mujahidin entered the capital and factions plundered all ammunition and wealth left behind by the communist government.

By now, Merza Kaka and Father had lost their jobs and spent much of their time with their families. Although many neighbours warned Father to get out of Afghanistan, for they knew that something terrible would happen soon, he did not take their warning seriously. Those people who sensed the coming of the dark storm began to leave Kabul for rural parts of Afghanistan. But Father ploughed most parts of the yard and grew different types of vegetables. He spent much of his time farming and hoping he would soon be able to get a job in the new army that the interim government would form. All Afghans were keen to see and to hear from the new government what their plans for the devastated Afghanistan were. How would they rebuild their ruined country?

On the TV, they did not show the face of the female presenter or anchor. People could hear the voice but instead of her face they were showing a flower. Showing the face of a female on the TV was considered immoral by the Mujahidin leaders. Indeed, they publicly announced a new set of rules governing the conduct of women called the 'Ordinance on the women's veil'. Their Ordinance on the women's veil is as follows:

1. They must not perfume themselves.
2. They must not wear adoring clothes.
3. They must not wear thin clothes.
4. They must not wear narrow and tight clothes.
5. They must cover their entire bodies.
6. Their clothes must not resemble men's clothes.
7. Muslim women's clothes must not resemble non-Muslim women's clothes.
8. Their foot ornaments must not produce sound.
9. They must not wear sound-producing garments.
10. They must not walk in the middle of streets.
11. They must not go out of their houses without their husband's permission.
12. They must not talk to strange men.
13. If it is necessary to talk, they must talk in a low voice and without laughter.

14. They must not look at strangers.
15. They must not mix with strangers.[19]

These were the people that the US government handed the fate of the Afghan women to. The United States government built a far more ferocious cage within the ferocious cage of old customs and traditions for the oppressed Afghan women. The US government handed the fate of Afghan women to the extremists as a gift and later justified its domination of Afghanistan by saying to the world that they were going to 'liberate Afghan women'. Those women who had torn apart the cages of old customs and traditions had been sent back. Gone were the glory days for those poor women who worked in public and studied at the university, those beautiful days when tidy men and women walked in the city of Kabul.

A fierce war broke out in Kabul amongst the Mujahidin factions. This war was far more brutal than any other wars that took place in Afghanistan. It did not take place in the valleys, mountains and rural areas; it took place in the densely populated city of Kabul. Showers of bombs, rockets and missiles fell upon Kabul residents day and night for four years. Tens of thousands of human beings were butchered by the Mujahidin factions.

Life Under a Rain of Rockets and Missiles

It was early in the morning and we all were awoken by an ear-deafening explosion. It was the first time I ever heard such a powerful explosion in my life. My ears stopped working. I was deafened. I could see my father's lips moving but couldn't hear his voice. Dust fell from the ceiling. Windows shattered. I saw my older brother's crying face. My mother ran and grabbed my newborn sister in her arms. I saw my father comforting my mother and my older brother. My ears started to pick up sounds around me again. I could hear Palang barking in the yard. My father again asked me if I was all right. I nodded. I suddenly remembered Telaa-e and ran to the chicken coop. When I got there the roof had collapsed upon the chickens. I screamed out and my parents both ran towards the coop and removed the debris. Some of the chickens had been squashed to death; some were badly injured and some slightly. Luckily, Telaa-e was not badly injured but one of her legs was bleeding.

A huge dark cloud rose towards the sky in a very ugly shape right after the explosion. It was a rocket that the Mujahidin had fired on one another but had landed in our village, crushing houses and families. After a few minutes we heard another gigantic explosion, this time it landed on a different village, but because the rocket was so huge and powerful, it sounded as though it had landed right beside us. Each explosion shook the earth. We could hear the cries of the other villagers. Everyone looked for sanctuary from the rockets, but nowhere could be found. Nobody dared go and help those villagers who had been crushed by the rocket. After a while, when no more rocket explosions were heard, my parents went to help the neighbours. When they came back, my mother's eyes were red and the tears were streaming down her face. She knew a woman who had been killed along with her family.

Several more rockets and missiles fell upon other villages and their nasty sound terrorised my little siblings, my parents and me. It was almost dark

45

before people were sure that no more rockets would come. All of the men in the village gathered together to bury the bodies that had been blown into pieces before they decomposed. My father joined them and they spent most of the night digging graves. Father later said that they'd buried children as young as Tariq.

As time went on the faction fighting became more ferocious. This war did not take place in the mountains, in the valleys and in the fields. It took place in the cities, the streets, the villages and the compounds and thousands of people were killed each month by the Mujahidin.

Rockets fell like hailstones day and night. I did not know what was going on. Father told me that the demons were angry and fighting one another and if I did not keep silent, they might grab me. I really believed that it was a fight between demons.

We all knew and took care of each other, but at that time nobody dared to find out who was alive and who was dead.

We could hear the cries of little children, poor women and men from all around our village. Some cried because they were injured and some because their family members were lying dead. All of the village men hid themselves during the day and collected the dead bodies at night, when the war cooled down. At night they dug graves to bury the dead. During the day, the rockets did not allow anyone to walk outside their homes. Afghanistan turned into hell. The extremist factions of Mujahidin, warlords and tyrants reigned everywhere.

The weather was unbearably cold at night. My brothers and I cried for our mother to keep us warm. She'd hold our hands and blow on them to keep them warm. I used to blow on the feet and face of Telaa-e to keep her warm and Tariq did the same thing to Palang, but Palang did not like it at all. One of our neighbours had no food in their house, so my parents shared the very little food they had left with them.

46

The rain of rockets and missiles and bullets intensifyied day after day. Father dug holes for us to hide ourselves in, to escape the shrapnel. Our parents dug from early in the morning until late into the evening as the rockets and missiles flew above our heads. Each hole was about two metres deep and became our new shelter. They were very tight and boring, but we had to get used to them. I shared my hole with Telaa-e and spent my time talking with her. Tariq forced Palang to live with him in the hole but it was not really big enough for both of them. Palang kept refusing to go in the hole until a close explosion frightened him and then he decided to live with Tariq.

We did not know what was happening with Merza Kaka and Simaa Khala, as they lived in a different part of Kabul. My parents did not know what happened to our maternal grandmother and uncles either.

We were all sitting in the holes in a state of constant fear and each time a rocket or a missile landed near us, my little siblings and I would scream to our parents. My helpless mother could do nothing but tell us to remain quiet and not raise our heads, and simultaneously the tears fell from her eyes. Sometimes I cried to Mother to take me out of the hole. She would say that the demons were very close and could see us if we got out of the hole. So, I would remain quiet with my heart full of terror and listen to the demons fighting each other.

The Mujahidin used anything to destroy one another and the civilians were trapped. Factions surrounded Kabul and were antagonistic with each other. There were so many factions: Hezb-e Islami, Hezb-e Wahdat, Jamiat-e Islami, Harakat-e Islami, itthad-e Islami, Junbish-e Milli. They all struggled to grasp the ugly throne of power. Sometimes two or three factions unified and fought others and sometimes they turned against each other. Almost all neighbouring countries interfered and funded their favourite faction. But, it was the helpless Afghans who were the victims. All factions were very vicious, but amongst all of them Hezb-e Islami of Gulbudin Hekmatyar was exceptional in its brutality. Gulbudin Hikmatyar considered Kabul inhabitants as the Russian collaborators and infidels. Therefore, he showed no mercy to them. The huge cargos of rockets and other ammunition that came from Pakistan to him were being used against helpless people who lived in Kabul. His rockets smashed Kabul day and night endlessly and killed thousands of civilians.

Months passed but the rockets did not stop falling on our village. We did not have enough food and my father could not go out to buy any because of the fierce war. Even if he could go, there was not a single shop left to sell food. One afternoon we were in our holes when four Mujahidin came to our house. It was the first time I had seen Mujahidin fighters. They were so different from the men I had seen before. Four Mujahidin covered their heads with *Pakul* and balaclavas and their hair came down to their shoulders. They had long messy beards, wore big baggy military coats and they all had different military uniforms. Two had rocket launchers on their shoulders and the other two had what I later learned were Kalashnikovs.

They entered our house without knocking on our door. Father asked Mother to go somewhere so that they could not see her. They told him that they needed food. Father welcomed them into our house. They did not go inside our room and said they were fine to stay in the yard. All we had potatoes, so he boiled potato for them while they waited in the yard. The Mujahidin fighters sat down not very far from our holes. They did not notice that we were hidden. I raised my head to get their attention. When one of them saw me, he was startled and reached for his weapon. He calmed down when my face appeared. They all came to see the holes. They saw me in the hole with Telaa-e and Tariq with Palang. One of them asked why one of us was holding a chicken and the other a dog. 'They will be killed if they do not stay here,' Tariq responded. The Mujahidin fighters liked Arif, my youngest brother. One of them said that Arif looked like his own younger brother. Their rifles caught my attention. One of them gave me his Kalashnikov to play with. I dragged it around until my father arrived and took it away from me. Father brought the boiled potatoes, which were cut into round pieces, and poured salt on the top of them. He placed them in front of them. The way they ate was as if their hands were fighting each other on the plate. They finished in the blink of an eye and got up to leave without expressing their appreciation.

48

Before they reached the door, they warned my father to leave, because the war will become much fiercer soon.

Time passed but the rockets and missiles and bullets did not halt. Every day huge crowds of helpless innocent civilians trapped in Kabul were killed. The sounds of sick men's weapons terrified the men, women and children. My little brothers and I too were frightened each time the rockets and missiles crushed our village and we knew that there was nowhere else to take refuge but in our mother's peaceful arms. Nobody knew which day would be their last in this violent world.

One day it was raining; all the holes filled with rainwater. My father got out and emptied the holes every hour. My siblings and I could not bear the coldness. We were screaming to our parents to get us out of the holes. Mother tried to scare me with the demons in order to silence me, but at that time all I wanted was to get out of that freezing hole. I was soaked in the rainwater and begged them to get me out, but they refused. I screamed as loud as I could until a huge blast of a rocket made me quiet. The rocket hit our neighbour's compound and killed several members of their family. After a few moments I resumed screaming. My brothers were in the same situation. Tariq was in agonising pain, but still he did not forget Palang. He worried about the dog and cried that Palang would die as he had not eaten anything for so long. All the food we had in the house was depleted. We began to eat our home grown vegetables and they kept us alive for a few days. My parents feared that we might not survive the war, cold weather and starvation. Mother often cried to my father. They were more anxious for my newborn sister, who was more susceptible to the cold weather. Mother wrapped her in so many clothes to keep her warm. She too cried all day long, yet there was no way to flee.

In our village there were more than four hundred families and many were crushed beneath the bombs and rockets. Some people buried their family members in their compound yards, as they could not walk outside. In each family, several members suffered from shrapnel wounds. Families could do nothing but watch while they suffered, and some died before their eyes. What can be more terrible than watching your children or parents struggling to die?

This factional war was an ethnic war, too. Pashtuns, Tajiks, Hazaras and Uzbaks killed one another in very terrible ways. There were terribly sick humans amongst them who committed crimes that are beyond imagination. They even hammered nails into people's heads. Faction fighters chopped the heads off their victims and poured boiling cooking oil over their severed necks. The oil would seal the veins so that their blood would become trapped within the body. The victim's body would convulse on the ground as the perpetrators cheered on. They called this grotesque act 'Raqse Murda' (Dancing of the Dead). They chopped off women's breasts. They sexually abused large numbers of tormented women. They took women from their families for themselves. They raped young boys. They killed and buried human beings in mass graves, of which some are being discovered now. These were the factions that the United States empowered and funded with the money of the American taxpayers and put the fate of a nation in their hands. The Revolutionary Association of the Women of Afghanistan (RAWA) has compiled some of the gruesome crimes of the Mujahidin factions in a book called *Afghanistan: Some Documents of the Bloody and Traitorous Jehadi Years 1992-1996*. Shockingly, many of those who perpetrated the most shocking crimes are busy today helping the United States and its allies bring freedom and democracy into Afghanistan and liberate Afghan women.

Kabul was divided amongst the ethnic Mujahidin factions. One faction committed terrible crimes against the people of other ethnic groups. In nation warfare, the nations do not live with one another; they destroy each other and then leave. But ethnics live with each other and war and hatred stays on amongst them.

Despite the fierce war in our village, my father went from house to house to find food for us. One family had buried turnips in the ground in order to use them in the winter. They shared them with us. Winter was not far away; we could see it coming towards Kabul. Mother suggested to Father to dig holes inside the rooms so that we could stay warm, but my father refused. He said if the rocket hit our house than we would be buried alive under the rubble, even if the rocket did not kill us. He believed the Mujahidin war would last for a short time and then it would fade away, but it was a mirage of hope. Now he wanted to escape somewhere else, but we were trapped in our village. So many people, including children and old people, had been injured either by bullets or shrapnel and left without treatment. At night our village turned into a horrifying place. All we could hear were the cries of wounded men, women and children who received no treatment, or the cries of those who had lost parents, children or partners, or the cries of those who watched family members dying from the wounds they had sustained.

There were several factories not very far from our village. Gulbudin Hukmatyar wanted to destroy them, before they fell into the hands of other Mujahidin factions. He fired his brutal rockets and missiles from an outskirt of Kabul called Chaar-Aassyaa. Only lucky shots hit the factories. Most rockets landed in the villages and massacred many men, women and children. After some months of brutal war every home, street, village, city was jammed with the civilians' dead bodies. The dead bodies of humans became dogs' food. The world's media was no longer in Afghanistan. All those western journalists who put their lives at risk to film the Soviet horrors in Afghanistan and to show it to the world had vanished. Afghanistan was no longer TV headlines in the west, but it still was the same human slaughterhouse. There was no one to report the horrors that had been committed by the US 'Freedom Fighters' to the world's citizens.

Time went by and we were gradually getting used to the sounds. Death roared at us day and night and nobody knew which day would be their last. One morning we had boiled turnips and my parents told us to go to our holes. My brothers and I refused to go, as it was freezing. Our parents knew that the shower of rockets would soon begin, so they put us into the holes by force. Twenty minutes after we hid ourselves something happened. It sounded like the earth and heaven were colliding into each other. I felt as if someone had lifted me high in the sky and then dropped me back into the hole. Shrapnel flew over our heads. A rocket had hit our well. Everything we had was gone. The room, kitchen, well and toilet were razed to the ground. All our clothes were buried under the ruins and we were left with nothing.

My father came to see if we were alive or dead. My brothers, my mother and I screamed. Father repeatedly said, 'It's gone! It is gone! Don't be scared we are going to leave this place soon.' We remained vigilant to see when the next rocket or missile would come and knew nothing of where it would land this time. We remained in our holes until afternoon, but after that my brothers and I could no longer remain silent. We cried for food. Our father asked the neighbours to give us food. Our mother tried to stop him from abandoning his shelter at that point. Bullets were flying in all directions like bees and there was a good chance of being hit. My father left the compound. We happily looked forward to him bringing food for us and our mother sat in tears watching him walking through the bullets. If something were to happen, it would have had terrible consequences for our family. Without my father, we would all die. My mother did not even know how to find her way in the village, she only knew a few places, the local shops and the bakery.

Miraculously Father came back after an hour. It was almost as if he had walked into a heavy rainfall and didn't get wet. He was clutching some very old and crunchy Naan bread. It was as dry as firewood. Mother gave a piece to each of us and told us to be careful not to hurt our mouth. I shared my Naan with Telaa-e as usual, but this time she could not eat it. My mother told me to chew the Naan first and then give it to Telaa-e.

Night came and the rockets and bullets ceased. My parents went to ask neighbours to give us shelter. There were a few compounds that had not been destroyed. Most people were sleeping in the freezing weather outside. Several children had died in our village, not by the rockets or starvation, but by diseases such as whooping cough that could be cured simply in peacetime. My father went up and down the village but failed to find anywhere for us to shelter from the cold night, so he came back and asked my mother to help him to remove the wreckage and find our clothes. They worked for several hours until they managed to get a few blankets out. We all slept close to one another to keep warm. The chilly weather did not allow anyone to fall asleep at night; instead we slept during the day in our holes.

Arif caught whooping cough. My parents knew that several children had died and they had to do something before Arif's disease intensified. A man introduced us to a drug that would protect children from dying and that drug was opium. He had opium in his house and he shared it with all of the parents. He recommended opium for all the children, regardless of whether or not they had whooping cough. Before we fell asleep, my parents gave each of us a very tiny amount. Although the amount we took was smaller than the size of an ant, it was still strong and made us sweat all night long even in the very cold weather. My parents knew that it could be harmful for children, but they had to keep giving it to us. Opium has a bitter taste and my little brothers and I refused to swallow it, but Mother forced us.

The Truce

Early one morning someone knocked on our compound door. A neighbour told my father that the Mujahidin had ceased fire so that civilians could flee Kabul. My father ran towards us smiling. He relayed his unexpected news to my mother, who thanked God so many times, and then she grabbed us out of our freezing sludge-filled holes. Tariq put a rope around Palang's neck and I took Telaa-e. My father put his money in an old bag amongst some clothes and blankets that had survived, so that the Mujahidin would not know that we had any money. We had managed a living before the war began, but now we were walking out of the compound with empty hands. We left everything behind and did not know where we were going. There was a time before the war that our village was full of people, but today only a handful walked out. Some were wounded and being carried by others; some were crying. Children had lost fathers and mothers. Mothers had lost husbands and children. Fathers had lost wives and children. Few people survived.

Nobody knew where to go, there were no vehicles to take us out of Kabul. Everyone decided to walk towards the city centre in the hope they could find a vehicle to take them out of Kabul. As we walked farther down the village we came to see the true horrors. Human bodies lay scattered like leaves in autumn. My parents knew all of those dead people – men, women and children. My father told my brothers, mother and me not to look at the bodies. I tried to concentrate on the chicken under my arm, but sometimes I slipped and would see the bodies; some had no legs, some had no arms, some had their faces covered with blood. Children lay face-down in the mud.

The streets were lined on both sides with high, muddy walls. Mujahidin fighters stood on both sides staring at us. The rain turned the earth to mud, which was hard to walk through. It was difficult for me to keep up with my family as everybody walked too fast. The ground was very slippery and people fell frequently. I too fell several times. My sandals got stuck in the mud, so I had to leave them and walk barefoot to catch up with my parents. Every few yards there was a dead body on the ground. Wherever one's eyes shifted one would see nothing but mournful people moving the dead or wounded onto wheelbarrows or carrying them on their shoulders. Tanks patrolled up and down. Unclothed and barefoot children ran with tearful eyes to catch up with parents who were in a hurry to leave their livelihoods behind and reach the safety zone. We walked for half a day on the streets of Kabul. My father wanted to go anywhere out of Kabul. As we reached Kabul city there was no sign left to show that this was once a beautiful city. All we could see were knocked down and burned buildings. All those restaurants, shops, buses, cars, beautiful buildings, cinemas, lights and, above all, all those beautiful people who walked in Kabul city had vanished. My father was very disheartened. The Soviet and US weapons had left no signs of the beautiful Kabul; Kabul used to be a dream place for all Afghans who lived outside. Now, if they came to Kabul, they might have thought that they had come to the wrong place. The ugly and savage Mujahidin factions had killed gorgeous Kabul in a very brutal manner. Once, beautiful men and women walked in every corner of the city; disciplined boys and girls walked towards schools and university. Now all one could see were wild and ignorant men with weapons, wandering around. Instead of cars and buses there were Soviet tanks that had fallen into the hands of the Mujahidin factions to destroy each other as well as innocent people. Tanks drove on Kabul roads and their tracks crushed the asphalt.

We could not find any vehicle in Kabul to take us out of the city, so we decided to go to *Pul Charkhi*, which was tens of miles away. The mud made walking very difficult for us. As I was walking barefoot I cut the soles of my feet very badly on sharp shards of glass on the ground. My father carried me on his shoulders but he was also struggling to maintain his balance as the ground slid away under his feet. He frequently fell down and dragged me with him. Once he fell and I landed straight onto my face and my nose began bleeding, but my chicken managed to get away before she got hurt. I cried as the blood flowed down my mouth, chin and onto my clothes. My mother cried too as she watched me. People around me thought I had caught shrapnel.

My father cleaned my nose but the blood didn't stop. He asked me to give my chicken to him so that I could hold my nose to stop it bleeding, but I refused to hand Telaa-e over. The soles of my feet were very painful. Each time I stepped on the ground it felt like I was stepping onto fire. Once, my family walked so far ahead that I thought I had lost them. They disappeared amongst other people who moved in the same direction in the hope of finding a vehicle to take them out of Kabul. I ran after them to keep up. Suddenly my feet slipped and I lost my balance and my chest hit the ground and Telaa-e was squashed. As I hit the ground, I heard Telaa-e make a noise. I stood up and saw that she was shivering. I watched her for a few moments and then she stopped. I thought she had fallen asleep. I tried to wake her, but she refused to wake up. My father came back for me. When he saw me with my bleeding nose, standing with my immovable chicken in my hands, the tears fell from his eyes. I told him there was something wrong with Telaa-e. He pulled me up on to his shoulders and said to leave her be, she was asleep.

We walked for miles, hungry, thirsty and exhausted until we reached a garden. Everyone rushed towards it and began searching the empty trees to find something to eat. My little brothers, mother and I wanted to rest, but Father did not let us. Palang created a lot of trouble. All the way he barked at strangers and scared them. Tariq was very angry with him. I was busy tapping and shaking Talaa-e, but she refused to wake up. We walked alongside a motorway for some hours and passed several dead bodies.

What a terrible day it was, some carried the wounded on their shoulders and some carried them in wheelbarrows while wounded people burned in pain. Tears fell from the eyes of men, women and children as they ran to find a way out of Kabul. Everyone was exhausted and could no longer walk. Therefore, my father let us rest alongside others beside the motorway. Most people immediately fell asleep. I put Telaa-e on the floor and lay down beside my mother and quickly fell asleep. At age four I had seen the face of war for the first time, and it was ugly and gruesome.

I was asleep when I heard a lorry engine. Everyone ran towards the lorry. The driver said that he was going to Jalalabad. People did not care where it was going; everyone just wanted to get out of Kabul. The driver was very opportunistic and asked everyone to pay a huge sum of money before getting onto his lorry. Those people who had money didn't hesitate for a second, but those who didn't begged the driver to let them onboard. The lorry could not carry all of the people, because there were thousands who were desperate to get out of Kabul. My father arranged our fare. He jumped into the back of the lorry and then helped us to climb up. My mother and Arif were the first to get onboard. Tariq was the last, but before he climbed up, he asked my father to help him to pull Palang up. As Tariq pushed Palang up, the driver came and pushed Tariq away, and shouted at him that there was little enough space for people and yet he was trying to get a dirty dog aboard. My father jumped off and told the driver he would pay for the dog as well. The driver did not accept. Surely, people were much more important for the driver than a dog, but Palang was a dear member of our family.

Father persisted but the driver became irritated and shouted, 'Take your family and filthy dog and find yourself another vehicle.'

All the people surrounding the lorry shouted at my father to either get on the lorry or get out of the way. Some said, 'You are crazy! People are leaving their family members behind to get out of Kabul and you are not willing to leave a dog.' My father knew if he missed this lorry he would never be able to find another. He finally backed down and had to leave Palang behind.

He lied to Tariq and told him that we would leave without Palang for now, because there was no space for him, but that he would come back to fetch him soon. Tariq knew if he abandoned Palang he would never see him again. He cried very loudly. Tariq begged Father not to leave Palang behind. But it was not up to him. He told Tariq to let go of Palang's rope so that he could get into the lorry, but Tariq refused. The driver ran out of patience and told my father to either get in or leave the lorry. So he grabbed the rope from Tariq's hand, picked Tariq up and forced him onto the lorry. The driver shouted at Palang to go away, but he refused. So the driver took a big rock and threw it at him. It hit him on the leg. Palang yelped and limped away, as he was badly hurt and could not run. Poor Palang was ignorant of what was happening. He stood 40 or 50 metres away from the lorry and barked. It was a bitter moment for us. Palang had no one else and we knew surviving was not easy in a world where there was no respect for human life let alone animals.

Everyone got aboard the lorry and it moved off. Space was very tight with more than eighty or ninety people squeezed in. I thought that I was going to die because two women sat on top of me and I couldn't breathe. I had Telaa-e in my right hand and a child stood on her. With my left hand I managed to pinch one of the women. When the woman looked down, she noticed that she was sitting on me. They both pushed other people away and I took a deep breath. I also managed to push the child away who stood on Telaa-e.

Tariq refused to sit with my parents, who were at the front of the lorry whilst he stood at the back. He fixed his eye to a hole and looked outside, shedding bitter tears. He was watching Palang as the lorry moved forward. Palang started to run behind the lorry despite his hurt leg. Tariq cried and begged Father to stop the lorry so that his dog could get on. A man who was crouched beside him shouted at him to keep quiet. He stayed there for a very long time and watched Palang running until he disappeared in the clouds of dust of the lorry wheels. We never saw Palang again.

The lorry was jam-packed and breathing was difficult. People sat on top of one another and some cried. My parents were very vigilant to keep my newborn sister alive. Everyone was hungry, thirsty and tired. People fell asleep in spite of all the difficulties. The driver drove all night long. Children cried for food, people were starving, but there was nothing for them to eat. Every few miles the lorry driver was forced to stop by the Mujahidin factions and two or three climbed up into the lorry and demanded money from the helpless people who were trying to flee Kabul. No one dared refuse. There were chains of Mujahidin checkpoints scattered all across the motorways, villages and cities and they robbed people. Anyone who had power could do whatever he wanted and those who were powerless suffered as a result.

The lorry drove almost all night through the mountains and valleys and deserts, while the flames of hunger burned inside of us. It was almost dawn when we stopped and the driver announced that we had arrived in Jalalabad city. We all got off the lorry and, luckily, there was a bazaar. My father told us to stay close to our mother and went to buy food. I still had Telaa-e with me. Mother sniffed her and took her away, telling me that Telaa-e was dead and decomposing. If I did not throw her away I may get sick. I snatched her back. My father came back and I ate a whole Naan on my own with some cheese.

The weather was warm in Jalalabad Province compared to Kabul. We sat next to the brook and ate until the food was gone. Our parents didn't know how to get to Khugyani. We sat there until the afternoon. My little brothers and I played while our parents contemplated how to get to Khugyani. We observed men and young boys who carried AK-47s and we wandered around the local bazaar. There were very few people who did not carry weapons that the US had brought into Afghanistan.

Before we left, my mother took Telaa-e from me once more and sniffed her. This time she did not give her back. My parents persuaded me to leave Telaa-e there. Father tossed Telaa-e in a brook and she floated on the water until she disappeared. A few minutes later she was gone. I wanted to jump in the water and get her back, but my mother held me in her arms and promised me she would get me a new chicken as soon as we settled down somewhere. I cried. After a while I went quiet, just like Tariq had.

Our father hired a Toyota vehicle to take us to Khugyani. The driver drove through the desert until at last he stopped his car beside the river and said we had to walk the rest of the way, as his Toyota could not cross the angry river of Khugyani. Khugyani was a marvellous natural world. My grandfather's compound was encircled by a beautiful hill, an angry river and a vast forest. As we entered the compound tears fell from our grandparents' eyes to see us alive. Merza Kaka and Simaa Khala were already there. They had luckily fled in the very first days of the war. Now Merza Kaka and Simaa Khala had four children, three sons and a daughter. Their second eldest son, Ajmal, was unique. He had blond hair and very pale skin. When children, in particular my cousins and my brothers, quarrelled or fought with Akmal, they bullied him by calling him *Shurawi* (Russian) or *Angraiz* (English).

My grandfather and uncles were still farming for landlords to feed their families. By now everyone grew poppies in Khugyani. Grandfather had cows, sheep and goats. They all helped him to make a living.

The CIA's weapons had also reached my grandfather's house. My paternal uncles filled the compound with CIA Kalashnikovs and mines and grenades. Khugyani was crammed with the US weapons like everywhere else and lawlessness and chaos were at their peak. Boys, adults and elderly people wandered about with the weapons with them; sometimes they carried weapons on their shoulders and sometimes turned them against each other. In the past when tribes fought one another, they beat each other with rocks and sticks and at the end a few would lose their lives. However, now they were killing each other in large numbers with US weapons. When the fighting broke out between the tribal people, villagers and families, it lasted for days and even weeks and they fired rockets and bullets at each other, not only in Khugyani but throughout Afghanistan. Communists were infidels to the local people in Khugyani and this is what Mullahs, Khans and Maliks alongside other social elites had told them. Many people thought Merza Kaka and my father were communists and they did not like them. Even their childhood friends were not very nice to them. My father and Merza Kaka left their village in search of a prosperous and peaceful living, away from the peasantry and the hostile way of life but instead they found the opposite. This is the horror of the Cold War, which turned brothers, friends, relatives, tribes and ethnics against one another.

In the capital of Afghanistan, Mujahidin factions were tearing each other's hearts out as well as devastating those helpless Afghans who lived in Kabul. The Afghan nation was shattered. All ethnic groups were at war with each other. The Soviet leaders who set this nation on fire were now resting in their luxurious houses enjoying a life of abundance. In the United States the people who poured fuel on the fire that Soviet leaders set were very proud of what they had done, and they even got rewards and medals for the crimes they had committed against the tormented nation and were plotting to pave the way for the occupation of the heart of Asia.

Food vanished from Afghanistan. Peasants grew poppies with little edible crops for themselves. Poor and landless people starved to death. Opium was good business for landlords and warlords. They were not concerned about the poor people. They wanted to make money out of this poisonous crop. However, they were not the real money makers. The real money makers were the ones who took it to the rest of Asia and Europe and the world. They were the ones who hid themselves behind powerful governments.

My grandfather and uncles were growing opium for someone else in return for food. They did not have enough food for themselves and now they had to feed us too. My grandfather and uncles looked after us and they gave us a room to sleep in and food to eat. They cooked bread made from wheat flour for us. They could not afford to eat wheat flour bread themselves; instead they ate cornflour bread. My mother noticed something very bizarre in my grandfather's family. My uncles' wives cooked food and they would serve it on the plates then they would all sit aside whilst the men came and ate. Once the men had finished, the leftover food was for the women. My mother had never experienced such an unfair custom in her life and was infuriated when she noticed it. She always argued with Zarmina Amma (my father's youngest sister) to put an end to this unjust custom. For Zarmina Amma this was normal and she did not see any problem with it. She said 'men deserve to eat first as they are working hard in the fields, and women should eat the leftovers as they are not doing the hard jobs'. However, I noticed women's work was even harder than the men's. Women had to wake up early in the morning to feed the cattle, clean the shed, light the Tandoor to bake Naan, sweep the yard and prepare breakfast. Once the men were served breakfast and went to the field, the women had to take the cow dung and flatten it into cookie shapes and stick it on the wall to dry out so that they could use it as fuel in the Tandoor. As they finished that work, they then had to light up the Tandoor and cook fresh Naan again to prepare lunch for the men. Women had to spread the fodder in the sunlight so that it would dry ready to store for the winter to feed the cattle and they would remain busy until late at night cooking, washing, cleaning and looking after the cattle as well as the men and their children. It was extremely difficult for Simaa Khala and my mother to adjust to the local culture. There was a water stream outside the compound, but Mother was not allowed to walk to it and wash clothes there, as other men would see her face.

After a while Rafi Kaka, who was a couple of years younger than my father, asked him for a talk beside the river. My father went down to the riverside and Rafi Kaka told him, 'Brother, I am sorry to tell you that we can't look after you and your children any more. We only earn enough to feed ourselves and if we allow you and Merza to eat that with our family then we shall be wasted with hunger in the winter. I hope you understand our concern but you should buy your own food.'

My father understood from the very first day of our arrival that people's lives in Khugyani were as bad as everyone else's in Afghanistan.

My father bought a bag of cornflour from a farmer after a lot of effort, because people were not used to money and did not want to exchange their goods for it; they preferred to trade their goods for other goods. There was only one small shop in the entire village but no one bought anything but chewing gum from there. People hardly ever went to Jalalabad city. The only reason for people to go to the city was to take a sick person to the hospital, since there was no hospital in the entire district.

My mother woke up early in the morning and lit the Tandoor, cooking corn-Naan. During breakfast time, everybody gathered and started eating. But I refused to eat corn-Naan. It was very dry and extremely hard to swallow. I cried and asked my mother to provide wheat-Naan for me. I kept crying and my cries annoyed my parents so much. Suddenly a slap hit me in the face so hard that I fell to the ground. It was my father and he kept slapping me all over. He said that he was sick of me and I had driven him and my mother crazy ever since I was born. My nose had not fully recovered yet, and it started to bleed again. When my mother saw what was happening, she jumped in between us to save me from my father's slaps. She cleaned the blood from my nose and her tears fell down on my lap. Father left the house and stayed away all day long. It was evening when he entered the compound with a bag in his hand. He came and told me that he had bought wheat flour for me.

In Khugyani, life was much more difficult for both us and Merza Kaka's family. We did not have enough space to live. After a great deal of effort, my grandfather emptied a room and Merza Kaka's family and ours had to share it. We did not have firewood to cook our food as it was difficult to find dry wood. The wood that my uncle and my father brought was wet and would not light, so Simaa Khala and my mother had to struggle to set fire to them. There were no jobs for Merza Kaka and my father for quite a while. The war in Kabul was still as fierce as we had seen. Pakistan still sent huge amounts of weapons and money to Hikmatyar to defeat other factions.

Since the fall of the Soviet Union the United States government decided to buy all the unused stinger missiles from the Mujahidin at any price. They had bought most of the missiles, but some fell into the hands of hostile nations, such as Iran. The Pakistani government already had plenty of these stingers. The US knew that if stinger missiles remained in Afghanistan, then it would cost them dearly when the right time came for their strike. So they managed to acquire most of them from Afghanistan.

In 1993 my father had no money to keep us alive. Therefore, he went to join Rabani's army in order to earn money to provide food for us. He left us in Khugyani and went to Kabul. Kabul was still under heavy fire from rockets and missiles, which were being fired day and night by faction fighters. Merza Kaka, too, left his family and headed to Kabul to join the army to save his family before they starved.

With my father gone we had no firewood to cook food. My uncles were busy in the fields all day long and could not help us. There was a huge forest on the other side of the river that we could collect firewood from, but the river current was too strong for me and Tariq to cross. My mother was not allowed to leave the house as she was a woman, and if a man she did not know saw her face it would embarrass my grandfather's family. Tariq was seven years old and I was almost six at the time. Our mother sent us around the villages to find anything that could be used to stoke a fire. Simaa Khala sent her eldest son, Akmal, with us. Tariq, Akmal and I went in search of wood from early in the morning until afternoon to find enough to cook our food on. Mother worried about the mines that were sown everywhere by the Soviet occupation force. She warned us every day before we left the house not to walk in the places where we couldn't see human footsteps or touch anything that was unfamiliar. Every day we heard that Soviet mines and unexploded devices had blown up someone somewhere. People in my grandfather's village knew that we had come from Kabul and adults and children called us *Camunistanu* (communists). We did not know what 'Camunistanu' meant. We asked our mother, she too did not know. My grandfather told us that it meant infidels. Whenever Tariq, Akmal and I went to collect firewood, the children began chanting *Communistanu! Communistanu!* Most people really hated us being there. They really thought we were infidels.

Children did not allow us to collect firewood around their compounds. We had to go far into different villages where people did not recognise us. However, after some time some people found out there too and began harassing us. While we collected firewood, children threw rocks at us. One day a rock hit Tariq's head, which started bleeding. When Mother saw his face covered with blood, she was terrified and took Tariq to my grandfather. Grandfather was in his late eighties, but still strong enough to walk. He had twenty-one grandchildren and had a lot of love for each one. He used to say, 'I love my grandchildren more than I love my own children.' When he saw Tariq's head bleeding he was furious. He took his walking stick and asked us to show him the place where Tariq was hit. Grandfather was a well-known person and people paid a great deal of respect to him. When we reached the place, the children who threw rocks at us were still there, but when they saw our grandfather, they scattered and concealed themselves in their compounds. Grandfather knocked on each one's door and spoke with their fathers to ask them to stop their children from bullying his grandchildren. Despite his warning, the children continued to cause us great harm. He taught us about Islam so that we could prove to the villagers that we were as much Muslim as they were. My grandfather began to tell me about God.

It is not an easy task to introduce someone or something to children when they cannot see it. I used to repeatedly question my grandfather about where God lives and why we can't see him, asking what he looked like. For days and months these questions were repeatedly asked by my cousins, brothers and me. We all loved our grandfather. When the moon and stars ousted the sun and its brightness, and the weather cooled down, we gathered on the veranda and my grandfather would tell us stories. Despite the fact that he was an uneducated person, he knew a great deal about Afghanistan's history and the empires that had invaded. He'd gather us all around him and tell fascinating tales. Aladdin was my favourite. I begged my grandfather to tell Aladdin's story over and over again. He knew several tales about the Mongol or Mughul Empire and their brutal emperor, Changaiz Khan. He said that when Chingaiz Khan invaded Afghanistan he completely shattered everything. He massacred people in every town and village, in particular the beautiful town of Ghazni, which was the centre of all knowledge at the time, and he massacred almost all of its population.

I spent most of the day in search of firewood and came home tired and hungry, but it was my grandfather's interesting tales that cheered me up for a few moments. However, he too sometimes told us demons' tales, which frightened me.

After a while Tariq, Akmal and I could not find enough firewood every day to cook our food. It became a huge problem for our mother. When she did not cook, my brothers and I surrounded her and cried for food. It was the same with Simaa Khala and my cousins. Simaa Khala and my mother suffered every moment of their lives. Their husbands were in the warzone trying to earn money to keep their families alive. They did not know what happened to their family in Kabul. Still Simaa Khala and Mother were amongst the luckiest in Afghanistan as none of their children had died yet. Tens of thousands of people were dying through war, famine and starvation, by very simple and preventable diseases, by unsafe water, lawlessness, hostility, drugs... We drank water from a stream near our compound and the colour was grey. It was muddy and filthy. When a flood came into the river, we had to drink floodwater as all the streams rooted from the river. This very same water killed Afghan children in large numbers.

Demons of Khugyani

In the summer of 1993, the river level dropped. Tariq, Akmal and I could cross it to the forest to find firewood. On the very first day when I stepped into the forest, I felt the presence of the demons there. I thought there were demons hiding everywhere behind the trees and bushes, staring at me. When the wind blew, the branches of trees, the leaves and the grass trembled. I too trembled with fear. I grasped Tariq's clothes tight as we walked in the forest so that I did not lose him. He did not like it. He wanted me to stay away from him, but I was frightened.

The climate was very hot, but we had to collect firewood under the burning sun. Sometimes I begged Tariq to take me home when I was hungry and exhausted, but he refused as he wanted to gather enough firewood to make our mother happy. He told me to go alone, but I could not because I thought the demons would eat me on the way home. Then I went to Akmal and begged him to take me home. He also wanted to collect enough firewood so that his mother could cook food for him, so he too refused. I cried for Tariq to take me home. Sometimes, my cries irritated him and he threatened to leave me in the forest all alone. That was my weakness, otherwise I could cry all day long. It took me several months to gain a bit bravery to let go of Tariq's clothes and wander a little further away from him, but I never gained the courage to walk alone from the forest back towards home. Sometimes, Tariq and Akmal terrified me by hiding themselves from me and I would scream and run in different directions to find them. I was even convinced that there were demons outside the forest and they were following me and concealing themselves behind the trees, watching me silently.

The moment came when I wore out my shoes and I had nothing else to wear. My mother had no money to buy new shoes or sandals for me, so I started walking bare foot. Khugyani was carpeted with splinters, like Soviet mines. As I walked in the villages and fields and forest, the splinters got into the soles of my feet and stuck in the flesh. My feet swelled up and walking became difficult. My feet felt like someone was injecting needles into my soles. Soon I was unable to walk and when night came, my feet were in agonising pain. I cried all night long and disturbed everyone who was sleeping. My poor mother was the one who suffered the most. Children think their mother can mend everything for them. I cried for her to free me from the pain. She put wild plants on the soles of my feet but whatever traditional drugs my mother used did not work.

One time Simaa Khala held my legs so tight that I could not move them whilst my mother forced a needle into my soles in the hope of pulling the splinters out. I screamed at the top of my voice, calling for Grandfather to save me. Several times my mother put the needle in and stirred it in the hope of finding splinters. Pus and blood surged from the soles of my feet, but no splinters were found. I was drowning in an ocean of excruciating pain and could do nothing but scream day and night, which upset my poor mother for weeks and months. One night the pain in my feet was intolerable and my cries irritated everyone, in particular Rafi Kaka who worked hard in the fields under the burning sun. He woke up in the night and told my mother to give him the needle. He asked my other uncles to come and hold me firm. He took the needle and repeatedly stuck it into the soles of my feet to pull the splinters out. Rafi Kaka spent over half an hour in search of the splinters. Every moment of those thirty minutes felt like an infinite time in the fiercest of fires. I screamed again and again. I asked for help from my grandfather, grandmother, mother, Simaa Khala and everyone else to save me, but none did. I screamed for my father to save me, but he was a world away somewhere in the ferocious warzone trying to earn bread for me. Rafi Kaka stirred the needle in every corner of my soles. At last, he found one huge splinter in my right foot and two in the left.

When Rafi Kaka had finished I looked at his hands; they were covered with my blood. My mother took a strip of cloth to cover my wounds. She looked at my blood-drenched feet, and she cried. She asked God to grant us death rather than the life we had. Rafi Kaka succeeded in taking a few splinters out, but there were several others hidden in the flesh. I remained in the most agonising of pain and kept screaming for days and nights.

Months passed, but we heard nothing from our father and Merza Kaka. We had eaten most of the food that Father had bought for us until he came back from Kabul. All we had in the house was wheat flour. My mother baked less Naan so that the flour would last longer. The Naan was not enough to satisfy our hungry stomachs. However, luckily, there were plenty of poppy seeds. It was the poppy harvest season and my uncles woke up early in the morning and went to collect opium until late evening. At the end of the day, they brought a bag of opium to the house and kept it in a special place.

I was a prisoner while the splinters were in my feet. I was no longer able to walk, so I sat beside my mother and Simaa Khala all day long. Simaa Khala and Mother spent most of their time cracking poppy pods and collecting their seeds to use as food. There had been a firm bond of friendship between the sisters ever since their childhood. They would not have survived the hardship of life without each other. Despite all the difficulties that entangled them from all sides, they still managed to make each other smile. They took refuge in their childhood memories. Sometimes they both sat in tears as they did not know what was happening to their family in the Kabul warzones. They were urban girls locked away in a silent corner of the world. They struggled for survival and saw nothing outside the encircled walls, but could hear the ugly weapons.

One day two tribes battled with each other. We could hear their rocket explosions and gunfire. They fired bullets and rockets that the CIA had left for them to kill each other with. Their fighting dragged on for many days. My mother did not allow us to walk outside since it was so dangerous. Hostile peasants planted the CIA's mines in each other's fields to kill them. They lay in ambush to kill each other. They threw grenades inside each other's compounds and killed children and women. The weapons made their survival extremely difficult. Poor peasants carried guns at all times on the farms, in the villages, at ceremonies, at home and even in their beds while they were sleeping. These ethnic and tribal clashes took place all over Afghanistan.

Simple Afghans sent each other to their deaths in large numbers every day. Soviet mines blew children to pieces every day. Countless young Afghans took their own lives by using heroin. Armed people looted and killed in all parts of Afghanistan. Warlords set up checkpoints in the cities, villages, highways, roads and streets taking money and other valuables from the poor and oppressed, and they killed and tortured poor people who did not give them what they wanted. Armed people broke into civilians' houses and abused their women. Most people who committed these heinous crimes were the Mujahidin who once fought for the United States, and the US government called them freedom fighters because they were fighting for the objectives of the US.

Among these brutal people was a commander whose name was Zardad. He set up checkpoints all across the Kabul-Jalalabad highways. He also had a very savage dog; his dog is more renowned than Zardad himself. Afghans called his dog *Sag-e Zardad* (Zardad's dog). This dog would bite people who refused to hand over money to Zardad. He was not a real dog but a man who pretended to be a dog.

Winter arrived in Nangarhar; luckily it was not as cold as we had firewood to burn in the house to keep ourselves warm. It did not snow in Khugyani, but it did rain a lot. Our accommodation was not safe in the winter. When it rained, the ceiling leaked and the whole room filled with rainwater. Simaa Khala and my mother were very anxious that the roof might collapse. They had taken our clothes out of the house and kept them with my uncles' clothes. The nights when it rained, Simaa Khala and my mother had to stay awake to keep an eye on the roof. One night as we were sleeping, my mother screamed and told everyone to get out of the room. She took my sister with her and I crawled along the floor towards the outside. We stood for a few moments in the rain when the roof suddenly fell to the ground. Grandfather told us to take shelter in my uncle's room. His rooms were crammed with his children and clothes. Despite this my grandfather forced us children in. Simaa Khala and Mother had to sleep outside. My uncle refused to let me sleep in their house amongst their children, as the pain in my feet intensified at night and I cried. So I had to sleep beside my mother outside. The nights were very cold. I not only cried because of the pain I had in my feet, but because of the cold weather too.

One night two men walked into our compound with huge bags on their backs. They put their bags beside the wall and came towards us. 'Where are my beautiful children?' My brothers, sister and I heard his voice. We knew who this man was. We all screamed because we were so happy. My brothers and sister ran cheerfully towards him. I began crawling on the floor towards him. It was my father and Merza Kaka who had come back home after months of being away. Father was extremely upset seeing us in such a dreadful state. He looked at my mother and asked what had happened? She cried but didn't say a word. She later told him that if she'd known they would have such an appalling life here, she would rather they all die by the Mujahidin's rockets in Kabul. Father reassured her that everything would be fine.

The bag my father brought was full of food. My brothers and I gathered around and searched inside to see what he had brought for us. There were apples, meat, vegetables, bread, and so on. Mother told my father about my feet. Father lit matches and looked at my feet and was aghast when he saw the wounds. In some parts the flesh had rotted. Our state of living saddened him.

That night was a very happy night for my family. The family all gathered around my father and Merza Kaka. Everyone's mouth was open, like a flower with the laughter. My grandparents thanked God for keeping their sons alive. The first thing my father did the next morning was take me to the hospital. He carried me on his back for several miles until we reached a point where we could catch a vehicle to take us to Jalalabad. In the hospital, doctors operated on my feet. Again I screamed. It felt like the doctors were doing what Rafi Kaka had done to me with the needle. By the time the operation had finished, I no longer had the energy to scream. My father took me to Jalalabad city and bought shoes for my brothers and me.

Mother told Father to take us back to Kabul. But he refused. She persisted. She said that she wouldn't stay in Khugyani any more and she would be happy to die in Kabul rather than live in Khugyani. Father described Kabul. He said it was much worse than we had seen. Those who were left lived in far more appalling conditions than us. Kabul was endlessly inundated with rockets, missiles and bombs. Tens of thousands had been killed since we'd left. People were starving and did not have water to drink. The Mujahidin were abusing women everywhere. Kabul was divided amongst different ethnic factions and if they caught one or another in their area then they were killed in the most brutal manner. Even going to Kabul from Jalalabad was not possible for women. There were so many Mujahidin checkpoints on the way. They were doing all sorts of evil things to people at these checkpoints; killing civilians and abusing women was very common.

It was here that my father first mentioned the name of Zardad and his dog. Nobody could believe how a human could bite off another human's flesh just for money. My uncles soon spread the news to their friends and this spread in the village. Men, women and children talked about him amongst themselves. My cousins, brothers and I made up different tales about Zardad's dog. I created all sorts of pictures of the dog in my mind.

Tariq asked my father about Palang. He was annoyed with him for not bringing the dog with him. At first, he wanted to go to Kabul with my father so that he could have Palang back, but after hearing about Zardad's dog, he never dared to ask our father to take him to Kabul. Our poor mother also gave up and did not want to go to Kabul any more. She sat beside my father in tears and asked when the situation in Kabul would improve. My father said everything was vague. All factions wanted to have Kabul under their control. All of them were determined to grasp power. Living in Kabul was not possible at that time.

One day we were all at home when someone shouted, 'Flood is coming, tell everyone to come and catch wood.' Before, when the river flooded my mother did not let my siblings and me observe it, as she was frightened that we might fall into it. But this time my father let us go with him. The flood destroyed the forest, people's fields and gardens on its way and by the time it reached our village it contained tonnes of wood, and wood played a vital role in people's lives. When my father and I reached the river I did not notice any flood. I asked why there was no flood. He said listen to the sound of it, it was coming. When I listened carefully, I heard the gigantic sound of it far away but getting closer. As it got nearer, it shook the rocks in the river and the ground beneath our feet. After thirty minutes, when almost all of the villagers were beside the river, the flood finally appeared. It was something that I had never seen in my life. I was expecting the water to come, but it didn't even look like water. It was yellowish, muddy water mixed with big trees. I couldn't believe that people would dare to stand against it and take big chunks of wood from its mouth. For the people of Khugyani it was normal, they were not scared of the flood as they had been doing this for centuries. As the flood reached where I was, people began jumping into the river to catch big chunks of wood. Merza Kaka jumped into the river, but the flood enveloped him along with the dirt and carried him down the river. Each time the flood came, it took several people's lives. Everyone thought that the flood had swallowed Merza Kaka and he might not survive, but miraculously he released himself from its jaws.

My father and Merza Kaka managed to take out enough wood to cook food on for several months. Merza Kaka and my father had to go back on their duty. They went to Jalalabad city and bought a food supply for us. Before Father left, Mother told him not to go to Kabul if the situation was too bad. He said he was working in the logistics branch, which is mainly in the office, and there was no fear for his life there. He promised he would come soon.

After a while, I was able to walk again. We did not need to go to the villages to collect firewood or get beaten by the children who thought we were communists. I was free! My brothers, sister and I spent most of our time playing with our cousins. I played with them from early morning until dusk every day. There was a big tawny-coloured ants' nest in our village and children would gather around it. Children believed that the ants were Russian ants and they would crush them to death to take revenge. There was so much hatred in people's hearts for the Russians in Khugyani, just like everywhere else.

One day Rahim Kaka, my father's youngest brother, whose part-time job was to herd the cattle in the forest every afternoon, picked me to help him. He carried me on his back to cross the river. The reason Rahim Kaka wanted me to go with him was so that he could sit on a boulder beside the river and play the flute. Playing the flute was his passion. When he sat on the boulder by the river, in the late afternoon, when the sun went down and a pleasant breeze picked up, his flute began to reflect upon nature with its marvellous sound. Stunning birds, the animals, the trees, the wild and angry river, the insects – everything – seemed to listen to Rahim Kaka's flute. I'd sit quietly beside him also.

Rahim Kaka did not like me because I was not useful when the cattle went deep into the forest. I would not dare to go and bring them back as I was so frightened of the demons that were waiting for me, so I refused to walk in the forest alone. Each time Rahim Kaka glared at me and jumped off his boulder. First, he kicked me hard in the backside and then slapped me on the back of my head, and then went himself to bring the cattle back. I would cry until he threatened to beat me again if I carried on.

Sometimes when the cattle did not leave the area, I would catch small fish and dig a hole beside the river to put them in it. I would pour water in for them and sit there and watch them as well as listen to the flute.

According to villagers, in the first Anglo-Afghan war, the British Empire's troops entrenched themselves in a hill that was beside our compound. There were rumours amongst the people in Khugyani that when the British troops were defeated they were unable to carry all of their precious objects with them, so they buried them in the hill. Several decades later, a team of Englishmen came back to Khugyani and told the people that they had buried their valuables in the various parts of the hill, among which was a queen's statue. If anyone unearthed it they would buy it at any price. I don't know whether it was true or not, but people genuinely believed it. Everyone used to climb to the top of the hill and dig in different places in order to find the queen's statue. People unearthed many statues (of which most were several centuries and millennia old) but nobody found the queen's statue. Many people used to smuggle the relics of old civilisations that they had unearthed into Pakistan and from there to other parts of the world

My uncles spent their free time digging the ground on top of the hill. My job was to supply them with drinking water. The hill was very steep, tall and rocky. It took me almost an hour to climb up, and another hour to climb down. I watched them searching for the English queen's statue. They dug deep and disappeared into the earth and I would be left alone on the surface. People did not inhabit the other side of the hill as it was a vast forest. I was frightened being on the top of the hill alone, as the jungle was full of demons and they would come and eat me. I shuddered until my uncles got out of the deep hole that they had dug. My uncles dug out so many beautiful statues. Amongst them was a bodiless head of a woman and my uncles kept it very carefully as they thought they would make a lot of money by selling it.

One day I had a jar full of water in my hand on the way to the top of the hill. I had almost reached the hilltop, when I saw a large dark snake in the bushes. I was awfully frightened and the snake was equally frightened of me. I threw the jar of water away and ran downwards and the snake fled into its hole. I came home and told the story to my mother. She knew that Khugyani was full of poisonous snakes and begged my uncles not to take me to work with them any more. But for the people in Khugyani, poisonous snakes were not as frightening as they were for us.

Simaa Khala and my mother did not know where their mother, brothers and sisters had fled until, one day, my father came back from Kabul with news that they were in Jalalabad. So he took all of us to Jalalabad to my Bebi's (maternal grandmother's) house.

When we stepped into Bebi's house, she and Soraya Khala (my mother's youngest sister) saw us. Bebi was enormously happy to see her daughter and her grandchildren alive. Tears of joy flowed from everyone's eyes. Several hours elapsed and still we did not see my uncles apart from my older uncle and his young and unhappy wife, Farzana. My mother asked Bebi, 'Where are the rest of my brothers?' She was again reduced to tears, but this time they were bitter tears. She said they had fled Afghanistan in the very first days of the civil war and went to Iran to earn bread. My mother's three brothers illegally entered Iran, alongside hundreds of thousands of Afghans in the very first days of factional war. Many Afghans had been tortured to death or injured by the human traffickers, Iranian border police or sent into cruel gaols. Afghans neither had a place in their own country, nor in anyone else's.

Later Bebi gave us some good news. She said that Soraya Khala had been engaged to a boy from a very good family who were their neighbours in Kabul. Soraya Khala's fiancé was not Pashtun. He was from Tajik ethnicity and he was born in the Herat Province and moved to Kabul when he was a child. At first Mother was unhappy that Grandmother had engaged her youngest sister into a stranger's family; Mother feared that she might never see her sister after her marriage. However, when she saw Soraya Khala's fiancé she calmed down. He was a very smart, courteous and eloquent boy. An arranged marriage appeared to work for Sorya Khala and her husband, they were happy with each other.

My mother's older brother now had two children (a daughter and a son) with his young wife Farzana. Farzana still hated every moment of her life with my maternal uncle. Farzana had no fear of telling people the truth about her marriage and her husband. She very boldly expressed to everyone that her parents forced her into marriage. My mother told her, 'Your marriage was God's will and you have to accept it since you have two children with my brother.' Nothing could convince Farzana. Life was futile for her; she was living and sleeping with a man she did not love.

We spent a week in Jalalabad and it was time for us to return to Khugyani. Bebi promised that she would come to Khugyani to visit us soon. I did not like Khugyani at all. There were always difficult tasks and I had very little time to play with the children or ask my grandfather to tell me tales. Back in Khugyani it was opium harvest time. In my spare time I would go to my uncles' poppy fields and copy them while they collect opium. I usually wasted my uncles' opium and they would chase me away from their fields.

I sometimes took poppy seeds and spread them around the riverside. They rapidly grew tall. Every day I went to the riverside and spent hours watching and cheering for my poppy plants, pretending to be a farmer like my uncles. My poppy plants would grow for weeks and sometimes even months before floods came and swallowed them all. Then I would cry to Mother and grandfather for the loss of my poppy plants.

I later found another form of amusement for myself and that was Gultair. Gultair was a huge dog. He was as big as a calf, highly aggressive and did not like people at all. He had been trained from a pup to be violent. When Gultair was young, my paternal uncles cut his tail and ears (as most people who keep dogs in Afghanistan do). They believe that by cutting the tail and ears off the dogs, they become cruel and that is what a lot of people want. The reason my grandfather kept Gultair was his cattle. There were many wolves in Khugyani and they frequently went after the villagers' sheep. Gultair hated strangers and loved to be left alone. Strangely, he and I became very good friends and he loved playing with me. When I wanted to leave, he didn't want me to; he held onto my clothing so tight with his sharp and tough teeth. Whenever I walked in our compound, and as soon as Gultair saw me, he began barking and wanted me to play with him. Everyone was amazed at our friendship.

One morning I woke early and heard that Gultair had killed a wolf. I ran to see what the wolf looked like, because I had heard many stories about how strong and brutish they were. When I got there, I saw a darkish grey mammal lying beside Gultair. The wolf was not as big as Gultair, but it looked how I expected it to be. Guiltair tricked the wolves, as he would hide amongst the cattle to disguise himself. When the wolves attacked the sheep, he then took them by surprise. My uncles would sometimes take Gultair for dog fighting. I once went to watch and was terrified when I saw the way he bit the other dog's throat. I thought the other dog was dead, but when Habib Kaka struggled to release Gultair's sharp teeth from the other dog's throat, the dog was still alive and managed to stand.

Animal and bird fighting have been widely practised in Afghanistan for centuries. People sit together in large numbers and let two birds or animals hurt or kill each other, and they would cheer them on. Each time my uncles took Gultair for dog fighting, he came back with so many wounds all over his body, bitten by other dogs. Each time Gultair fought, it took him so long to recover and as soon as he recovered, he was taken again for a new dog fight. Each time my uncles took Gultair for dog fighting, I would cry to my mother to stop them.

The Cruel Bull

One day Rahim Kaka and I were deep in the jungle when we heard the roaring of the flood. Rahim Kaka grabbed me and ran towards the river and the cattle followed us. He carried me back to the other side of the river before the flood caught up with us. As I walked along the riverside, the flood swallowed the ground and expanded. Rahim Kaka appointed me to lead the cattle back to the compound as he went to catch wood alongside my other uncles. My grandfather sent everyone back to the riverside to bring the wood into the compound that my uncles had taken from the river. I clutched a long and weighty stump and walked back. In fear of the river, as it was expanding, I walked close to Habib Kaka's cattle shed, which was beside the riverside. I was watching the river, the way the flood waves raised up and down, then I spotted a snake on the surface of the waves, stood upright. The fear once again crept through my body when I thought of the dark snake I had seen on the hill. Suddenly I was struck very hard on my left side and thrown almost into the river. When I opened my eyes I saw Habib Kaka's bull; he was the one who butted me so hard that I nearly fell in the river. The bull was charging for another strike, but his rope was nailed down and he couldn't reach me. The pain was severe on the left side of my body. I began crying. I struggled to stand up. I tried to move my left arm but failed. There was excruciating pain in my elbow. I left the wood there and walked back to the compound. I could not endure the pain and cried for my mother. She put my arm in a sling and wiped away my tears. I wanted her to go and punish the bull for hurting me so badly.

Day concealed itself into the darkness of night and the pain increased so much that I could not stand it any more. Mother was trying different methods to help me, but none of them worked. Again, she remained awake all night long sitting beside me in the darkness while the pain in my left elbow forced me to cry. The morning arrived, but the pain did not abate. My mother begged my paternal uncles to take me somewhere to fix my arm, but there was no doctor in the entire district. Mother did not have money to give them to take me to the Jalalabad city hospital because my father only earned enough to satisfy our stomachs. I stayed in the house for four weeks without any treatment. My mother spent her nights sitting beside me and listening to my unpleasant cries. She would take mountain plants, boil them and put them onto my elbow every night or boil a costly chicken egg and put it onto my elbow, but nothing helped to ease the pain. She sat beside her sister and best friend, Simaa Khala, and cried with her sometimes. Simaa Khala heartened my mother all the time. She would say have faith in God and pray to Him and He would make everything right. After a while, my arm began swelling and the skin turned dark. Mother was frightened and ran to Grandfather and begged him to help. He didn't have enough money himself, but he feared that if anything happened to me he would have to answer to my father. He took his entire life savings and borrowed some from his friends, and gave it to Rafi Kaka, and told him to take me, along with my mother, to Jalalabad hospital.

Rafi Kaka shouted at my mother to throw her headscarf away and wear a Chadari (burqa). My mother had never worn a Chadari before in her life. Rafi Kaka took his wife's Chadari and gave it to my mother to put on. She refused to wear it. Her refusal shocked the men and women in my grandfather's family. Neither my grandfather nor my uncles beat my mother, but if it was their wife or sister the case would be different. They knew that my mother had spent most of her life in Kabul and did not understand the rural culture properly. Rafi Kaka refused to take us to Jalalabad hospital unless my mother wore a Chadari. My mother had no other choice but to lock herself in the cage of Chadari.

We crossed the river. I walked a short distance, and then I cried to my mother that I couldn't walk any more. But we had a long journey before we could catch a vehicle. My mother pleaded with me to walk until we reached the bus. But after a while I was entirely unable to walk. I asked her to carry me on her shoulders. She already felt drowsy inside the Chadari and repeatedly beseeched me to walk on my own two feet, but I refused. Rafi Kaka did not walk with us since he was embarrassed walking alongside a woman in public.

He walked 60 or 70 metres ahead of us. My mother had no choice but to carry me on her shoulders. She rode me on her shoulders for a short distance, lost control of her balance and we both fell to the ground. My left elbow was already broken and again I landed on it. I screamed and she was horrified. She shouted at Rafi Kaka to help us. He gave me a ride for a mile and then asked me to get off his shoulders and walk. Once more, my mother had to carry me. She walked for some time, but suddenly began vomiting. She became irritated with her vast Chadari and took it off and walked bare headed. She walked for a while, until Rafi Kaka looked back to check where we were. When he saw my mother walking bare-headed he couldn't believe his eyes. He ran towards us and grabbed me away from my mother. He shouted, 'Are you crazy? Do you know what you are doing? Put your Chadari on and cover your face before someone spots you.' Mother said that the weather was burning and she couldn't breathe under the Chadari. 'I will only go with you if you have the Chadari on or else I will go back home,' said Rafi Kaka. My mother did what he demanded.

When the doctors inspected my arm at the hospital, one of them shouted, 'What kind of mother are you? Why didn't you bring your son earlier? Your son has a severe bone fracture in his elbow and if we fail to fix it we may have to amputate.' When my mother heard this, she cried and begged them not to amputate my arm. The hospital was filled with injured people from local hostilities and children who were blown apart by mines and explosive devices. The doctors took me to an operating room, where there were two dead bodies and an injured person who was screaming. When I looked at the dead bodies, I was terrified. Their wounds were open. One of the dead persons had a stomach that was badly ripped apart and it disgusted me. The doctor told me not to look at them. For several hours they worked on my arm. I stayed for a week in the hospital and then the doctors asked us to leave.

One problem had vanished when another one emerged. Arif, my youngest brother, and Zakia, Simaa Khala's only daughter had been diagnosed with typhoid. Soon the state of both was terrible and yet there was nothing my poor aunt or mother could do. Survival of my cousin and brother did not seem possible. Children died in their tens of thousands each year from petty curable diseases across Afghanistan, but typhoid was not a petty disease. After a while, the flesh vanished from the bodies of my little cousin and brother. Their hair began to fall out and their skin turned pale. They were unable to eat food. Simaa Khala and my mother forced them to eat. They could do nothing but weep and watch. There was nothing left of them apart from bones covered with pale skin. Everyone thought they both would die soon. Merza Kaka and my father returned from Kabul. Each time they came back, there was another shocking surprise for them. They took both of them to Jalalabad hospital for treatment and spent all of the money that they had earned to feed their family. Merza Kaka and my father remained in Khugyani for a while until my cousin and brother recovered. Death did not come to take our lives, it liked to play with us. It was always around us, roared at us, intimidated and frightened us, but it did not take our lives.

Merza Kaka and Father left us yet again in the harsh Khugyani. A month after my father's departure, my sister Sarah began to suffer from a very peculiar disease. Giant, painful spots grew on her head. After a few months her head was covered, each as big as a walnut. She could not sleep at night they were so painful. Our mother stayed awake as she held Sarah's head with her hand while Sarah slept. As the days went on, Sarah started losing her hair. The spots grew bigger and began to bleed. The blood ran down her face and clothes. Her head became twice its normal size. She was transformed into a creepy looking child. When I looked at Sarah I remembered the demons, as they were described almost in the same way as Sarah looked. Once, Habib Kaka burst the spots. He took a sharp knife and cut them. Several men and women held Sarah tight while my uncle did this. Sarah screamed and struggled to release herself and she begged our mother to save her.

'Mother, save me! They are trying to kill me!' Her agitated state made me cry and I charged towards my mother and started kicking her legs and pushing her away to leave Sarah alone until I received a slap on my face. My brothers and I all began screaming, as we thought they were trying to kill our sister. Tariq, Arif and I tried to get them to leave Sarah alone, but we were too small to push them away. There were more than twenty spots on Sarah's head and all had been cut out. She lost lots of blood. Sarah's wounds bled for several days and after a few weeks the spots grew again. Sarah lost so much weight and changed into a bony and pale-skinned child. Mother always cried to Simaa Khala that her daughter might die soon. Simaa Khala as usual heartened her and would frequently say 'Have faith in God'. Blood and pus flowed from Sarah's head. Mother ripped up clothes and used them as bandages to cover her wounds. Poor Sarah was in a dreadful condition for months. She was in violent pain and children were scared of her.

One day Rahim Kaka came and said there was a doctor who had recently opened a private hospital in the district centre. My mother immediately asked my poor grandfather to find money. She took my little sister there with the little money he had given her. We met the doctor who was in his late twenties. His hospital was attached to his house and he did not look much different from other peasants. He took my sister into a room, called his brothers from the backyard and asked them to hold her tight, the same way my mother and the other women had done previously. He did what Habib Kaka had done before. The only difference was he cut the spots with scissors. He cleaned the blood with thick paper. Sarah again screamed, but this time neither of us dared to stop the doctor, as we were so scared of him. When he had finished cutting the spots off, his hands were covered with Sarah's blood like an Afghan butcher's hands. The spots grew as before and nothing had changed.

My mother prayed constantly and asked God to help her daughter. Simaa Khala and Mother had made their minds up that they were going to leave Khugyani and go to Kabul when their husbands returned. Mother desperately prayed for God to return her husband alive otherwise without him we would all be wasted in Khugyani. When my father saw Sarah, he was traumatised. The next day he took Sarah to Jalalabad for treatment. He came back after three days and Sarah's head was bandaged and the doctors had given her medicine to take. But, the doctors warned my father to take Sarah to a better hospital. It took years before Sarah fully recovered. However, Father had brought Bebi back with him from Jalalabad.

Bebi loved to see her grandchildren and spent time with them. She was very sad seeing the way we were living there. We were sleeping outside and had no room, no kitchen and no bathroom. Most of our clothes were scattered all around the yard. My cousins, siblings and I wore ragged clothes. The next afternoon my Bebi took me to the river and washed me, and then she gave me a new set of clothes and let me put them on. In the evening I begged her to tell me the *Kalbacho* tale and she agreed. The *Kalbacho* tale was my favourite. Sometimes I insisted on her telling me the tale twice. She spent six days with us. It was six happy days for me.

On her last day, she looked at Simaa Khala and my mother and said 'I pray for God to give you two all the happiness in the world'. My mother went inside the room to get a teapot and make tea for Bebi, when she came back Bebi had left this world. I was on the way back from the hill when I saw Simaa Khala, my mother, brothers and cousins all with tearful eyes. I saw Bebi lying on the floor, wrapped in a blanket. I asked Tariq, who himself was crying, 'What is wrong, why is everyone crying?' He sobbed as he answered 'My Bebi has died'. Bebi had left this world for good. I cried, but that changed nothing. Villagers gathered and helped us to carry Bebi to the point where we could find a vehicle to Jalalabad. Once there, close and distant relatives, neighbours and community people gathered and prayed for her. Her brothers cooked food and invited everyone to share the feast. After a week, we left Jalalabad to go back to Khugyani. Everyone was very dismal after her death. My father tried to keep everyone happy, so he took us to the river to swim.

Simaa Khala and my mother cried all the time after the death of their mother. My father repeatedly told them that everyone dies, some sooner and some later and we must not let the tears flow from our eyes constantly. It was time for him to go back to Kabul. Simaa Khala told my mother to pack her clothes and leave Khugyani for Kabul. My mother asked my father to take us with him. Once again he refused.

'Then I am going to leave your children here and go back to Jalalabad and live with my brother!' shouted my mother. This was the first time she had spoken with a loud voice to my father. In most Pashtun families, women would not dare to challenge a man's decision. However, my father didn't beat my mother; instead he agreed to take us back to Kabul. We packed our clothes and were ready to leave Khugyani. Mother was anxious for Simaa Khala as she would be left behind. Simaa Khala told her that once her husband returned she would ask him to take her to Kabul too. Rafi Kaka came with us, as my father could not carry our clothes alone. Father was fearful of the Mujahidin's checkpoints, which were throughout the Kabul-Jalalabad highway. I was scared of Zardad's dog and was filled with fear. However, I was not the only one who was terrified, my siblings and my mother and even my father were terrified of Zardad's checkpoints.

We took the bus from Jalalabad city and drove towards Kabul with our hearts filled with terror. The bus was crammed with people. Every few miles there was a Mujahidin checkpoint. Two or three Mujahidin fighters got onto the bus and demanded money from every passenger. Those who did not have any or who refused to give up their money were taken away. The bus kept stopping at checkpoint after checkpoint and everyone gave their money to the armed men with their long filthy hair. Poor passengers were reciting verses from the Quran in order to pass safely.

We drove through high mountains and long tunnels, until we arrived at the Mahi par checkpoint. I was sitting between Rafi Kaka and a woman whose face was covered. Two Mujahidin boarded our bus, searched everybody and took money from everyone. They thoroughly looked at everything to find excuses to take people and loot from them.

As they reached Rafi Kaka, one of them asked, 'Why are you sitting so close to the woman?' despite the fact that I was sitting in between Rafi Kaka and the woman. Before Rafi Kaka could reply, the other one slapped him in the face so hard that his head banged against the bus window. The two Mujahidin dragged him off the bus to their checkpoint and locked him up. Father ran after them and begged them to leave Rafi Kaka alone.

There was a nomad outside the checkpoint who had several camels with him. The Mujahidin were demanding lots of money from the poor man and it seemed as if he refused to give them any, so a Mujahd smashed him on the head with his Kalashnikov and the blood poured like rain onto his clothes.

My father disappeared inside Zardad's checkpoint for tens of minutes. My mother cried and begged the other passengers to go and ask the Mujahidin to leave my father alone. My siblings and I too were crying. They could have killed Rafi Kaka and my father if they felt like it. The bus driver waited for a while. My father at last appeared, but without Rafi Kaka. He walked onto the bus with his sorrowful face. He told Mother that the Mujahidin were asking a huge amount of money that he did not have. Passengers collected together some money and handed it to my father to give to the Mujahidin so that they would release my uncle. My father again went into the checkpoint for quite some time. The driver told us that he had to leave. Mother begged him to wait. Passengers talking about the cruelties that were taking place at these checkpoints and that made my mother more anxious. At last, Father and Rafi Kaka appeared. My father managed to get Rafi Kaka out with all the money he had and there was no more for my father to buy food for us. Our stomachs cried out for food throughout the journey.

Death Chased Me Around

It was late afternoon when we arrived. Kabul was a ghost town. There was not a single undamaged building in Kabul. Everything was shattered. The elegant residents had vanished. Some had been killed, some had fled to Pakistani and Iranian refugee camps and a few lucky ones to other countries around the world. The only people who could be seen were beastly looking men with an AK-47s or RPGs over their shoulders, orphaned children and widowed parents. Kabul's gardens, parks and fields had been turned into graveyards. The city was brimming with graves. We had no choice but to live in this ugly Kabul. Still the war was being fought in the streets and villages. Still the Mujahidin fired rockets and missiles at each other day and night. Still Gulbudin Hekmatyar, the favoured man of the Pakistani government, was determined to ruin the already ruined Afghanistan.

My father chose to live in Macroryan, which was under Burhanudin Rabani's control. The buildings were concrete and had basements. They were slightly safer than the rest of Kabul's muddy houses. My father told us that if we heard explosions, we were to hide in the corners of the rooms, which were safer.

It was morning when two missiles landed outside our apartment block near our water pump. I panicked and smacked my forehead against the edge of a cupboard and cut it so badly that blood flowed everywhere. My parents were terrified, as they thought I had caught shrapnel. A man who had gone to fetch water for his family was killed and several others were injured. The next day missiles hit another house and killed and injured more innocent humans. Rockets and bullets were nonstop. People who lived in the apartment blocks decided to live in the basements of their houses, as it was safer than living above the ground. The basement was very dark and cold so we would wrap ourselves in thick blankets and remain there, often hungry. Life was terribly boring there. Children cried for food. Weeks passed but the missiles did not stop, their aim was to hit Kabul airport. Macroryan was located near to the airport. However, more than 90 per cent of the rockets and missiles hit civilians instead.

The Mujahidin fighters were more fearful than their rockets and missiles. They constantly broke into houses to plunder and abuse honourable women and young girls, and nobody was there to stop the United States freedom fighters. They took people's wives and daughters by force before everyone's eyes!

There was a decent family who had a young and beautiful daughter and who lived on the sixth floor, in an apartment behind ours. One day their daughter was washing clothes outside when a Mujahid spotted her. In the evening the Mujahid came back with his comrades to take the girl for themselves. The poor girl was with her mother in the house when they broke in. She knew what would happen to her if the Mujahidin took her. She jumped from her family's balcony and said her farewell to this wild world. The Mujahidin had failed in their purpose, but they certainly took her life. Her death terrified everyone in our block. Men, women and children all sat in tears. I watched a few men washing away the innocent girl's blood where she had landed. They buried her behind the apartment block and people went to pray for her.

The United States government created, trained and funded guerrillas in Asia and Latin America and even inside the United States in SOA, or Schools of Americas. These guerrillas committed horrible crimes in their own countries, including massacre, rape and severe torture. However, none was as barbarian as those they had created in Afghanistan. It seemed the CIA had painted every single Mujahid's heart with hatred, violence and brutality and then gave them weapons. Afghans had experienced lawlessness numerous times during the British-Russian rivalry over Afghanistan from early 1800 until early 1900, but Afghan did not humiliate Afghan. Afghan men did not abuse and humiliate Afghan women. The Afghan did not ruin his own home, village, garden, city and country.

Months had elapsed since our return to Kabul. Gradually our eyes got used to the human blood, torn apart bodies, the explosions and the dark smoke. Our ears got used to the cries of the orphans and widows, and the sound of weapons.

Nobody knew when the next rocket or missile would hit their house and kill them all. The smell of power blinded as well as deafened the Mujahidin factions so that they could neither see the streams of blood that were flowing nor hear the cries of their victims. Kabul's sky and air was dark with the smoke of rockets and missiles and bullets. We breathed the smoke.

My father began thinking about going back to Khugyani before something terrible happened. Everything seemed wrong in Kabul. Bullets, rockets, missiles, lawlessness, the Mujahidin's brutality, famine and disease did not leave any hope in his heart. No one knew when the Mujahidin factions would stop their vicious war. No one knew when the cargos of weapons would stop coming from Pakistan and other neighbouring countries.

Merza Kaka by now had brought his family from Khugyani and my mother was reunited with her sister and companion, Simaa Khala. Merza Kaka and my father decided to move out of Macroryan to a remote part of Kabul in the hope it might be safer there. We moved into a vast, crushed village. There were around five hundred ruined compounds and nobody lived there, but a few families who did not have money to escape. My uncle and my father chose a compound that was less damaged for us to live in. Mujahidin fighters wandered in the village and took any valuables they found in the houses. Here, too, we were not immune from the torment. Rockets landed all around us as usual and we were more vulnerable in the mud house than we were in Macroryan. We had to take shelter inside the compound all the time. Our parents did not allow us to play outside the house. All of us were crammed into a small room that our parents thought safer than the rest. Day and night we heard the Mujahidin's rocket explosions that they fired at each other. After a few weeks, Mujahidin fighters were closing in from all sides of our village.

The village was a good sanctuary for them. Father was very fearful that we might be trapped just like at the start of the Mujahidin war.

One day we were eating lunch when a rocket hit our yard. The explosion lifted all of us up and then dropped us back to the ground. Everyone disappeared in the dust that fell from the ceiling of our mud house. Nobody knew who was alive and who was dead. There were several trees in our yard, the rocket landed amongst them. All of the trees were broken into pieces; all of the compound walls had been reduced to rubble. But we survived yet again.

The next day, early in the morning, we fled the war-ravaged village as the rockets and bullets were passing and landing around us. Again we had to walk several miles before we found a vehicle to take us back to Jalalabad. Merza Kaka and my father managed to find a vehicle to take us away and we went to Jalalabad, the capital of the Nangarhar Province. They rented a house for us and left us there while they went back to war-torn Kabul to earn bread.

Our life was miserable in Jalalabad without Father's presence. Mother could not look after us on her own, as she was a woman. Sometimes we had food to eat and sometimes not. When we had food, my siblings and I ate, but when we did not have any, we surrounded our mother, cried to her and demanded food. One night we cried for several hours for food. But there was no food. She took us out into the yard with her. Then she told us to look at the moon. When we looked at the round and bright moon, my mother said, 'The reason it's so white is that it's full of milk. And now I want all of you to ask the moon to drop milk.' My little siblings and I stood outside and screamed at the moon '*Maataw! Maataw! Sheer Partu*', Moon! Moon! Drop milk'. For hours we screamed at the moon to drop milk, but the moon refused.

All sorts of fatal and preventable diseases took the lives of countless Afghans as most hospitals had been reduced to dust by the ignorant men's disease, war. There was a stream outside our house filled with stagnant water where mosquitoes lived, and I was bitten by a malaria-carrying mosquito. Malaria is one of those terminal diseases that killed and is still killing countless Afghans every year. My little body had no resistance against and I was soon in a severe condition. At first my mother thought I had caught a fever and I would recover soon. But as time went on she realised it was more serious than that. She could do nothing but watch me while I suffered. The village women warned her to check in case I had malaria. She knew that malaria sent so many Afghans to their deaths every day, so she soon sold her only treasure, a golden ring my father had bought for her when they got married. She took me to the only hospital that was semi-active. I was hospitalised for some time but, yet again, survived.

One day my father came back from Kabul. When he saw our living state, he once again chose to take us back to the warzones of Kabul and have us under his protection. My mother too said she could not look after us alone. However, Merza Kaka decided not to take his family back, as the war was still fierce in Kabul. Once more we moved to Macroryan. We had to accept the war and the brutality as everyday components of our life.

My mother's youngest sister (Suraya Khala) had married and her husband decided to leave Afghanistan as there was no sign that the war would end any time soon. He took Suraya Khala and tried to cross the border between Afghanistan and Iran illegally. Thousands of Afghans fled their homes into Iran and Pakistan every day without knowing how they would survive there. My mother had to watch with tearful eyes while her younger sister left home and walked towards an unknown land. Soon after her sister left, another terrible event occurred to their eldest brother. Farzana was not happy with her husband. Farzana had a romantic relationship with a young man who lived in her neighbourhood. After some months he asked her to elope with him to Pakistan, and he would marry her and bring her two children along later. Farzana was too young to know the repercussion of deserting her husband and going with someone else. She believed the young man and ran away from her husband. However, the young man just wanted to take advantage of her. Soon rumours spread everywhere that Farzana had disappeared. Most believed that the Mujahidin had kidnapped her and some thought she might have run away from her husband. This devilish man kept Farzana for a few days with him and then one morning ran off and left her alone. She had nowhere else to go but to her husband's house. It was obvious to everyone that Farzana would be killed either by her husband or her father or brothers. Everyone considered that she should be stoned. The Imam too confirmed that Farzana should be stoned in public. Everyone tortured and beat Farzana day and night for what she had done. She left no honour for her family. Women refused to talk to her or look at her face as they considered that she was sinful.

However, Farzana's mother knew that this was her and her husband's fault because they had married their extremely young daughter to an elderly man. She cried and begged her husband not to allow anyone to kill their daughter. After a while Farzana's father also accepted that it was his fault.

My uncle took his children and moved from Jalalabad to Kabul and pretended that he would not hurt Farzana. Farzana and her parents also moved to Kabul since Jalalabad was no longer safe for her, and they rented a house in Macroryan. Everything seemed fine for a while. Farzana's parents believed their daughter would be safe now. However, my uncle first claimed that Farzana had no rights to see her children and warned everyone not to allow this to happen any more. That was the only punishment that he had given so far and then he remained silent. My uncle's behaviour seemed peculiar to everyone. His wife had brought enormous shame into his life and yet he was silent. Some considered him a coward for letting his wife live.

The war did not end. But, in 1994, Pakistan was fed up with its favoured man. Gulbudin Hekmatyar with all his brutality wasn't even good in a battle either, despite the weapons that flowed to him from Pakistan. He lost almost all of the battles to other factions. So Pakistan looked elsewhere for someone to achieve its nasty ambitions in Afghanistan.

A GIFT FROM EMPIRE OF AMERICA FOR ME

A Gift from the Empire of America for Me

In the spring of 1994, my father enrolled Tariq, Arif and I into a war-torn school. The war was not over yet, but our father was very concerned about our education. My parents were not the only ones who decided to send their children to school in the warzone: so many people began sending their children to the ruined schools, as they realised that there would be no end to the war in Afghanistan.

Our teacher was a woman. She told us to stand before the students and introduce ourselves. Tariq introduced himself then it was my turn. As I stood I said, 'My name is Laiq.' (Intelligent). All my classmates burst into laughter.

The teacher looked at me and said, 'Who chose this bizarre name for you?' I replied that it was my parents who had chosen it. She said 'Ask your parents, was that the only name left in the world?' The students ridiculed me and called me Tanbal (lazy or idle), the opposite of my name.

For the first time ever I held a book in my hands. I opened the book and saw pictures of weapons on most pages. Afghan children were the only ones whose books were filled with pictures of weapons and terrible ideas and these books came all the way from the land of democracy, freedom and human rights – America! The millions of books that the United States government created in the university of Nebraska for Afghan children to radicalise them against the Soviets in the 1980s were now used all over Afghanistan and in Pakistani refugee camps. All the books that existed before the war had vanished and these new books took their place because they glorified Mujahidin and their medieval ideology.

School was very interesting for me. Girls and boys of my own age studied with me in the same class. I'd to go and stand behind the school door an hour before other children turned up. I loved school more than home, until one day when the teacher asked me to repeat the previous lesson and I failed.

Teachers carried fresh tree branches with them. Our teacher had a thick, long branch. When I failed to repeat the lesson, she hit me with the branch. The pain was great and I burst into tears before my classmates. All of them laughed at me and some called me a coward. The teacher no longer called me Laiq. Now the teacher called me the very same name that my classmates addressed me as – Tanbal.

My father could only earn enough to feed us. The winter was about to arrive and we needed firewood to survive the extremely cold weather. My mother asked Tariq and I to collect wood, just as we did in Khugyani. When Tariq and I came from school, we had to take our bags and go in search for firewood. We spent the rest of the day searching for wood.

We wandered far from home in search of firewood every day. Our heads were down, our eyes fixed on the floor so as not to miss a single piece. Several other neighbouring children went with us and we became very good friends. In our spare time we played marbles and football. I loved to play football and marbles, they were my favourite hobbies. I had worn-out my shoes playing football and had no others. My father could not afford to buy me new shoes. I had to walk barefoot. I even played football barefoot. Often there were several wounds all over my feet.

Each time when I went to school, the teacher would ask me to repeat the previous lesson, I could not. There were times when the teacher's tree branch broke in several pieces when she hit me with it. Gradually I began to dislike school, the books and the teacher. I no longer woke up early in the morning and ran to school. Now my mother forced me to go. I fought with the children who called me Tanbal. I enjoyed collecting firewood more than going to school.

Merza Kaka finally returned his family from Jalalabad to Kabul. This time Simaa Khala had painful news to share with my mother. Merza Kaka had changed completely since we left Jalalabad. He began to beat and verbally abuse her on a regular basis. He encouraged my cousins to verbally abuse her, too. He repeatedly told her that she was not good enough for him and he was going to marry a new wife. Simaa Khala was afraid of nothing as much she was afraid of sharing her husband with another woman. She burst into tears and said, 'He is constantly punishing me, without any wrongdoing.'

My parents knew that Merza Kaka was an ill-tempered man. My mother told her that Merza Kaka might be distressed because he was struggling to find bread for them; he would be a nice person once the nasty war came to an end. My mother shared this subject with my father, who was also very anxious about his brother's behaviour towards his wife. In addition to this, my father paid a great deal of respect to Simaa Khala as she was older than him. When Father spoke with Merza Kaka about the subject, my uncle was irritated to talk about his private life with his younger brother. He said that Simaa Khala was his wife and he could do whatever he wanted. He even warned my father not to meddle in his life. This was the start of a break in my father and uncle's brotherhood. Merza Kaka refused to live with us and found a house several miles away.

It was the end of 1994 when my mother gave birth to my second sister. Again, Father was disappointed that she had failed to give him another son. Mother was lucky that at least he did not blame her. A woman who lived a few houses away gave birth to three daughters in succession. The fourth time she gave birth to a female child, her husband blamed her for failing to give him a son. So he used that as a pretext to marry a new wife.

One day my maternal uncle (Farzana's husband) secretly bought a huge machete from a butcher, disguised it under his clothes and went to see his wife. Farzana's father was not at home. My uncle told her mother he wanted to talk with Farzana in private. When she heard this, she became so happy and thought that he might forgive Farzana and take her home, for she was a burden on her parents. So she left them alone and went to a neighbour's house. Poor Farzana also considered that her husband might forgive her and reunite her with her beloved children. However, when my uncle was sure there was no one in the house, he took the sharp machete out and slashed at her until he thought she was dead.

It was afternoon when he entered our house. His clothes were covered with blood. He told my mother that he had just killed Farzana. Mother began screaming and told him to get out. My uncle told her to look after his children until his return and then he left. He went straight to a Mujahidin checkpoint and told them what he had done to his wife. When the Mujahidin heard his story, they told him 'well done' and refused to punish or imprison him at all!

After an hour or two, Farzana's mother decided to check on them. When she put her ear to the door, she failed to pick up any sound so went back in. All she found was her daughter in a pool of her own blood. She screamed and the neighbours came to help. Farzana was taken to the hospital in time but had lost almost all her blood. Her parents gave some of their own blood to save her. Still some of our relatives were angry that Farzana had not died. Women gossiped that Farzana had had an affair with the doctors while she was in the hospital. Poor Farzana was young and did not understand that one mistake could ruin her life forever. She lost her children, her family and almost her life. There was no sympathy for her at all. The worst thing that could happen to someone is to be born female in Afghanistan. Tormented Farzana recovered and continued a life of agony, separated from her two children.

One day Tariq broke his hand in a fight with a boy. Our father took him to the *Charsade Bester* hospital, the only properly equipped hospital in the entire country that was funded through foreign aid. The hospital was crammed with the victims of the Mujahidin factions' war. Tariq was hospitalised there for three months. One day Father took me to the hospital to see him. I was revolted by so many young and disabled children who had been blown up. The hospital was overflowing with wounded people; some by the mines that the Soviet military had sown everywhere and some by the bullets, rockets and missiles that the United States and Soviet Union spread all over Afghanistan.

There was a child in the bed next to Tariq who had lost both his legs from his thighs down. Tariq complained that the child cried very loudly at night when he couldn't bear the pain in his thighs. I greeted the child and he smiled and gave me one of his apples. I asked him how he lost his legs. He said he stepped on a mine in their garden.

Each time I visited Tariq, the child shared his fruit with me until one day there was another child who had lost both his arms and legs in a rocket explosion. There were so many injuries on his face. When I looked at him, he frightened me. The next time my father told me to go with him to see Tariq I refused.

The neighbourhood children stole copper and aluminium cables from the ruined factories to sell. Most of the children stopped collecting firewood and started plundering cables from factories and power stations instead. Father warned me not to play with those children any more. Because Tariq was in the hospital, I now went alone to collect wood. One evening, when I returned from searching for firewood, I spotted some people who had gathered in one of our neighbour's house. I knew at that time that all neighbourhood men gathered around when someone was killed. A child used to collect wood with us but when he started to steal copper and aluminium, he stopped collecting firewood. One day he mistook an explosive device for copper or aluminium and hoped he could sell it. But the device blasted him apart, tearing him into pieces and badly injuring three other children who were nearby.

Every day many Afghans were killed either by mines or unexploded devices, in addition to those killed by the Mujahidin. A mine awareness organisation came into our school to warn children against the toy-shaped mines that the Soviet military sowed into Afghanistan in their millions. They issued leaflets to all students in our ruined school. There were mines in the shapes of butterflies, pins, nails and other children's toys. There were stories and pictures of Afghan children who had lost parts of their bodies because of these mines. The teacher read a story of a girl who was six years old who had lost both her arms and the sight in both her eyes when she picked up a butterfly-mine. There were so many heart-wrenching stories of Afghan children who were victims of Soviet mines and other explosives. They showed us a movie of children who had been injured.

Each one of those Afghan children permanently maimed by mines and explosives had long lives to live. The people who did this were enjoying their comfortable lives far away so that the cries and pains of these children did not reach them. Not even those civilised nations who elected these monsters as their leaders could see what they had done. Some spread mines all over Afghanistan, and some brought propaganda textbooks that were filled with violence to radicalise them. Their weapons killed or maimed millions of men, women and children without them knowing of their wrongdoings.

The Taliban

It was one evening in mid 1994 when we were eating dinner and, for the first time, my father mentioned the word 'Taliban'. He said the Taliban had taken Kandahar Province from the Mujahidin and were growing rapidly in the southern part of Afghanistan. Soon this would free the whole of Afghanistan from the cruelties of the Mujahidin factions. In the following few months everyone was talking about them. There were different tales about Mullah Mohammad Omer, the invisible leader of the Taliban. The story that people told each other in our area was that he fought very bravely against the Soviet Union. When the Soviets had been defeated he put his weapon down, as he was also an Imam, and went to the outskirts of Kandahar and began guiding people towards Islam, teaching children the Quran. One day, when he was walking from the mosque towards his house, he noticed a group of Mujahidin had taken women by force to their base and sexually abused them. Mullah Mohammad Omer went to his house and slept. Then the Prophet Muhammad called upon him to stand against this evil force. He told this story to his fellow clerics and they all decided to assault the Mujahidin base. They killed them all. And that is how they started fighting against the Mujahidin. Afghans considered them as their saviours from the cruelty and barbarism of the Mujahidin.

Who really were the Taliban and who created their empire? Who funded this huge organisation and its wars for years? It is widely believed all over the world that the Pakistani and Saudi governments and their secret services formed the Taliban. But, is it true? Benazir Bhutto was the prime minister of Pakistan when the Taliban empire first appeared. A lot of people accused her regime of creating the savage empire of the Taliban. Some people even call her the mother of the Taliban. But she herself crudely said that the Taliban had been established and emerged according to the United Kingdom's plan, US directorship, Saudi money, and Pakistan was the executor.[20] In 2009 Asif Ali Zardari, the current president of Pakistan, said in his interview with an

American TV channel that the ISI and CIA created the Taliban.[21] Today, if one asks an Afghan child, 'who created the savage empire of the Taliban?', the Afghan child would point its finger at the United States government and its allies. Powerful intelligence services of the United States, Great Britain, Saudi Arabia, Pakistan and several other western and non-western allies of the United States were the architects of the Taliban, to achieve their objectives in the region. Long before the catastrophic events of 9/11, the US and its allies were working for the domination of the dreamland of the empires.

Most of the Taliban fighters were those children who fled their country during the Soviet-Afghan war into Pakistan, where they had been radicalised into the Pakistani Madrasas for over a decade. They were all completely brainwashed and their minds had been filled with a perilous ideology. Most of them did not even have a glimmer about Afghanistan and its past. However, everyone was happy for the Taliban to come and save them from the Mujahidin's brutality and oppression. Pashtuns welcomed the Taliban into their villages. They wanted rid of the militias and warlords who had oppressed and terrified them on a daily basis. Most warlords shifted from the Mujahidin to the Taliban side everywhere the Taliban went. The Taliban were defeating the Mujahidin in most battles. As they were swiftly expanding everywhere in Afghanistan, the Mujahidin began to tremble at their arrival. Gulbudin Hekmatyar no longer received the cargos of weapons from Pakistan; now these weapons went to the Taliban.

My father could not afford to pay the house rent. So we found a semi-ruined house just beside Merza Kaka's house to live for free. My mother was once again very happy to be reunited with Simaa Khala, her best friend. We hired a donkey cart to carry our clothes to the new house. The donkey was very young and feeble. It seemed like it had not been fed properly. Our clothes overloaded the cart. The owner of the donkey had a thick cable with him and reminded me of my teacher. The donkey owner was much heavier than the poor and malnutritioned donkey but he jumped on top of the donkey and lashed it on the back with his cable, and the donkey began to tow the cart, but with a lot of trouble. It seemed like the owner was pulling the cart, not the donkey, as he was so big that he concealed the poor donkey underneath himself. My family and I followed them. After some time, the donkey would not move unless the owner flogged it several times on the back with his heartless cable.

After a while the donkey fell to the ground. The owner forced his donkey to stand up. He once again began flogging the poor donkey to move. The donkey began moving once more, but this time the owner did not sit on top of it. The donkey could not tow the cart any more unless the owner flogged it viciously. Again, the poor animal fell to the earth and was not able to stand. The owner flogged the poor donkey again and again to make it stand and move on, but it did not have enough energy to do either. Therefore, it remained on the floor and had to endure the painful blows from the cable. Its owner was determined to force it to stand and move by repeatedly flogging the poor thing. The owner terrified me; I thought he was going to kill the donkey the way he was flogging it. I began crying and told my father to stop the man. My father told the man to stop flogging the donkey and they would pull the cart together. My father and the man carried the cart for the rest of the journey.

Our new house was only 15 or 20 metres away from Simaa Khala's. The villagers welcomed us and help us unload the clothes. A woman brought food for us. She said to my mother that the whole village was very friendly and nobody ever quarrelled with others, apart from one family. She pointed at Merza Kaka's compound.

My mother was surprised and asked her, 'Why aren't they good?'

The women said, 'The man beats his wife perpetually and all the neighbours hear her cries. Several times the village men gathered and went to talk with him and told him not to beat his wife, but he did not listen to anyone. He even sometimes threw his wife out of the house onto the street and locked the compound door. She stayed outside the door for several hours and begged her husband to allow her inside the compound. Nobody knows why he beats her all the time.'

Hearing this, my mother began crying, and ran towards Simaa Khala's house. When she reached her, she began shouting at Simaa Khala, 'Why do you sit quiet in the fire and let it burn you?'

Simaa Khala understood what my mother was talking about. She replied, 'Then what else could I do apart from sitting quiet?' Simaa Khala told her sister that sometimes Merza Kaka told her to leave his house and children. Simaa Khala burst into tears and said, 'They are my children too, how I can leave my children and where would I go?' She showed my mother the scars and bruises all over her body. She also talked about the long and chilly nights that she spent outside the locked door of the house. She asked Mother to ask Father to speak with his brother to stop beating her all the time for no reason. She warned my mother that if life carried on like this, then she would prefer to pour fuel over herself and set it alight.

My father sat with Merza Kaka and asked him to stop beating Simaa Khala. However, once again Merza Kaka told my father not to interfere in his life. Merza Kaka repeatedly warned Simaa Khala that he would bring a new wife into the house. Each time he said this she was terrified. Merza Kaka did not have enough money to buy a new wife for himself, but the never-ending war produced innumerable widows all across Afghanistan and he could easily bring one into his house.

Our new house was miles away from school. We had to walk for more than one-and-a-half-hours to get there. Our class started at ten o'clock in the morning and finished at one-thirty in the afternoon. It was not a problem getting to school; I would leave at eight o'clock when the weather was cooler. However, on the way back home it was very difficult for us to walk such a long distance in the summer when the climate was very hot. I did not have shoes or sandals so the hot earth burned the soles of my feet. It took us more than two hours to get back home from school. I did not like school at all because my classmates and teacher mocked me. Everyone forgot my real name; they all knew me as Tanbal.

One day I told my parents that I did not want to go to school any more. It really roused their anger. Both my parents tore at my hair. My mother was illiterate. She told me, 'Study my son, if not you will regret it when you are older.'

My father said, 'Knowledge is a sea of wealth, take as much as you can out of it. The more you take the better your life will be.'

Tariq, my older brother, was the one amongst us who really had a passion for school. Arif and I did not even like to walk in the direction of the school. There were too many students in our class, so the headmaster decided to split us into two classes. Arif and I remained in the same class, but Tariq had been picked for the new class. Now there was no one to tell our parents how badly we were doing.

Merza Kaka and my father left home at seven o'clock to go to work. Once they had gone, Simaa Khala prepared a big pot of green tea and came to our house for half a day talking, laughing and drinking tea with my mother. There were no good moments in the Afghans' lives since the arrival of the Cold War. Simaa Khala and Mother usually took refuge in their childhood memories. They would talk for hours about their lives then and make each other laugh. Sometimes they would shed bitter tears for their siblings who fled the country into Iran.

A bitch and her puppies all starved to death in my father's working place, apart from one. My father brought the only surviving puppy home. He had an arrow-shaped marking on his forehead. There is a widely superstitious belief amongst Afghans that a dog should not be kept in the house, as angels come down from the heavens on Thursday nights into peoples houses to bring blessings, but they do not come into the house where there is a dog. This was because dogs could see them.

But my father did not believe that angels would not come down into our house if we kept a poor and hungry puppy. Tariq, Arif, Sarah and I spent much of our time looking after him. Tariq chose the name of our previous dog– Palang. We all had to take turns to play with him. He was a very charming puppy that everyone wanted to spend time with. We could not afford to buy meat very often, only once every one or two months. When my mother cooked it for us, everyone, apart from my parents, gave half of their meat to Palang. He learned something amazing that entertained my siblings and me. When someone threw something away, he went to bring it back. So we threw our hats away and he would bring them back for us. When my siblings, cousins and I fought or quarrelled with one another, Palang would come and bark and even bite us if we did not stop fighting.

One evening my siblings and I were playing with Palang when our neighbour knocked on our door. She said to my mother that Simaa Khala was being beaten by her husband. My mother ran towards Simaa Khala's house, by the time she arrived to her compound Merza Kaka had already thrown Simaa Khala out. Mother did not dare to ask Merza Kaka why he beat her sister constantly; she knew he was a very bad-tempered man. She took her sister's hand and brought her into our house, asking her why she was being beaten.

Simaa Khala had several chickens in their compound; one of the chickens slipped out of the coop and ruined a few tomato plants that Merza Kaka had planted in the yard, so Merza Kaka blamed Simaa Khala for being irresponsible. She had several wounds on her body, but the one she had on her hand was the most extreme. Her hand was covered in blood, as if she had dipped it into a bucket of red paint.

Merza Kaka had entirely changed. He no longer paid respect to anyone. All the village men and women hated him. He was impatient to marry a new wife. Day after day, the fresh air of remarrying entered Merza Kaka's nose. All my siblings and I were so scared of him. When we played with my cousins, it sometimes ended up in fighting and then they complained to their father and he would come and beat us. When we complained to our father, he would say that it's fine, children do fight sometimes, but he did not like Merza Kaka beating his children.

One day Tariq and Akmal fought with each other. Tariq scratched Akmal's face. That night my father did not come home, as he stayed at work one night a week. When Merza Kaka came back from work, Akmal cried and told his father that Tariq had beaten him. It was almost evening; Tariq and I were playing marbles with the other village children in the fields when Merza Kaka shouted at both of us to come to him. I did not know what was going on, but I did know that Merza Kaka only spoke with us when he wanted to beat us. Tariq knew what was going on, so he told me to run away. Tariq was in front and I was following him and when Merza Kaka saw that we had disobeyed him, he became more frustrated. He chased us for quite a long distance until we were far away from home. We did not know where we were. We concealed ourselves in a compound that had been destroyed by a rocket, but someone had turned it into a pottery. Merza Kaka came and looked around, but he failed to find us. When we were sure that he had gone, we tried to find our way home.

We were on the way out of the ruined pottery when we heard a voice ask, 'Who are you?' I was scared as I thought it was Merza Kaka, but when I turned my face I saw that it was an old man who had lost his sight in a Mujahidin bomb explosion. He was the owner of the pottery and he regularly came to our village with his young son holding his hand to sell his marvellous pots. Tariq replied that we had lost our way and by mistake had entered his compound. By this time his son had arrived too. He knew us because when he came into our village with his father, my cousins, siblings and I used to surround them and look at their remarkable handmade dishes. Sometimes we tried to touch their pots and the boy became irritated and chased us all away.

Tariq asked his son how to find the way back to our village. He was such a brilliant boy; he walked with us for a great distance and guided us. It was nine o'clock in the evening by the time we arrived home. My mother was looking for us everywhere, checking all the neighbours' houses. The kids told her that Merza Kaka chased us away somewhere. It was the first time we had gone so far from the house and remained outside until late at night. We entered the house and my mother beat both of us for fighting with Akmal, despite knowing that Merza Kaka was a very ill-tempered person. Tariq and I went to bed without any dinner.

Early in the morning, while everyone was asleep, we heard knocks on the door. The door was locked. We all knew who was knocking so my mother refused to open it. Tariq, a very brave boy, asked, 'Who are you?'

'It is me, open the door!' It was Merza Kaka.

Tariq said, 'I am not going to open the door for you, since you are going to beat me.'

'If you don't open the door, then I am going to break the door down and get you!' shouted Merza Kaka.

This time we all sensed the anger in his voice. None of us wanted him to break down the door, because without a door it would be very hard to live, as there were so many burglars looking for an opportunity. Therefore, my mother went and opened the door for him to come in and she knew that Merza Kaka only wanted to come to punish Tariq and perhaps me too. However, as Merz Kaka entered the compound, he saw that Tariq was standing right before him. Without saying a word, he slapped Tariq in the face. Merza Kaka kicked him with his boots again and again. We could do nothing but watch.

Whenever my siblings and I were faced with any kind of difficulty my mother would help us. So Tariq went hid behind our mother, but she could not save him this time. He was trapped in the compound and Merza Kaka beat him with his punches and kicks and slaps. Mother told me to run away, otherwise, when he had finished with Tariq it would be my turn. I did as I was told. I ran towards the fields, but Tariq's cries followed me. I heard Tariq's cries for a long time. Merza Kaka beat Tariq until he got too tired to carry on. When I came back Tariq was black and blue around his eyes and face and my mother was putting a hot cloth onto his bruises. My father came home in the evening and as he entered the compound I told him what had happened. When he looked at Tariq's face he was so enraged that he dropped the bag of food on the floor and ran towards Merza Kaka's compound. He entered Merza Kaka's compound, but found that Merza Kaka had not come back from duty yet. My father wanted to beat Akmal to take out on him his own son's revenge. When he found Akmal, he controlled his wrath and did not harm him.

One afternoon we heard a massive explosion, it sounded like the entire sky had fallen down. All our window glass shattered into pieces and we all took cover. After a few moments we went out and saw a dark, dusty cloud rise from the direction we had escaped on that day when Merza Kaka had chased us. Everyone from our village ran towards the explosion to help those who had been killed or injured. Tariq and I asked for permission from Mother to go and help and she allowed us. We ran towards the scene of the explosion. When we reached it, we found that the rocket had ruined the entire village. People were searching for survivors who were buried under their homes. The rocket landed exactly where Tariq and I had hidden ourselves the other day. The blind man was screaming, 'Where is my family!' He had been in the mosque when he heard the explosion. Nobody knew what type of rocket it was. Some said that it was a scud missile, since it had wiped out a whole village. No one knew why, as there was no presence of any faction groups. Kabul airport was also miles from the village.

I stood near the blind man, who was screaming for his family. The rocket had killed them all, including his son who ran the pottery as well as being the eyes of the blind man. Nevertheless, I took his hand and sat him down on the dirt. I did not know whether he was crying or not, since I could not see any tears falling from his eyes, so I asked Tariq. He said he is crying, but because he is blind his eyes cannot create tears. I left the poor blind man there with his own pain and went to see what else had happened. That was when I saw the most shocking and painful tragedy that any human being could ever see. My eyes widened and the tiny hairs on my body stood on end when I saw a man holding a little girl's headless body. He was screaming and repeatedly saying 'Oh, God what was this little girl's fault!' When I saw that terrible scene, my body refused to listen to my mind and my legs ran back towards our village. I was so frightened that I could not tell my mother what I had seen. The headless body of that little girl was before my eyes all the time. At night I could not sleep; my mind was locked on that horrific scene. A few days later we were playing in the field when another rocket hit a house in our village. Miraculously this time nobody was killed.

A month later I saw the same old, blind man struggling to find his way to our village alone, with a bag fastened to his back. The children in the village ran towards him and guided him. He sat where he usually sat with his son and the people came to buy his pottery from him. I told my mother about the poor man. My mother took cooked eggplant with Naan and gave it to him. From all over the village people came and expressed their condolences. Women even cried for the elderly man's state. However, at the end of the day, he walked back towards his village. I was thinking in bed before I slept: How hard must it be for this old man to live alone? Who will cook for him? Who will guide him around? Who will show him the mosque? How painful is it for him to sit in the room and not hear the voices of his family?

The Mujahidin filled men's, women's and children's hearts with horror and terror. I was awfully scared of them. Whenever I saw them I would run towards my home. The textbooks that the United States provided for us lied to us. They said good things about the Mujahidin. The books praised Afghan Mujahidin, but I knew that it was not true as I could see what they were doing in Afghanistan. People were tired with what the Mujahidin were doing. We were living under their violence, but no one knew how long their oppression and brutality would continue.

My Feeble Body Trembled All Winter Long

The weather was cold and Afghans were extremely anxious as to whether they would survive through the vicious winter or not. My father somehow managed to buy a bag of coal to keep us warm. The firewood we had collected would not last more than a few weeks, but the winter lasted for three months. Winter was another killer of Afghan children. Gas and fuel was scarce. People began to destroy Afghanistan's gorgeous jungles and use them as fuel. Wood was highly expensive so only the Mujahidin's family could afford to buy it. My mother was anxious for all of us. She had already kept enough opium for us to take in the snowy nights. I did not have shoes or sandals. I could no longer walk outside the house, as the earth began to freeze. My mother repeatedly sewed my other siblings' sandals. Sometimes I begged Tariq and Arif to lend me theirs so that I could play with the children in the village. Mostly they refused, as they were worried that they too might be imprisoned in the house like me if they wore their sandals out.

It was late one afternoon when the snow began to fall. Each flake brought another chunk of misery and sorrow into this war-torn country. Most mud houses could not resist the snow or the rain, as they had already been worn out by the previous bombardment of rockets, bombs and bullets.

When it snowed in Afghanistan, before the arrival of the Cold War, Afghan children ran into the streets and cheered and played in the snow. Men and women stared at snowflakes through their windows and the elders said that snow brought more water and prosperity. Peasants were as jubilant as they were in the harvest time. My family cooked *Shurwaa-e-Gusht-e khushk* and sometimes *Shalgham Shurwaa* to celebrate the coming of the snow.

Since the empires of the Soviet Union and the United States came into Afghanistan all those beautiful customs and visions had melted into the flames of war. New, brutal practises took their place. Nothing but pleasing tales left from the peaceful Afghanistan.

Parents sat with their children and talked for hours about the Afghanistan that had not seen the ugly face of war and violence. My parents too sat with us as we gathered around them and they told us wonderful tales about the peaceful Afghanistan for hours. My father described with so much clarity each beauty of the Afghanistan he had once known that, when I closed my eyes, I could picture them all through his colourful words. I could see its beautiful cities, gardens, villages, farmlands, valleys and high mountains crammed with flowers and elegant people. I was in the peaceful Afghanistan for as long as my father's tales lasted.

Once he stopped telling those tales and I opened my eyes and looked around, I could no longer see it. There was not a sign of the peaceful Afghanistan left to support my father's tales. His stories were about a different Afghanistan located somewhere else; not where I was born. My Afghanistan was different and I could see its ugliness through my own eyes. Its mountains, hills and valleys were crammed with mines, painted with the blood of people, and the dark smoke of the sick men's weapons rose from them. Its gardens were burned and filled with graves. Its air was packed with the dark clouds of rockets and all sorts of brutal weapons that sick technologists had invented. Its inhabitants were terrifyingly oppressed and tormented. Hearts were filled with pain and sorrow. The people who lived in my Afghanistan were those beastly looking men who had Kalashnikovs and rocket launchers on their shoulders and those who were maimed or mournful or who had lost parents or children in the endless war.

Three weeks passed, but the snow refused to cease. My father went looking for food for us, but someone had to climb on the rooftop and sweep the snow off before it collapsed and buried us all alive.

My mother could not climb onto the rooftop to sweep the snow off because she was a woman and if strange men saw her face it would become a problem. Tariq had to climb and sweep almost a metre of snow from the rooftop every morning and evening. Mother would ask him to climb down and then ask me to put Tariq's sandals on my feet and sweep the rooftop. The pain that coldness inflicted upon all of my body was really intense. I screamed for my mother to bring me down. Tariq had to climb back up and sweep the rest of the snow off while his tears turned to ice on his face. This suffering lasted almost every day for three months. My teeth chattered and my body trembled incessantly during that harsh winter.

We could not warm the house with the firewood Tariq and I collected as it was not much and we could only burn very little of it during the night. The temperature reached 18 to 20 degrees below zero. Mother asked us to sit closer to one another and cover ourselves with the blankets to keep warm. Our cousins also came into our house and sat amongst us to keep themselves warm and sometimes Simaa Khala and Mother told tales to entertain us. Tariq sometimes insisted on bringing Palang into the room as it was very cold outside. Although Palang had a den in the corner of the yard, Tariq could not see him suffer. He sometimes cried that Palang might die in the snow.

Sometimes Tariq and Arif went outside and played snowball fighting with the other village boys and I'd to cry to my mother to buy shoes for me so that I could play with them too. She asked me a question each time I cried for shoes, 'Your father does not earn enough to feed your stomach; so how can he buy shoes for you?'

In the midwinter, apart from Tariq and my parents, everyone caught whooping cough. My father collected a type of mountain herb in the summer, which he believed healed whooping cough. Mother boiled it in water and forced us to drink its juice. It was awfully bitter, which none of us liked. All sorts of herbs failed to heal our whooping cough, but there was a drug which my mother believed could cure any winter disease, opium. My father was very anxious about this wonderful drug, since he knew how harmful it could be for us. He only suggested opium when our illness was intense. As we took opium, our bodies began sweating and it felt like we were sitting beside a fire, despite the weather being freezing cold.

At last the winter circle passed and we prepared for it to come again. The New Year arrived in Afghanistan, but it was just any other day accompanied by the same bloodshed, hunger, disease and brutality. The Taliban rapidly moved towards Kabul and the Mujahidin tried to stop them. However, the Taliban's rockets arrived in Kabul first. Their rockets fell everywhere and killed powerless Afghans. But, people's hearts were filled with hope that the Taliban would come and save them.

School started and I had to go again to a place I despised. This time Tariq, Arif and I were not the only children to go from our village. A new boy whose parents recently returned from Pakistan's refugee camps joined us. His name was Hekmat and he was slightly older than me. His father enrolled him in our school and he chose to join my class.

When I walked to school, it felt like someone was taking me by force into a prison. Sometimes I refused to go. Mother did not get mad at any of the mischief that I committed as much as she got mad when I refused to go to school. She first begged me to go to school or if she had food in the house, she would offer it to me to bribe me. When nothing worked, she would take a tree branch and flog me until I ran to school. Arif too was like me. He hated school even more than I did. We tormented our mother every morning. She had to deal with us individually. She tried to avoid flogging us, but when nothing else worked, flogging was the last option. Arif and I were doing badly in school lessons. When the teacher gave us homework, we never fulfilled it. Some children learned reading and writing in the second grade, including Tariq, but Arif and I could not even write our own names. Every day our teacher tortured us with the tree branch, usually twice in the same day: once, when the teacher checked all students' homework, which we did not complete; and the second time when she asked all students to read the previous lesson. After a while neither our teacher nor students bothered to call Arif by his name. They called both of us Tanbal, even outside class and school, which embarrassed us very much. Hekmat was the only one who called us by our true names. And that is how our friendship began. He even quarrelled with others who called us Tanbal.

My mother prepared for the following winter from the very beginning. She sent Tariq and me to look for firewood as soon as we arrived home from school. The sun was burning, but we had to wander about in fields and villages and pick up tiny bits of wood. Many times we came across mines and unexploded devices, but Tariq knew what to do in this kind of situation. First he would shout very loudly, 'Mine! Mine! Mine!' And then he would trace back over his own footsteps and inform the elders of the location. He learned this in school from a mine clearing organisation. What we were doing was highly dangerous. Kabul was filled with mines and unexploded devices, and every day large numbers fell victim of them.

My mother was not the only one who sent her children under the burning sun in search of firewood, every mother in our village sent her children to find wood, plastic and old clothes or any other material that could be burned. As there were so many children who were in search of the very same items that Tariq and I were, we could find very little, or sometimes nothing. We explored every corner of the villages and fields for almost two months, but we found very little. We went many miles away from our house in the hope that we could find wood or some other burning materials, but everywhere had been searched by others.

We told our mother that we could no longer find firewood anywhere and there was no reason we should look for it. My mother knew that the entire village's parents sent their children after firewood. So she told us not to go in search for firewood any more. We were free! For several weeks we could play in the village with the other children after we returned from school. I was amongst the very few children in our village who had mastered marble playing. I won almost every child's marbles when they played me. My marbles were priceless and I kept them close at all times.

One day Tariq and I were playing marbles when our mother called us. She had made two buckets out of two old oilcans, one for Tariq and the other for me. We did not understand what she wanted us to do with the buckets. She told us that we have to look for a new burning material that others do not look for.

Mother told us to go and gather cattle dung. At first we thought she must be joking, but soon found out that she was not. She told us that if we did not collect cattle dung then we might freeze to death in the coming winter.

Both Tariq and I refused to start this disgusting job. But after a while we agreed. We took our buckets and walked towards the fields. After looking for several hours, Tariq at last found a huge, fresh, cow dung. Tariq asked me to pick it up. The greenish colour was disgusting. I refused. Tariq and I argued with each other over who should pick it up. Neither he picked it up, nor did I. We both sat beside it. After some time, Tariq came up with an idea. He said if I was to find a piece of plastic or a plastic bag then he would use it as glove and pick up the dung.

We were in a field and it was not possible to find any plastic, so I had to walk all the way to the village to find some. I found a plastic bag and took it back to Tariq. He covered his hand in the plastic bag, using it as a glove. He closed his eyes, dipped his hand in, picked up half, and put it in his bucket. He suddenly threw the plastic bag away and ran away from the dung, complaining that it smelt terrible. He then came back and told me to put the used plastic bag on my hand and pick up the rest of it. Once again I refused to pick it up. This time Tariq ran out of patience and threatened to beat me. I had no option but to pick the rest of the dung up. At first it really was hard for us to do, but we got used to it. Just in the same way we got used to the war, hunger, bloodshed, suffering and other miseries.

At the height of the summer I had to walk over the burning earth barefoot to school and chase cattle. One day my father promised that he would buy a pair of shoes for me for the coming winter, if I studied my lessons and achieved good grades in my exams. What my father demanded from me was close to impossible. Day after day, the gap between me and school and books became wider. Arif and I really were tired of being bullied by the students and flogged by the teacher every day.

One day our teacher came into the class with a thick power-cable. She said that from now on she would no longer punish lazy students with a tree branch; instead she would punish them with her new cable. The teacher asked me to hold out my palm. I opened the palm of my right hand and the teacher struck it with her cruel cable. I thought every single bone in my hand had broken into pieces. I began weeping, but it failed to soften her heart. She asked me to hold out my left hand palm. I refused to do it, which irritated her, so she began lashing me all over. Each time the cable struck me it felt like the flesh was falling of my body. I screamed and cried so loud that it brought other teachers into the classroom to see what was going on. The other teachers asked my teacher to forgive me this time, but she refused. She once again asked me to hold out the palm of my hand. I much preferred to be flogged on the palm of my hand rather than all over my body. She gave me ten flogs on the right hand and ten on the left hand. The pain remained in both of my hands for the rest of the day.

It was then Arif's turn. As the teacher flogged him, he began crying and also refused to hold his palm out again. The teacher lashed him all over too. Arif tried to escape from the teacher's cable blows and ran towards the end of the classroom. He trapped himself in the corner of the class and had no way to escape, which made it easy for the teacher to whip him.

Our teacher was really angry at us. We never completed our homework or managed to learn everyday lessons. The teacher warned us that if we did not do our homework and learn our lessons, then she would punish as until we 'vomited our mother's milk we had drunk when as babies'. We could not fulfil our homework since we did not know how to read and write. We did not tell our father, since he too would tear at our hairs. The next day Arif and I refused to go to school. My mother, as usual, first peacefully told us to go to school. When we refused, she took the tree branch that she kept for us. But before she flogged us, we decided to go. Arif and I knew what the teacher would do to us again, as neither had done our homework nor remembered the previous lesson. We certainly did not want to taste the pain of the teacher's new cable again. As we got closer to school the fear of the teacher's cable grew bigger. An idea floated into my mind, but it seemed too wicked so at first I did not mention it to Arif, but as we were nearing the school I decided to share it with him.

I said, 'Let's not go to school, instead let's roam the villages.' Arif was ready to do anything to avoid the teacher's punishment. So, for the first time in our lives we played truant. We spent half of the day wandering from one village to another until one o'clock in the afternoon, and then walked back towards home alongside the other students. The second day we did the same thing. We wandered around until it was the right time to return home so that Mother did not suspect anything. We did not go to school for a whole month. Arif and I became anxious. We were afraid of Hekmat, because he was our classmate as well as living in our village. We were concerned that he might tell our parents.

Hekmat himself was equally as idle as Arif and I were in school, and he too was punished by the teacher almost daily. But he did not think of playing truant. Arif and I warned him not to tell our parents what we were up to. To some extent Hekmat was afraid of Arif and me since he was alone and we were two, so he remained silent. After a while Arif and I visited the school to see what was happening there. As we entered the class, we caught everyone's attention. The teacher looked at both of us and asked, 'Why are you two cheating your parents? Why didn't you tell your parents that you are not capable of learning? Ask your parents to take you both to a mechanic or a carpenter to teach you a skill. It will be better for both of you to leave school and learn a craft; otherwise, if you don't learn the lesson that I teach you and don't fulfil the homework I give you, I will keep punishing both of you every day until you run away from my class and never come back.'

In 1995 the emergence of the Taliban planted a new seed of hope in the hearts of the most exploited and oppressed nation on the planet. Once again millions of mothers whose hearts were badly wounded wiped their tearful eyes and eagerly looked forward to the arrival of the Taliban. Even some refugees began returning home in the hope of starting a new life under their protection. Thousands of students who studied in Pakistani Madrasas flowed back into Afghanistan and took up weapons to fight the Mujahidin. The Mujahidin factions trembled at the swift rise of the Taliban. Once again they gathered together to fight their new enemy.

It was an era of hope. Children flocked together in the villages and made up tales about the generosity and heroism of the Taliban. Children in our village would divide into two groups and play the role of the Taliban and the Mujahidin. The Taliban were the good guys and the Mujahidin the bad. Women talked amongst themselves inside the compounds. Men in mosques talked for hours. It seemed that this endless night of oppression had come to an end.

Mothers began to sing to their thirsty, hungry and unclothed children:

> *My children cry not, Uncle Talib is coming!*
>
> *Sit silent, endure the pain of hunger, Uncle Talib is coming!*
>
> *The dark night of oppression and bloodshed is almost over, Uncle Talib is coming!*
>
> *My children look, it is dawn, in the morning Uncle Talib is coming!*
>
> *Fear not the demons, for Uncle Talib is coming!*

Tariq carried his textbooks and notebooks with him when we were in search of cattle dung. So he could study and do his homework. I had made so many friends since my mother gave me the task of following the cattle. Most were cattle-herders. These boys had an old ball so we played football or *Tup Danda*. Football and *Tup Danda* made me hungry as I was running a lot during the games. Food was not available in our house all the time. Mother baked few Naans and cooked vegetables only once in twenty-four hours. We had to eat half of the vegetables at lunch and the other half at dinner. For breakfast, we had Naan and tea (*Naan-e Chai*). My mother kept the leftover Naan in a basket and hung it from the ceiling so that my siblings and I could not reach it, and she would save it for the next lunch. There was no eating in our house apart from those three particular times. Sometimes I had to sit quiet beside Tariq and refuse to play with the kids, as I did not want to get hungry after the game. Sometimes walking itself was a big problem with a starving and shrunken stomach. In the morning the *Naan-e Chai* we ate did not give enough energy to our body to keep us strong enough to get back home from school at one o'clock in the afternoon. On the way back from school, our heads were dizzy, our stomachs shrunk like empty plastic bags and our legs refused to carry us home. I was in love with food. Food was always on my mind and most of the time I could not think about anything else but food. I dreamed about food at night. My stomach perpetually cried out for food.

At the end of the school term, Arif and I achieved the lowest score in the exams. However, Tariq became the top student in his class. When our father looked at Tariq's exam result, he was very happy. When he looked at Arif and my exam results, he overfilled with pure wrath. We could see the bitter anger in his face, eyes and body. He asked Tariq to go out and break a fresh tree branch to punish us with it. It seemed that Tariq too was very angry. Our father usually punished us at night for our mischief. Neither of us knew what kind of punishment he would give us. We spent whole days filled with fear. That night, our father asked Tariq and my mother to help him with the punishment. Arif and I wondered what sort of punishment he would give us that needed our brother and mother to help him. Mother was more than happy to help, as she was also disenchanted with our school results.

The punishment is called *Qafaai*, very well-known in Afghanistan. Tariq and my mother forced me to lie on the floor, than Tariq sat on top of me and my mother held my feet up for my father. My father flogged me on the soles of my feet with the branch. When they had finished with me, it was Arif's turn. We received this type of punishment twice a year, once in the middle of the year and once in the end of the school term. My father said that we were the luckiest children in the whole of Afghanistan that we could attend school and not have to undertake difficult work from early in the morning until late into the evening like most other Afghan children.

It was autumn and our parents already were anxious about the arrival of the winter. Mother prepared a new bucket for my younger brother Arif so that he too could go alongside Tariq and me to collect cattle dung. Arif took his bucket and walked with us very cheerfully. When we came across the first piece of cattle dung, Tariq asked Arif to pick it up. When he looked at it, he refused to pick it up. Tariq forced him to pick it up. Arif finally picked it up while the tears were falling from his eyes.

By the end of the autumn, the earth was very cold and I could not walk barefoot any more so I refused to collect any cattle dung. I stayed inside and listened to Simaa Khala and Mother's many conversations. Simaa Khala mostly complained about her mistreatment by Merza Kaka. She told my mother that Merza Kaka looked for the slightest excuse he could find to beat or curse her. She did not mind much when he physically and verbally abused her; she was used to it. However, she hated when Merza Kaka verbally abused her dead parents and would come early in the morning to our compound and weep. Mother always said that God would punish Merza Kaka for his madness.

I got really bored sitting all day long, so I asked my aunt to tell stories. Sometimes she refused as I was not doing well in school lessons. But, I persisted, sometimes even cried, until I obliged her to narrate a pleasing tale.

Mother, Taliban Has Arrived!

There were a few weeks left before the winter of 1995. I spent every day crying to my parents to buy a pair of shoes for me, as I was gravely bored sitting in the room like a prisoner all the time. Occasionally, my moaning irritated my mother and she tore at my hair, twisted my ears and threw me out of the house. One day before my father left home for work, he took a length of string and called me to him. He measured my foot with the string and told me that he would fetch a pair of shoes for me. I spent the whole day cheering. In the evening when my father returned, he truly did bring a pair of shoes. As soon as I slipped my feet into them, I ran outside. It felt like I had been kept like those striking tiny birds that Afghans keep in cages and unexpectedly release. I played with the village children until the day ended and the night was born. All of the children went to their homes and I was left alone. I played alone until Tariq forced me back into the house. At night my father warned me not to play football, *Tup Danda* or any other game that made me run, because my shoes would wear out and he would not be able to buy any more.

Most of our village had been reduced to rubble during the Mujahidin conflicts and it was a perfect playground for children. Late in the afternoon when we finished work, I joined the others, including Hekmat and played hide and seek. As children scattered into the wrecked compounds to hide, so did I. But soon I became frightened of the demons inside the dark wrecked rooms and came out. I truly felt the presence of the demons in those rooms. Demons changed my life into one of hell. My heart was filled with fear all of the time. I could feel their presence everywhere.

The unwelcome snow began to fall and in a matter of hours painted the earth white. Again, Tariq and I had to wipe the snow off the rooftop day and night. This winter I did not have to spend all day in the house like a jailbird. I could go with the village children into war-torn compounds, climb onto rooftops and jump down on the snow or build a gigantic *Santi kulunta* (snowball) in the village or play snowball fighting. In less than a week I had caught whooping cough and flu. Yet I still wanted to go out and play with the other children. My mother was so angry with me that she hid my shoes to stop me going outside. Again, she boiled the bitter mountain herb and forced me to drink its juice, and at night time I had to take a pinch of opium.

Winter was enjoyable for me because I did not have to go to school or get beaten by the teacher. Simaa Khala and Mother narrated enthralling tales for us every day. However, most people did not have anything to burn and a large number of children lost their lives. Winter snow buried families alive beneath their war-ragged mud houses. So many people were frostbitten and lost parts of their bodies. Winter brought catastrophes each time it came. But that year my siblings and I survived again!

It was the spring of 1996, our school's door opened again. I even loathed the name of school when someone mentioned it; I remembered my teacher's cable and my classmates' bullying. Arif and I from the very start played truant. We spent the first two weeks wandering the villages and streets. Our teacher knew our parents were sending us to school every day, but we did not go. She preferred us not to even bother coming to. She once said to us, 'Leave the school so that I can bring two new students into your places that are keen to learn.' We didn't want to attend school, but our parents were the ones who were very keen for us to become doctors or engineers in the future.

On 27 September 1996, at around one o'clock in the morning, we heard gunfire nearby. We didn't bother to get up as we were used to the sound of weapons. In the morning I heard chants of *Zinda Baad Taliba* (long live the Taliban) in our village. I ran outside to see several pickup trucks loaded with scary-looking men. At first I thought they were the Mujahidin as they had the same weapons as them. However, they were not the Mujahidin. Most Mujahidin had *Pakuls* on their heads and wore military trousers and coats, but the Taliban wore black and rather long traditional turbans and they did not wear military coats or trousers like the Mujahidin. It seemed that the Taliban never shaved as they had dark and bushy beards. They were all young men in their twenties and some even younger, but their leaders were older. They looked friendly and were talking with the elders and the children. They asked the elders to show them the location of the Mujahidin commanders. I moved closer to their vehicles and said *Salam* to one of them who was speaking to the children. He bent down and replied *Walaikum Asalam*. He was so close to my face that I could smell the *Naswar* (snuff) that he had in his mouth. He asked me in Pashtu language with a smile, 'Where are you from young man?' I gave no response to his question as my parents had never told me where I was born. Hekmat too came to see this new faction as the rumours of their existence had long been spoken about in people's houses. The Talib asked the same question of Hekmat. He knew where he was from, so he replied straight away that he was from the Farah Province.

I ran toward our house and screamed, 'Mother, Taliban has arrived!' My siblings stormed into the village with joy. Mother walked towards our compound door and peeped out to see the saviours of the Afghans.

Within a few moments, all of the village men and children surrounded the Taliban fighters. My father too came to check up this new faction. They behaved very well with everyone in our village. The Taliban commander made a promise that from now on no bullets, rockets or missiles would hit our village or any other village in Kabul. Our village was filled with happiness and joy. After a remarkably long time, men, women and children were laughing and their hearts were filled with hope for a peaceful future. My little brothers and I also joined the crowds and began chanting, *Zinda baad Talibaa! Zinda baad Talibaa!* Long live Taliban! Long live Taliban! And we marched from one village to another.

Kabul inhabitants welcomed the Taliban with joy and cheerfulness, with love and generosity. Kabul inhabitants considered the Taliban as their saviours and liberators.

The Taliban decided to open a checkpoint a few miles from our village. Back in the house, my father turned the radio on and tuned it to the BBC channel. There were male and female anchors reading the news saying that the

Mujahidin had fled Kabul without any resistance and the Taliban had taken control. Later on they said that the Taliban had captured Dr. Najibullah, the last president of the communist regime. First it said on the news that Dr. Najibullah was in custody, but later they said that he had been murdered by the Taliban. There was love in the hearts of most urban Afghans for Dr. Najibullah. Afghans who witnessed and lived under the oppression of the Mujahidin factions considered life under his regime as a golden time. This was particularly true for the women. Everybody was saddened in our village when they heard about his death.

Dr. Najibullah had tried a lot to compromise with the Mujahidin during his administration in 1986-1992, to form a coalition government or hold elections and let the Afghan nation choose their leader. But the United States, Pakistan, Saudi Arabia and others who were the masters of the Mujahidin factions would not let them. His regime fell apart after the fall of the Soviet Union. In 1992, he was left with no choice but to peacefully hand over power and the fate of Afghans to the beastly factions of the Mujahidin, who drowned Kabul under the blood of tens of thousands of innocents. After Dr. Najibullah handed over power, he attempted to flee Afghanistan but was stopped at the airport by one of the Mujahidin factions. He then took refuge in the United Nations compound in Kabul. He remained there for four years. During this time he would listen to the radio and hear about the calamities of the Mujahidin's factional war. In the last days of his life he endeavoured to translate Peter Hopkirk's book *The Great Game* into Pashtu. The reason he was translating Hopkirk's book was to help Afghans understand history and avoid repeating the mistakes of the past. But, Death did not let him complete the translation. When the Mujahidin departed from Kabul, they made an offer for him to leave with them, but he did not trust them and rejected their offer. His brother was murdered alongside him by the Taliban.

The barbarous Taliban first castrated both of them then tied their bodies behind a truck and dragged them through the streets of Kabul. They later hung their bodies in the *Aryana* square for several days. Almost all of Dr. Najibullah's prophesies turned out to be true and Afghans are still witnessing it today. He warned the Afghans and the Mujahidin leaders repeatedly that if we did not unite and end this appalling war, then Pakistanis, Arabs and Americans would come into our country. How right he was!

He once, after the Soviet withdrawal, said that the United States government wanted to turn Afghanistan into Vietnam for the Soviet Union, but by continuation of such assistance and the supply of mass murdering equipment against the people of Afghanistan, Afghanistan would turn into a second Vietnam for America.[22]

The very same people whom the United States government empowered and supplied with the most ugliest of weapons worth billions of dollars turned against them, such as Gulbudin Hekmatyar (the leader of *Hizb-e Islami*, which received half of the billions of dollars that the US spent to make the Soviet Union bleed in its Afghan-Trap), and Jalaludin Haqani (the leader of the Haqani network that now kills young Americans in Afghanistan). Today the Afghan war has become the United States' longest war.

Dr. Najibullah's death was the first appalling violence of the Taliban that Kabul residents witnessed. All of the men from our village went to see his body hanging in the square alongside that of his brother. When village men came back everyone was shocked and dismayed by what they had seen. There were people who shed tears for the death of Dr. Najibulla. There were women who refused to eat food for days and cried loudly over his death, even though he was accused of torturing people when he was the head of *Khadamat-e Aetla'at-e Dawlati* or KHAD, which was the intelligence agency of Afghanistan during the communist era. I did not know much about Dr. Najibullah at that time. As I grew up, I saw the love for him in the eyes of tormented Afghans. Today his pictures are sold in the streets of Afghanistan with some calling him a hero and others calling him a martyr.

After my father came back from seeing his body, he said to my mother, 'I can't imagine why the Taliban has done this to human beings.' He sat by himself in the corner of the house lost in his own thoughts. He later came back and said Afghanistan was once again in the hands of wild people.

A short while after the Taliban had seized Kabul they announced their cruel and medieval laws. Some are listed below:

The Taliban declare that women are not allowed to attend school or university or work in public. Women must cover their face and other parts of the body that attract men's attention. And women must be accompanied by men when they are in the public.

All men must grow a beard. If anyone attempts to shave they will be punished and imprisoned. (My father shaved his beard every day and he was appalled when he heard this news.)

TV, music, films, etc, are banned. (Luckily I knew nothing about TV, music and films so at that time I did not understand what they meant.)

Murderers will be murdered in public. A thief's hand or other part of his/her body will be amputated in public.

Adulterers will be stoned in public.

All men must attend the mosque five times a day for prayers. Those who do not attend will be punished.

Students of all ages must wear traditional clothes and turbans in school. (My siblings and I were very excited to wear a turban.)

Celebration of Nawruz or New Year is prohibited.

Boys must not grow western-style hair.

Gambling and kite-flying, are prohibited.

There were several other idiotic rules that were also imposed upon the tormented people of Afghanistan.

MOTHER, THE TALIBAN HAS ARRIVED!

An ignorant man is a dangerous man. But an ignorant man with an ideology is as dangerous as a wildfire, storm and tsunami. He clings to his ideology like a raw fruit in the tree and kills, suppresses and imposes his ideology upon others. Sadly, the Taliban had an Ideology, an Ideology that someone else planted in their minds for their goals, and they imposed it upon us.

People throughout history have devastated each other in the name of religion and in the name of God. Man has committed horrifying crimes in the name of God. He justifies every form of cruelty, suppression, injustice and exploitation in the name of God. Religion has been used as a means to brutally exploit humanity. Women have been suppressed in the name of God. Progress and development have been stopped in the name of God.

The savage and intolerant empire of the Taliban has also tortured Afghans so terribly in the name of God. They denied women, men and children their basic human rights. The dictates of the Taliban killed freedom, if there ever was any freedom in Afghanistan. One of the major reasons that Afghans remain backward and miserable, becoming the prey of savage, regional powers and international superpowers is because of the lack of freedom in Afghan society. Where there is no freedom there is poverty, ignorance, war, intolerance, violence, backwardness and chaos. Where there is freedom, there is progress, invention, creativity, peace and prosperity. A mind without freedom is worthless and barren. Mind only thrives when it's free. And it is only the free mind that can invent and solve human problems. The mind that is not free and is shackled in ideologies is violent, destructive, intolerant and reactionary. In some parts of the world there is a little bit of outward freedom, but outward freedom is futile without inward or psychological freedom. There is no psychological freedom in this world at all. Psychologically a free human being is a dangerous human being for society. How rightly philosopher Jean-Jacques Rousseau says, 'Man is born free, and everywhere he is in chains.' Through education, culture, dogmas, media and various other powerful establishments, our psychological freedom is being taken from us. Psychologically we are slaves. We are nationalists, but we can't see the danger of nationalism. Nationalism divides humanity and division breeds appalling wars and violence. We can't see the danger of military and weapons; a huge chunk of humanity's wealth is wasted on the military and weapons. Tens of millions of young human beings are being turned into soldiers and being programmed to kill, destroy and be killed – and humanity is so indifferent towards this barbarism. We cling to ideologies, but we can't see the danger of clinging to any ideology. When one clings to an ideology then one divides oneself from those who do not cling to the same ideology and thus conflict rises. Human beings are blindly following leaders and they can't see the danger of following someone else. If one cannot lead himself, how can someone else lead him? If human beings were psychologically free, the world would not be the savage and chaotic place that it is. A world with psychologically free human beings would look utterly different. One does not know himself unless one is psychologically free. The one who is psychologically free knows what love and kindness are.

These new dictates of the Taliban certainly brought misery upon urban people, but it was not such a surprise for rural peasants, especially for the Pashtuns who lived in rural areas. It is a mistake to say that the Taliban oppressed all Afghans. Yes, they oppressed urban people alongside Tajiks, Hazararas and Uzbaks, but they had almost the full support of the Pashtun ethnicity. As a result of Pashtun support the Taliban rose rapidly. Why were the Taliban widely supported by the Pashtuns? For many years, militias and warlords and Mujahidin commanders plundered, tortured and killed people in Pashtun areas like everywhere else. They were fed up with it and were looking for anyone to come and rid them of them all. When the Taliban rose from Kandahar Province they brought peace and stability to the Pashtuns, which they desperately needed. A poor Pashtun peasant did not want anything more than security and the Taliban provided it for him. Since the arrival of the Taliban, all Mujahidin and militia checkpoints that committed all sorts of horrible crimes had been wiped out. Crime itself vanished. Weapons that were everywhere and in the hands of almost every Afghan male were taken from them. They have established peace and stability in nearly all parts of Afghanistan under their control. They provided justice for the victims. The cruel dictates of the Taliban had very little effect on the daily lives of most

Afghans who lived in rural areas as they had been practicing most of the Taliban's laws for centuries. They did not allow their women to go out alone or without a veil. Most of them did not shave their beards off as they did not have the facilities to do so. Most did not have a TV, cassette tape player or radio, so they did not mind these prohibitions. They did not mind the prohibition of women not working in public or attending school or university as there was no work for women outside of the compound and no school and university for their daughters to study in. So, all of the regulations that the Taliban imposed upon people did not affect most of the Afghans who lived in rural areas. Therefore, it would be a mistake to say that all people did not like the Taliban in Afghanistan. The reason I mentioned this, is that it helps us to understand why today some Afghans prefer the Taliban and their medieval laws, than the extremely corrupt government which is being propped up by the West.

After a couple of weeks, those who did not take the Taliban's new regulations seriously in Kabul were severely punished. Among them was a man who lived not far from our village who shaved his beard off for his wedding. He was on the way to a shop when the Taliban spotted him. They beat him viciously and then blackened his face and sat him on a donkey and took him around the villages, as a lesson for others. They brought the poor man into our village and it was enormously exciting for the village children. The Taliban seized burglars, chopped their hands off and displayed them to the public. Those who committed murder, the Taliban murdered in public before thousands of horrified Afghans. Adulterers were stoned to death. Women who did not cover themselves properly were brutally whipped.

Once again, the plant of hope that grew in the hearts of broken Kabul residents was dead. The streams of joy that flowed in the hearts of Afghans after the arrival of the Taliban dried up. Before the arrival of the morning of peace came another night of oppression! Once again Afghan women were imprisoned within the brutal confines of old customs. Unhappy parents broke another promise to children that they would have plenty of food to eat when the Taliban arrived. Once again the bird of despair sat on the tree of the Afghans. New beastly-looking men wandered the streets of Kabul whose task it was to harass poverty-stricken people.

Merza Kaka and my father instantly lost their jobs after the arrival of the Taliban. They did not know what to do, they had families to feed. During this miserable time, my mother gave birth to Tamim, my third brother. Tamim was welcomed into this cruel world by misery, hunger, danger and pain, like all children who were born in Afghanistan.

Merza Kaka and my father decided to start a business with the little money that they had. Father bought two sheep so that he could fatten them up and sell them. Merza Kaka bought goats for the very same reason. Now we had a new chore besides collecting cattle dung. We had to take the sheep every day into the fields so that they could feed. It was hard for my brothers and me to lead our two sheep under the burning sun, looking for grass and cow dung, but we had no other option. Soon Tariq and I became known as shepherds everywhere. I loved my sheep and I loved watching them regurgitate their food. I spent most of my spare time with them and Palang. At first Palang was frightened of the sheep and barked at them, but later he was on good terms with them and would sometimes even played with them.

Simaa Khala and Mother rarely spoke about poor Farzana, whose life had become so bitter after she attempted to elope with that young man. Rarely did any news of Farzana come into our house. She was separated from her two children by my maternal uncle. My mother was fearful that the Taliban might stone Farzana to death if they were to find out about her case. However, Farzana had no fear of death. Every breath in and out was for Farzana like an eternal life in a fierce fire. Her eyes and face were wet with tears, her heart filled with hatred for men. She was even fearful of men's shadows and ran from them like a wild animal. After all, it was men who injected their poison into her life and destroyed her once and for all. She had nowhere to escape, just like a caged bird. She begged her parents, brothers and relatives to let her see her children if only once. She tore at her hair and beat herself as she could not endure the pain of separation. Some men called her cunning and some called her crazy. She wanted to take her two children and follow a path that would take her far away from the men's world until she reached one where men could not reach her, or take her children away from her. It was a dream. God had not built such a world.

News of her suffering arrived at our home. When my mother heard it she felt sorry for Farzana and told her older brother, 'You have punished Farzana for her mistake. You have chopped that feeble woman like a butcher, but she has survived. Now let her see her children as she is their mother.'

But my uncle had a hard heart and he refused and said, 'No one has the right to show my children to Farzana. Farzana has no right upon my children. She lost her right on the very day she started an unlawful relationship with another man.'

Farzana's children had a miserable existence without their mother. My uncle had not only tortured Farzana, he punished their children too by depriving them of her love. He could neither look after the two poor children nor let their mother take care of them. The children constantly cried for her, but my uncle did not feel sorry for them. The children were hungry, unclothed and filthy as nobody washed them, and they wandered in the village under the burning sun in summer and in the brutally cold weather in winter.

Later on my uncle married off his daughter when she was around fourteen years old, without Farzana even knowing about it. He did not look after the boy, who became a tramp and turned to drugs. Now he is a drug addict and wanders the streets of Kabul. Poor Farzana still lives with her parents, drowned in despair and agony.

School started again in 1997. In the first two weeks, luckily, they did not allow Hekmat, Arif and me to enter school since none of us had turbans. The Taliban forced all school children to wear turbans and those who didn't were not allowed inside. My father could not afford to buy turbans for us, nor could Hekmat's. So we were free and played for half a day in the village with other children and spent the other half working. By now Hekmat had become a good friend of ours. He preferred to wander about with us rather than with other children. However, my mother panicked when she noticed that it had been two weeks since my brothers and I had attended school, so she made turbans out of my father's clothes for us and sent us to school. Hekmat's mother was also very anxious for her son, so she made a turban out of her headscarf for him. We used to make fun of Hekmat by saying to him, 'You wore your mother's scarf and you are a woman.' And he would cry to his mother to buy a proper turban for him. However, his poor parents were as poor as mine. They had the desire to educate their son but could not afford to provide the education cost.

All of our female students and teachers had disappeared since the Taliban came into power. Our classes looked hideous without them. It must have been a terrible feeling for those female teachers and students and all other Afghan women to be suddenly imprisoned in their houses by the Taliban.

It was interesting for us to wear the turban at first. In our free time we would play a game where Arif and I were the Taliban and Hekmat was the thief, and we would chop his hands off. The Taliban had introduced new textbooks for students, so now we had to study these alongside the US government's propaganda books. Most scientific subjects had been eliminated from schools. Our new books were written in Arabic and had weird names such as *Noor-il Iza, Shama...* Now Arif and I were not the only lazy students in the class. All our classmates did not understand what was written in the new textbooks. The new teachers were all male, mostly Taliban members, and far more brutal than our previous teachers. Arif and I chose to attend school every day as we liked to wear our turbans in school and play with them in class, and in the streets we pretended to be Taliban.

One day our new teacher came to our class with a black cable, which was much thicker and longer than the one our previous teacher had. He read the Arabic texts from the book and then translated it for us, but no one understood his lesson. At the end, he warned everyone to remember the lesson and he would ask us tomorrow about it. The next day when everyone arrived in the class, our teacher was already there. He asked all the students about the previous lesson. Those who failed to repeat yesterday's lesson had to stand in the corner of the class. Almost everyone failed to repeat the lesson. We were not sure how our new teacher would punish us. The entire class gathered in the corner of the room. Each student tried to hide himself behind the others, so not to be the first to be punished. Finally, the teacher turned his face towards us with the snake-shaped cable in his hand and asked one student to come forward.

We all expected that he might whip us on the palms of our hands like our previous teacher. But he flogged him all over, just like the Taliban who flogged Afghan women in the streets. Our previous teacher gave us ten lashes on each hand, but nobody was sure how many lashes the new teacher would give us. Each student screamed when they felt the first blow of the cable. He kept lashing until no part of the student's body was left untouched. It was then Arif's turn. The teacher looked at Arif and asked him to come forward. He lashed Arif all over. Arif fell to the floor and screamed for help as usual from our mother. The heartless teacher did not stop. I thought he was going to kill poor Arif. The teacher kept on beating Arif until his Turban fell from his head. He punished a few other students and then he picked me to come forward.

The first blow of the cable hit me on the head. For a brief moment I thought someone was sawing my head in half. Before the teacher threw another blow, I took the chance to check my head to see if it had cracked in half. Happily it hadn't. The second blow hit me on the back and forced me to scream. Then the cable blows fell upon me like flames. I closed my eyes and covered my head with my hands and was not sure when the teacher would stop lashing me. I thought he had gone mad and would kill me. He kept on lashing me until he got tired. Hekmat too screamed once the teacher's cable stung him. On the way home the three of us compared each other's bruises; our bodies were covered with marks. When my parents saw the bruises they were traumatised and my mother cried and cursed the teacher.

We were running out of food in the house and Father had no money to buy any. Every day he left the house early in the morning until late evening in search of a job. Merza Kaka could not afford to provide food for his family either. Both were anxious, distressed and angry all the time and did not know how to provide food. Day after day they both became touchy. Father sometimes shouted at Mother over petty issues and sometimes beat my siblings and me for the smallest mischief we committed. Merza Kaka relieved his anger by beating and abusing Simaa Khala and his children. Simaa Khala and my mother sat together, both haunted by thoughts of what their children would eat once they consumed the little food that they had. We were not alone in this neverending journey of war, brutality, hunger, disease and suffering; all Afghans accompanied us. The problem was not only the lack of jobs for Afghans; there was very little food in all Afghanistan. The fields were crammed with the poppy crops.

Merza Kaka and Father went to the Taliban and asked for a job. The Taliban told them to go to the front line and fight against the Mujahidin. They both knew that fighting on the front line was suicide and if they got killed, their children would starve to death. So they both looked for a different job. All we had in the house was a bag of rice and a little flour. My mother began to add a little rice to the big pot filled with water, and she boiled it and prepared rice soup. She called it *Shurwa-Berenj*. We had to search the bowl to find the rice in the water. Each time we finished our food our stomachs were packed full with water. After one or two hours, we were hungry again and demanded more food. We were lucky to have a mother to ask for food from. There were countless children whose parents had been killed. They ran in the streets of Kabul unclothed and barefoot after the Taliban vehicles, begging for a loaf of bread. The very same sick people responsible for the misery of Afghans were enjoying living free of worry in Russia, the United States, other western countries, Pakistan and Saudi Arabia.

Palang, our lovable dog, suffered the most from hunger as he received far less food than everyone else. At first, when he received enough food, he was very healthy and stunning. But since then he had lost so much weight and we could easily count his bones. My brothers and I looked in the villages and streets on the way home from school to find food for Palang, but people had eaten it before we could find it. There were children scavenging everywhere for food and, later, both Arif and I joined them. Poor Palang no longer had the energy to play with us. However, he became a good excuse for Arif and me not to attend school, instead we searched for food. My father did not bother to force us to go to school, as he knew the state of the education system in Afghanistan during the Taliban regime. Mother wanted us to go on any condition.

One morning a scorpion slipped inside Arif's clothes and stung him several times. He cried and told our mother that he had been stung by something. She did not believe him and thought he was trying to make excuses to avoid school, so she forced him to go to school. Halfway to school Arif lost consciousness and fell to the ground. I thought he had died so I screamed and asked for help. Our mother was horrified when she saw him unconscious. She took his clothes off and found a squashed scorpion in his clothes. She had a strong faith in the Mullah's treatment, like most Afghan women have in Afghanistan. She took Arif to our village Mullah to cure him. The Mullah read a few prayers and then he was done. Arif remained in the same condition until Father arrived home from job-searching in the late afternoon. He immediately took Arif to hospital. When my father came back from the hospital he was furious with Mother. He said that if he hadn't arrived when he did Arif might have died.

Farmers decided not to allow us to leave our sheep in their farms to graze, as the sheep ruined their crops. There was no other place where we could feed them. I found out that the Taliban checkpoint, which was not far from our village, produced a lot of rubbish every day. Consequently, I woke up early one morning and headed there. When I arrived I noticed all the Taliban were awake and preparing for morning prayers. They threw their rubbish just beside their checkpoint. It was like a shop. I collected vegetables, half-eaten fruits, Naan, animal bones and even animal meat and fat. The food I collected from there was more than enough for my sheep and dog. Now Palang spent most of his day eating and playing with the bones. My mother fed us twice in twenty-four hours. My stomach was empty and shrunken most of the time. My siblings and I cried for food day and night. She had nothing to give us. We'd eat at ten o'clock in the morning and five o'clock in the afternoon; sometimes our parents gave their own share of food to us in order to keep us quiet. Sometimes our mother had no energy to walk or do the chores, instead she slept. This was the only way for her to escape the hunger. Mother slept for most of the day. Simaa Khala did not have any energy either. She came into our compound and slept beside her sister. My cousins, siblings and I surrounded them and cried for food. They did not wake and listen to our cries, as they were used to them. Mother still tricked us at night. We spent hours looking up at the moon screaming for it to drop milk.

One day when I was picking the Taliban leftover food, I found an intact onion. I kept it so that my mother could cook it for us, but on the way home my hunger was so intense that I did not have the energy to walk back home so I ate that raw onion. My eyes began streaming tears. When Hekmat saw me, he thought someone had beaten me.

With my hungry stomach I used to sit beneath the basket of Naan hanging from the ceiling it and look at it, wishing I was tall enough to reach. When the food was ready, everyone tried to eat faster before the food disappeared. Rice soup was usually very hot and we all burned our mouths. We'd fight for the pot because there were pieces of rice stuck to the bottom of it. Tariq was the strongest amongst us and usually won. One day I stood up against him and tried to take it from him. We fought and I scratched his face with my fingernails and he tore at my hair. When I screamed, our mother came and punished both of us, and neither of us had the pot.

We had a widowed neighbour whose husband was killed by Soviet soldiers. She had four daughters and two sons. One day our neighbour's younger son, who was roughly six years old, entered our house with tears in his eyes, and told us while he was sobbing, 'My mother sold two of my sisters this morning.' Hearing this we were all shocked and ran to the neighbour's house.

MOTHER, THE TALIBAN HAS ARRIVED!

We entered their room, usually it was very full and noisy, but now it looked empty. The two daughters who were left were crying quietly. My mother shouted at our widowed neighbour, 'Why did you do such an appalling act?' She looked at my mother; her eyes were red as if she had been crying for a long time. She did not answer, so my mother shouted again at her, 'You are the cruellest mother in the world. Everyone is hungry all over the country, but no parents sell their children for money.'

This time she did not remain quiet. She said with a loud voice and tearful eyes, 'Yes I am a vicious mother, and sold my daughters because I could not see them dying before my eyes from hunger! Tell me, what else could I do? They did not eat for two days and were all dying right here in this room.' More village women found out and asked the same question from her. All the women sat in tears in her house. No one had anything to offer her. Everyone was in the same boat.

My mother cried and said, 'This is what will happen to us soon.'

My father went in the morning, sat until late evening behind the Taliban's base gates, and begged them all day long to give him job, but not in the front line, somewhere else. Once a Taliban commander asked him; 'If you are going to die tomorrow, why not die now?' Human life was as worthless to the Taliban as water for someone whose neighbour is a river.

Taliban supply convoys passed through our village to the front line full of heavy and light ammunition and food. Most of their vehicles were pickup trucks with dark windows. Their vehicles were so new that our village children used them as mirrors. Sometimes, when their convoys stopped in the road, we children asked them to give us some food. Most of the time they chased us away, but once a Talib gave everyone a 1,000 Afghani note, which we could barely buy half a Naan with. Men and children asked one another, 'Where do these pickup trucks, ammunition and money come from?' No one had an answer.

One day a convoy came and we asked for food, but these Taliban, who were going to the front line, looked different from the Afghan Taliban and some could not speak Pashtu, instead they spoke a language that was unfamiliar to me. Some village children who had spent some of their lives in the Pakistani refugee camps said they were speaking Urdu.

Murder Before My Eyes

One day, before I went to the Taliban checkpoint to collect their leftover food, I cried for my mother to give me something to satisfy my stomach. But she had nothing to give me. So I cried even more loudly. I knew she did not want the neighbours to know we had nothing in our house to eat; this was something our mother was greatly ashamed of. So, when my mother could not provide food for me I would scream at the top of my voice, 'I am hungry!' But that day, when I screamed, she grabbed me by my hair and dragged me into the room so that neighbours couldn't hear my cries. She slapped and pinched me. Because I had been beaten at school and by my parents, it no longer hurt me as much. For that reason, she looked for something that would cause me proper pain. She locked me in the room and went out. She came back with a thick wire and flogged me just the way my teacher did. She flogged me all over until she became too exhausted to flog me any more. She cursed my siblings and me. She prayed for God to take all her children from her one after another. I cried for a long time and then walked to the Taliban checkpoint with my shrunken stomach and legs like jelly. I had to force them to carry me. I collected the Taliban rubbish and spotted a half-eaten apple covered with grit and thousands of ants. Hunger is a very callous evil. I picked the half-eaten apple up and shook it, but had to pick the ants off one by one and throw them away. Then I ate the apple, but it did not satisfy my hungry stomach.

I returned to the village. Hekmat was leaning against a wall. He was as hungry as I was and asked me to go and bring a piece of Naan for him, as he thought there was food in my house. I could not tell Hekmat that my house was as empty as his house and that my family was as hungry as his family was, because our mother warned us not to dare talk about what went on in the house. I told Hekmat that we had loads of food but our mother did not allow us to give it away.

A farmer grew tomatoes in one corner of his field. Hekmat told me to steal a tomato from the field. I knew that it was terribly wrong and if my parents found out they would beat me to death. But I was hungry. The farmer never left his field. During the day he worked on his farm and then he stayed until midnight to guard against hungry village children. When Hekmat and I arrived the farmer was in a sweet dream under the shadow of a cherry tree. He had fenced his tomato fields with barbed wire, which he had stolen from a ruined radio station. The farmer was known for his brutality. Any children who touched his crops would be beaten badly. He had lost the sight in one of his eyes during the war. His name was Anu, but village children called him Anu-e Koor (blind Anu). I refused to cross the barbed wire into the tomato field because I was so scared of him. Hekmat crossed the fence and helped himself to the ripe tomatoes, and he passed them to me. He stole enough tomatoes to put out the fire of hunger inside our stomachs and we started stealing from that day onwards.

We went miles away from our village into the peasants' fields to steal anything we could eat. When Arif found out how Hekmat and I got rid of our hunger, he joined us. An old man sold food outside our school from a small cart. Hekmat, Arif and I stole biscuits and dry fruits and nuts from him. We then went on to stealing from shops. So many shopkeepers knew us and as soon as they spotted us, they chased as away. We were frequently punished by the peasants and shopkeepers and yet we could not stop stealing their food.

The Taliban had no plans for rebuilding Afghanistan or finding any solutions for the misery of the Afghans. They said God would solve everything. They did not care whether Afghans lived or died. So many people had lost their lives in the famine. No one knew what their misdeed was; no one knew why all these catastrophes were falling upon them. First it was the Soviet Union who came with their deadly and sophisticated weapons. They took husbands from wives, fathers from children, brothers from sisters. Then came the United States proxy Mujahidin, who devastated the Afghans. And now it was the Taliban with their brutalities. Kabul's ruined roads, streets and city were filled with beggars. Most were poor women whose husbands had been killed.

Each woman had more than six or seven children who demanded food from her. I was amazed by those mothers' patience and strength. Their little starving and unclothed children would encircle them and demand food while they were sitting under the burning sun in the summer and in the brutally cold weather in the winter begging for food. Children as young as five ran after the Taliban's new pickup trucks and begged for food. Parents sold their children in order to feed the rest of their family.

Early one morning as I arrived at the checkpoint to collect the leftover food, I noticed that there was nothing. I looked around and thought they might not have thrown their rubbish away yet. I sat and leaned against the wall and waited for several hours. Taliban were stepping in and out, but none of them threw rubbish out. I was worried that someone else might have taken it already so I asked a Talib. Most Taliban claimed they were Mullahs and they preferred to be called *Mullah*, *Mawlawi* or *Imam*. So I called the Talib, Mullah Sahib.

He seemed happy, and said, 'What is wrong *Bachaya*?'

'Do you know where your leftover food is?' I asked him.

He looked at the place where they threw the rubbish and said, 'I am not sure, but I think my men threw it out early this morning when we woke for prayer. What do you do with our rubbish?'

'I feed my sheep and dog,' I said.

He leaned his AK-47 against the wall, sat beside me, looked at my ragged clothes and then my bare feet and asked, 'Why don't you change your clothes?'

I was embarrassed and said, 'My father doesn't have enough money to buy new shoes and clothes for me.' He spat out his *Naswar (*snuff*)*, which looked like chicken dung, and then spat out the bits that remained in his mouth. He asked me what my father does. 'He is jobless,' I said.

'How many brothers and sisters do you have?'

'I have three brothers and two sisters,' I said.

'And how many mothers?'

'Only one.'

He took his AK-47, stood up and told me to stay there and he would find out where their rubbish was. The door opened, I thought the man who went to find the whereabouts of their rubbish was coming back. But it was someone else and he glared at me, almost as if I had killed his father. He told me to go away.

I started walking back towards our home, when someone shouted at me, '*Wurkya*! Child! Where are you going?' I looked around, and it was the first man who went to find out about the rubbish. This time he didn't have his AK-47 on his shoulder, instead he had a piece of Naan in his hand. He said that his man threw the rubbish out this morning and someone else had collected it already. 'If you don't want someone else to take the rubbish, you'd better come early in the morning,' said the Talib. He put the Naan in my hand and said 'Go home now.'

I ate the Naan in a second. On the way home I saw Arif playing outside with a new neighbour's children. They were quite well off because their father worked for a mine clearing organisation that was funded by foreign aid.

I entered the house and saw everyone was in the compound yard including my father, who had not gone job searching. My mother was lying beside him. I told my father that I could not bring food for the sheep and Palang because someone else had already taken it. He cursed me and blamed me for not bothering to wake myself up early enough in the morning to collect the Taliban leftover food before others got to it. I preferred being beaten by my father than being cursed. His curses stung and were more painful than his slaps and punches.

My father suffered from diabetes and he had kidney problems. He pretended that he was in good health, but he was suffering silently. He knew that there were more than enough problems in the house and even if he shared his health problems there was nothing that could be done. We did not have enough food to satisfy our hunger let alone have money for my father's treatment. His diseases were not the only pain he endured. He was the father of six children and had the responsibility of feeding them. He suffered when he looked at his children, who surrounded him and his wife demanding food, when he saw his wife spend most of the day sleeping because she was hungry, when he saw his country being destroyed, and when his compatriots died because of war, hunger, disease, drugs.

An hour later, someone knocked our door very hard. It was the new neighbour's wife. She was holding Arif by his collar and there was a piece of Naan in Arif's hand. Before I could open my mouth to ask why, she grabbed Arif and told me to fetch my mother. When Mother came the woman released Arif's collar but still held him by his hand to make sure he could not escape. Before my mother said anything, the woman said, 'Why can't you control your children?' She pushed Arif towards her and said, 'He is cheating my children by giving them petty toys and in return taking their Naan. It is better to sit in the street and ask for food than leave your children to rip off others.'

My mother slammed the door on her and refused to listen to anything else. She slapped Arif very hard and then took her tattered sandal off her foot and began beating Arif with it on the head, face and back. At the same time she shouted, 'You have left me with no dignity in this village.' Arif screamed and tried to extricate himself, but she had him by his collar. Finally, he managed to get away when his clothes slipped away from his body and remained in her hand.

The next morning I woke when it was dark and headed towards the checkpoint. It was cold; my body trembled. As I approached I saw four goats eating the leftover food. I ran towards them and just as I was about to reach them realised that they were three goats, and the fourth one was their owner, who was bending over to collect the food. I shouted at him not to collect because it was mine. He was slightly older than me.

'It's not yours it's the Taliban's leftover food,' said the boy. I could not bear watching his goats eating all of the food, so I ran towards them, and pushed his goats away. His goats were as hungry as everyone else and would not leave the food. Finally, I kicked the goats in their bellies. When the boy saw me beating his goats, he became annoyed and pushed me hard – so hard that I fell over the rubbish and my clothes got soaked. I stood up and grabbed the boy by his clothes and tried to force him down onto the rubbish so that I could take out my revenge. As I was forcing him down, I lost control and we both fell down onto the rubbish. I grabbed his hair and pulled it as he was struggling to grasp mine.

Suddenly a huge hand appeared and picked us both off the ground. He was one of the Taliban who had seen us fighting. He slapped us both and said, 'My slap will remind you for the rest of your life not to fight again'. Then he asked why we were fighting. I told him that the leftovers belonged to me since I had been collecting them from the start.

'No Mullah Sahib, it does not belong to him,' said the boy. I cried to the Talib that my sheep and dog would die if I didn't take the food.

Before the boy opened his mouth to say something the Talib said, 'Share it, between yourselves.' Then he shouted at me not to cry. I took the Taliban's food and went straight to Hekmat's house and told him about the goatherd. He promised that he would go with me tomorrow and teach the goatherd a lesson.

As I returned to the compound I rushed to Palang's den. He had no energy to stand; his stomach was shrunken. I gave Palang two big chunks of cow bones. Palang was so hungry that I thought he was trying to swallow the bones. He badly hurt his gums and teeth with the bones and the bones were encrusted with his blood. I tried to take the bones away from him but he wouldn't let me. I put some burned rice on his plate and left him there. I did not bring enough food for the sheep since the goatherd had taken most of it.

Arif and I often went to find food for our animals. Melon, watermelon and banana skins were our sheep's favourite food. It was only the Taliban who could afford to eat fruit. Arif and I went miles away from our village in search of Taliban checkpoints. We came across some but other people had already looted the rubbish. We searched every corner until, at last, we reached a checkpoint that nobody else had looted. There was everything we needed. Food for our sheep, dog and even for Arif and me, too. Arif found a piece of Naan to eat. As I was picking melon skins, I spotted a 10,000 Afghani note. I was about to burst into cheers, but remained quiet. I did not even tell Arif what I had found. I thought if the Taliban found out they may take it from me.

As we collected the Taliban food and walked away, I shared the news with Arif. The money may sound a lot, but with a 10,000 Afghani note one could hardly buy one meal. Money had lost its value in Afghanistan, inflation was at its highest level and people had to pay more than 100,000 Afghani to buy 7kg of wheat flour. Ten thousand Afghani certainly was a lot of money for Arif and me. We went home but did not tell anyone in the house, instead we went straight to Hekmat. He too was so excited when he saw the note. Arif and I were too young to have it; we feared that shopkeepers might take it from us. So we asked him to go and buy food. He boldly walked into the shop in our village as Arif and I stood outside. Hekmat came back with five pomegranates in a plastic bag. We could not eat the pomegranates in the village in case other children begged us to share them. We had to go somewhere nobody would see us, so we decided to go to the nearby fields. My family had not tasted fruit since Ronald Reagan's freedom fighters entered Kabul.

The next morning I collected Hekmat and we went to the checkpoint. When we arrived, the boy and his goats were not there so I began collecting the rubbish swiftly. Hekmat collected all the stuff he thought he could eat. He told me that his mother secretly collects grass from their yard and cooks it for them. He said, 'My sisters don't know it and are eating it like fools, but I know what my mother cooks. I have eaten it and it tasted disgusting. Taliban leftover food is much tastier in comparison to the grass my mother cooks.' Hekmat's mother was not the only mother who cooked grass for her children. Countless parents cooked grass for their children in order to avoid starvation. We saw the boy with his three goats walking towards us. I thought if Hekmat clashed with the goatherd, the Taliban might come and share the rubbish with the boy as well as give me another hard slap, so I asked Hekmat to flee. He wanted to teach the boy a lesson. I told him what the Taliban would do if they caught him fighting and it was then he was ready to run away.

Hekmat, my two brothers and I loved football. One day Hekmat asked me to go with him to Kabul stadium to watch football. I did not know how far it was as I had never been there in my life, so I refused to go. However, Hekmat was a smart boy. He looked at me and said, 'Do you know Karim-e Pajero?'

'No,' I said, 'who is he?'

'He is the top footballer in all of Afghanistan. He runs faster than a Pajero vehicle. That is why people named him Karim-e Pajero. He is playing in Kabul stadium today.' I asked how far the stadium was. He said it was one or two hours away. I could not dare go that far.

Since Hekmat had mentioned Kabul stadium, football and Karim-e Pajero, I could not stop thinking about them. I wondered how the stadium might look, but Karim-e Pajero was of most interest to me. 'How could he run faster than a Pajero vehicle?' I asked myself. After a while I decided to go to Kabul stadium. Now it was my turn to persuade Arif to go with me. If Arif did not go then my family would look for me as we were together at all times. When Arif heard about the stadium he also became excited. Arif and I told Mother we were going to collect food for the sheep and Palang.

Hekmat was so happy when he found out that we were willing to go with him. We walked for an hour to get to the main road, and the main road was covered with holes from explosions. It was empty and hardly any vehicles passed through it. Hekmat waved at every single vehicle that did pass, but none gave us a lift. We saw a lorry approaching us, so we secretly ran behind it and clung to the back without the driver knowing we were there. At Kabul stadium we all jumped off. The lorry was going too fast, though, and as we all rolled in the road we each hurt something. We were all bleeding, but Hekmat had hurt his knee so badly he couldn't even walk properly.

At Kabul stadium we jumped over the fence before any Talib spotted us and we waited for the football to start. We were hungry and needed something to eat. We knew that we could only find food in one place – where the Taliban were. Hekmat pointed at a group of Taliban who were sitting on the pitch eating melon. We sat silently, not too far from them, and kept an eye on them to see when they were leaving so we could take their leftover fruit. After some time they stopped eating, but they did not leave. Instead they lay on the grass and started chatting and laughing. My stomach was crying to me; it could no longer remain quiet. Hekmat and Arif's eyes were fixed on the Taliban's leftover melon like a predator's eyes on its prey; their lips and mouths were as dry as tree bark. Suddenly a group of *Spandi* kids came and sat opposite us and their eyes too were fixed on the melon leftovers.

Many Afghans smoke a herb called *Spand* in their houses occasionally and they believe that the smoke annihilates all evils and bad luck and brings blessings and good fortune, so *Spandi* kids would run after people and vehicles and smoke *Spand* in return for money or food. Their target was the Taliban, who were the only ones who could afford to give out money. Luckily, however, after a while the *Spandi* kids got bored and went to prey on someone else. At last, the Taliban left and we rushed towards the melon. We ate what was left but it was not enough to satisfy us. Arif began eating the melon skin. Hekmat watched, then he too began eating the skin, and so did I. Our stomachs were full and after some time we even played on the pitch.

The football was about to start, but there were more Taliban in the stadium than spectators. We were sitting in a place where we had a very good view of the pitch. I was excited at the prospect of seeing Karim-e Pajero, when three

Datsun vehicles suddenly entered the stadium. Each vehicle was packed with Taliban. They took out a man whose eyes were covered with a black strip of cloth. I had no idea what was going on. People around us anxiously looked at the Taliban and the blindfolded man. I asked Hekmat what was going on, but he didn't know either and asked the man next to him

He said, 'The blindfolded man has committed murder, so the Taliban are going to kill him.' I looked at the man who was going to be killed. The man who sat next to Hekmat went on by saying, 'You are not allowed to watch a *Qasasi* (execution) as you are too young.' We moved away from him and sat somewhere else.

Hekmat had lied to me about the football match. Arif and I quarrelled with Hekmat for his deception until people who sat around us told us to shut up. Arif repeatedly begged me to take him home as he was frightened. I was frightened too. But, in another way I was keen to watch a *Qasasi*. The three of us anxiously remained quiet and tried to mask our fear from one another and pretend we were bold and not afraid of what we were about to see.

A Talib began reading Arabic verses – probably from the Quran – and then talked for a while and everyone else was silent. My hands trembled, my whole body started to sweat, and my heart raced faster. I looked at the blindfolded man who was surrounded by Taliban and about to be killed before our very eyes. I could not imagine what that man was going through knowing he was about to be killed.

Hekmat and Arif appeared to be more scared than I was. The Taliban gave a Kalashnikov to a man who was a close relative of the person who was killed by the blindfolded man. Some shouted from the crowds, 'Forgive him!' The man walked towards the blindfolded man and pointed the gun at him. I did not dare to watch, so I shut my eyes and then heard the familiar bang that I have heard from the day that I was born.

When I opened my eyes I saw the blindfolded man lying on the ground with blood streaming from him in all directions. Two of the Taliban grabbed the body and put it into the back of a Datsun. People were leaving with shock in their eyes. The three of us were terrified and wanted to leave the stadium as quickly as possible. So we headed home. There was not much talking, joking or laughing among the three of us.

By the time we arrived home it was evening. It was the first time Arif and I had ever gone that far from the house. We had no excuse to offer to our parents. As we arrived, my father began tearing at our hair and slapping us, but that was not the end of the punishment. He deprived us of our dinner. Arif and I went to sleep without any food. I was lost in the thoughts of the man who was killed before my eyes. I could not sleep that night.

In the morning someone knocked our door. When I opened it I saw that it was the new Mullah, who himself was an influential Talib. He asked me to call my father, so I did. Father greeted the Mullah and his fellows. 'We have come here,' said the Mullah, 'to ask you why you don't attend the mosque for five times prayers and why your children don't come to learn the Quran?' They did not give an opportunity for my father to reply. The Mullah said 'I want to see you at the next congregation and your sons in the Quran class.' Then they walked towards our neighbour's door.

Back inside, Mother asked who was at the door. Father smiled and said, 'The Mullah came with his stomach full of food and wants me to attend the mosque for five times prayers.' My father could not fulfil five times prayer in the mosque as he was so desperate to find a job that he left the house early in the morning and searched until late evening.

The Mullah had an extraordinary life. The mosque was his home and villagers had to provide his three times food and wage. His stomach was satisfied, but he did not put his smooth and warm feet into the worn out shoes of the ordinary Afghans to know how it feels to be hungry and thirsty. The Taliban ordered him to force the village men into the mosque. The Mullah and his fellows did not beat and drag my father into the mosque, but some were not as lucky. Several village men were beaten and dragged into the mosque. My father told my brothers and me to attend the evening Quran class in the mosque when we returned home from cattle dung collecting.

I went to collect the Taliban leftover food. The boy and his goats were already there. Before I started to quarrel, he said we should share the leftover food between us rather than fight over it. I was embarrassed. He was not a bad boy at all. He could have fled as I did the other day, but he did not. We shared it amongst us. He too ate Taliban leftover food and his pockets were filled with it. We gradually became very good friends and never fought over the leftover food ever again. However, more children found out about the checkpoin and they too came to acquire it. The two of us had to stop other children and their cattle. We had to deal with each cattle herder separately and they did not all back down without a quarrel or a brawl. We sometimes hurt each other and our clashes dragged on for tens of minutes until the Taliban saw us, separated us and gave us hard slaps.

Since I had started sharing the food with the boy there was not enough to feed our sheep and dog. My brothers and I had to look somewhere else. We learned how to climb into the trees to collect leaves for our sheep. I was prepared to do anything to feed my animals and it was extremely hard, not only for me, but for all of us watching them burning with hunger. Many times Tariq and I fell from the trees. We hurt ourselves but luckily not so badly as to severely damage ourselves. Palang did not eat grass or leaves and we could not find food for him, so he was hungry day and night. Poor Palang looked at me to feed him, but there was nothing I could find. When my brothers and I failed to resist hunger and couldn't find anything to eat, we would look for tree-gum. We moved from one tree to another in search of it. We could find more tree-gum in cherry trees than in others. But, there never was enough food to kill the hunger. I was perpetually hungry. Life for everyone all over Afghanistan was a struggle for survival.

Since the arrival of the Taliban very noticeable good and bad changes emerged into the lives of people in Kabul. All militias and their checkpoints had disappeared. Thieves, murderers and all other sorts of criminals had disappeared. Rains of rockets and bullets almost ceased to fall. The Taliban were a force of good for some people, since they provided what the average person needed the most – peace and order. The Taliban had vanquished the brutal Mujahidin commanders who killed, tortured, looted and abused poor Afghans on a daily basis. One of the greatest changes the Taliban brought into Pashtun lives was more or less the evaporation of the tribal, village and family hostility. No central government ever dealt with this issue as effectively as the Taliban did. Large numbers of tribal people were killing one another, especially since the United States poured huge cargos of lethal weapons amongst them.

After the arrival of the Taliban, hostile tribes, villagers and families did not dare to kill or harm one another: for there was a severe punishment for murderers. But the lives of Tajick, Hazara, Uzbek ethnicities who lived under the Taliban were bitter. As the Taliban forced the Mujahidin out of each province in central, south-eastern and northern Afghanistan, they suppressed other ethnicities. Wherever their enemy resisted them, once they had defeated them they would then turn their guns on poor civilians and destroy their livelihoods. The crimes that the Taliban committed in some parts of Afghanistan are far beyond belief. Hazara ethnicity had suffered the most. The Taliban's slogan was Peace and Justice, but their deeds were in contrary to their slogan in many parts of Afghanistan.

One morning my cousins (Akmal and Ajmal) entered our room. Akmal said that his father was sending him and his brother to Pakistan to work for a man who owns a carpet factory. Merza Kaka had failed to find a job like my father. There was no food in their house and my cousins cried for food all the time. Sending Akmal and Ajmal to Pakistan was the last option that remained with Merza Kaka. However, Simaa Khala was ready to perish from hunger alongside her children, rather than send them far away into another country at a very young age to work. She first quarrelled with Merza Kaka not to send her children to an alien land, but that only infuriated him. She begged him not to send their children away, but failed to change his mind.

There was one day left before Akmal and Ajmal were to leave Kabul for Pakistan, Simaa Khala wandered around with tearful eyes and repeatedly hugged them and kissed them on the forehead and cheek. She came to our compound and cried a lot to my mother. She said that she would be happy to die rather than her children be separated from her. Simaa Khala and my mother both cried for so long and asked for God's mercy. The next morning it was time for Akmal and Ajmal to leave. We all walked with them to the door for a final farewell. 'Poverty took both my sons from me,' Simaa Khala said. My mother sat beside her to comfort her. Simaa Khala's face was wet with tears watching her children walk away from her in search for food. As Akmal and Ajmal walked away, they reduced everyone to tears. Jamaal, Akmal's younger brother, ran with tearful eyes and begged his older brothers not to leave.

In the mosque, the Mullah was fed up with Arif and me, neither of us had learned the lesson he taught us. The Mullah had a long tree branch and flogged us each time we did not understand the lesson. One day, when I failed to read the previous lesson, he flogged me but the branch broke into pieces. He tore at my hair but that didn't seem to satisfy the Mullah, so then he grabbed my ears with his powerful hands and lifted me from the ground like my mother used to do when I was a kid. I did not cry, since I was used to it, and that aroused more of the Mullah's anger. He shouted at me, 'Why don't you feel the pain and why don't you cry!' Hekmat, Tariq and Arif cried instantly when the Mullah or the teacher flogged them. They advised me to cry while the teacher or Mullah were punishing me, for if I cried they would not punish me any more.

My father had to wake up early in the morning and attend prayers in the mosque, and when he came back from his job search in the evening he was exhausted; but he had to go straight to the mosque. The Mullah repeatedly complained to my father about Arif and me not learning the Quran. Father forced Arif and me to sit with him at night and learn the Quran from him. There was no passion in my heart for learning. My passion was to play football and marbles with the village children. I would have played day and night if I were allowed to. Father behaved like my teacher and acted as the Mullah when he taught me the Quran. Each night he tore at my hair as I failed to learn the lesson he was teaching me. The more I was tortured by the teacher, Mullah and my father the more I hated learning.

Palang Had To Leave

In the summer of 1997, Hekmat, Tariq, Arif and I were bold enough to climb trees. There was a time each year that *Toot* (berry) trees could feed most of our villagers. Each year the villagers passionately looked forward to the *Toot* season to come. During *Toot* season, I spent most of my spare time climbing trees. First I ate as much *Toot* as I could and later I collected them for my mother and little sisters. *Toot* trees belonged to the farmers and most of them did not allow others to consume their berries as they wanted them for their own families. Sometimes, when they caught me, they would beat me badly. But nothing would stop me as my stomach forced me to accept abuse and punishment to satisfy it. There was plenty of food during the *Toot* season, so one day we thought of eating a little bit of meat too. Hekmat, Arif and I built a slingshot to hunt birds. Once we had fed ourselves on the trees we climbed down and looked for the little birds. We spent hours shooting stones at the birds on the trees, but the birds were very smart. As we fired stones at them, they flew away before the stone could reach them.

After several weeks, when we were about to give up bird hunting, Hekmat eventually shot a tiny bird and it fell down like a leaf from a tree. The bird had been hit in the stomach and blood was flowing from its mouth and it reminded me of the man who was shot in Kabul stadium. The bird was alive when we got to it. However, Hekmat put his knife into its neck. Shooting the bird, watching the blood flowing from it is mouth and Hekmat's knife, the whole process seemed very cruel to me so I refused to eat it. Hekmat asked me to collect firewood so that we could light a fire and cook the bird, but I refused. Hekmat and Arif quickly collected wood and lit a fire. When the bird was cooked they tore it in half and in a second it had disappeared. From then on I refused to take part in bird hunting. Hekmat and Arif spent more time hunting and went on to become good hunters. They killed three or four birds a week and sometimes even more, and Arif brought his hunt home to share with our sisters. Arif would carry his slingshot even when he was collecting cattle dung. Whenever he saw them, he would put his bucket down and fire several stones.

Palang could no longer endure starvation and I could no longer deceive him with the bones and the very little leftover food I collected. He started barking day and night but there was nothing we could give him. He disturbed our neighbours when he barked at night. The neighbours told us, 'People can't feed themselves, but you keep a dog to feed too.' Tariq was anxious for his pet as day after day Palang was getting thinner. He looked everywhere to find food for Palang, even on the way to and from school.

Palang was a good friend to everyone, but there was a special bond of friendship between him and my sisters. As he was so hungry he could no longer play with them. Days, weeks and months elapsed but Palang did not stop crying for food. Neighbours frequently complained. One day my father decided to throw Palang out of the house so that he could find his own food before he died. Tariq protested against our father's decision, but after some time he too agreed and knew that Palang would eventually die inside our compound. Our father tasked Tariq and I to take Palang and leave him far away somewhere so that he couldn't find the way back home. However, there was no safety for a poor dog in Afghanistan. Children threw rocks at dogs in the villages, streets or anywhere else.

We tightened a rope around Palang's neck. Our sisters screamed while Tariq and I dragged the dog from the house. We walked for miles into the fields until we reached a bushy forest in an area called *Qabulboy* and tied Palang's rope to a tree and left him there. Tariq was extremely upset, all the way home he did not say a word. Surprisingly, Palang somehow reached home before us.

A friend of our father was a driver. He took people from Kabul to Ghazni and from Ghazni back to Kabul, so Father asked him to take Palang and leave him somewhere in Ghazni. The driver accepted and said, 'Bring the dog.' Tariq put a rope on Palang's neck again and took him out of the house. Again, our sisters began crying.

My youngest sister asked me with her tearful eyes, 'Where is Tariq taking Palang again?' I told her we did not have food to give him so we were going to send him somewhere far away where he could find plenty of food. With Palang gone our compound yard looked empty. The first few days were really difficult for us. I was scared of the darkness of the night, but walked fearlessly in the yard when Palang was there. Once Palang had gone, the fear of the demons once again emerged in my heart. I could no longer walk boldly in the yard at night.

Simaa Khala was disheartened with her life once her sons had left for Pakistan. She no longer talked with my mother about any other subject but Akmal and Ajmal and whenever she mentioned their names she began weeping. Mother tried a lot to comfort her by saying she was not the only parent who had sent her children to provide food for them all. Her children weren't just earning money, they were learning a craft as well. Many were forced to send their children to unknown places.

My mother was anxious that my father might also send their children to Pakistan in search of food. Father began moaning about what would happen with our futures. He said that we were not learning anything in school but we needed to train for a profession so that when we grew up, at least we would have a craft and through that could feed our family. My mother warned him not to even think about sending her children to Pakistan. She even cried and said, 'I can endure hunger and suffering, but I am going to die without my children.'

My father did not mind if he had to send us to Pakistan for work, but he was scared of one thing and that was drugs. He was anxious that we might get hooked on heroin if we didn't have him to look out for us. In every ruined house there were groups of young Afghans who became victims of the drug. Thousands lost their lives each year. It really was a serious threat, even to the farmers who grew it. Their sons became haunted by heroin and their children smoked it to their death, like so many other young boys, even though the Taliban prohibited the use of drugs and alcohol. But they did not mind poppy cultivation since they profited from it. The Taliban were not the only ones behind opium production in Afghanistan. Many powerful people were behind the business; powerful governments too.

One day I woke up early in the morning to go and collect the Taliban leftover food. As I opened the door, I saw Palang standing there. Seeing him at home, I was amazed. Ghazni Province was more than 80 miles away; it was not possible for an animal to travel through those wild mountains and deserts all the way to Kabul, but Palang did. He had wounds on his tail and back. He jumped up at me and sniffed and licked my hands. I took him in and called everyone to see who was back. Palang greeted every single one of us by rubbing himself on our legs and sniffing our clothes and jumping around us merrily. I saw in his eyes how much he had missed us. We were his family and he considered us his family and yet it was poverty that blinded us to see his love for us. He saw my parents as his parents, my siblings as his own siblings. His world was our compound and we were his family as well as his everything. We sent Palang over 80 miles away and yet he came all the way back to us.

My father said he would no longer send Palang anywhere. 'If we are starving, let us starve together,' he said. My sisters were extremely happy when they saw that the dog was back. There was a firm bond of friendship between them and Palang.

Amongst the Taliban was a special group called *Amre bil Marouf, wa nahi az munkar*, but most people called them *Amre Bil Marouf*. They were religious police and their job was to force people to comply with the harsh laws of the Taliban and they hold the record for brutality, especially in Kabul. They beat women who did not comply with their rules. They shaved the heads of boys who dressed their hair in western style. They forced men to attend prayers in the mosque. They imprisoned those who listened to music or watched films. They beat and imprisoned those who cut or shaved their beards.

One day we were on the way to school when two pickup trucks packed with *Amre Bil Marouf* stopped and caught three boys who had dressed their hair like Leonardo DiCaprio in the film *Titanic*. At that time the film was at its height in Kabul. Boys secretly watched the film and copied Leonardo DiCaprio's hairstyle. The men half-shaved each boy's head and then blackened their faces. Then they put the three boys in the back of their new pickup trucks and drove them through the streets and bazaars. We decided not to go to school and instead followed the *Amre Bil Marouf*. We followed them street by street and village after village. They had caught so many law breakers that they could no longer fit them into their pickup trucks, so they shaved off half their hair and then marched them through the streets. Some had a patch of hair in the front of their heads and no hair on the top and some had hair on the back of their heads and none in the front.

Amre Bil Marouf spotted a woman who wore a barque and it seemed that she had complied with the Taliban rules for women. A Talib began lashing her. The woman started crying. She fell to the floor. I thought that as she had fallen to the floor the Talib would stop lashing her, but he didn't. He carried on whipping her like our teacher used to do. As the woman cried, she also begged the Talib to stop lashing her. She even promised the Talib that she would never walk out of her house ever again if he put an end to the whipping. It seemed as if the Talib enjoyed whipping women. The helpless woman attempted to escape from the cruel lash, but there was nowhere for her to go. The unlucky woman went through all those pains for two absurd reasons: Firstly she wore sandals, men could see her fee and secondly, she had painted her fingernails.

Only once or twice did Hekmat, Arif and I attend school, the rest of the time we chased the *Amre Bil Marouf* and watched them beat and humiliate men, women and boys. There were times when the *Amre Bil Marouf* chased us away, yet still we followed them. They had an expert with them who looked at men's beards and could predict whether one had cut it or not. Those who had cut or shaved their beards were ruthlessly beaten and imprisoned.

One day they caught a man who was in his mid-thirties who had cut his beard. Two Taliban began lashing, punching and kicking the man. Surprisingly, the man fought back. He was a strong man that managed to beat both Taliban before the rest of their comrades came to their aid. This man was in deep trouble, for he had dared to raise his hand on the Taliban. More Taliban grabbed the man and beat him viciously with their Kalashnikovs. The two Taliban who were beaten by the man took their Kalashnikovs and wanted to shoot him. Hekmat, Arif and I, including everyone else who had witnessed the scene ran away in order to avoid being shot. Luckily, the other Taliban did not allow their two comrades to shoot the man. However, they had beaten the man to the limit where he was lying on the floor covered in blood. The Taliban dumped him into the back of their vehicle and drove off.

We went on watching the *Amre Bil Marouf*. They went around Macroryan's market and destroyed the poor people's shops as they considered them to be illegal. Tens of boys would go to help them in shop demolition. Hekmat, Arif and I too joined them. Poor shopkeepers would not dare to tell the *Amre Bil Maaruf* not to destroy their shops, but the *Amre Bil Marouf* were heartless. There was a disabled shopkeeper who had no legs, and he begged the Taliban not to tear down his shop. He said, 'This is the only source of income for my family and my family will starve to death if you tear my shop down.' Nothing could stop the *Amre Bil Maaruf*, not even the disabled man's tears.

We enjoyed watching what the *Amre Bil Marouf* were doing, but people were tired of them, yet the helpless people of Kabul could do nothing to stop them. The *Amre Bil Marouf* seemed like a drunken gang who went around hurting poor men, women and boys for petty reasons. One day, a bunch of women were washing clothes in the stream outside their house. (The Taliban banned women from washing clothes outside of their compounds.) None of them wore a burqa. Suddenly, the *Amre Bil Marouf* caught them by surprise. The women panicked and scattered in different directions. Some even entered other people's houses to hide themselves. But the *Amre Bil Marouf* went in different directions and caught them one by one. The whole village heard the poor women's cries while they were being beaten.

It was almost evening and I was playing marbles with the village children when the *Amre Bil Marouf* appeared out of the blue and encircled us. They considered marble-playing as gambling and gambling was outlawed by the Taliban. One of them picked up all of our marbles from the ground and the other began to search everyone's pockets. I had hundreds of marbles and it took me over a year to win them from the village children. They were too precious to me. I couldn't just let the *Amre Bil Marouf* take them from me, so I decided to flee. I ran as fast as I could and two of the Taliban chased after me. They caught me and brought me back to their commander. The commander took all of my marbles and then asked me to stand up straight. Then he slapped me several times in the face. It was so painful – not the slaps, but the loss of my marbles. I could not sleep for several weeks as I was thinking of my lost marbles. On many occasions I secretly cried for them.

Hekmat, Arif and I did not know how to live with shrunken and empty stomachs. When there was no food in my stomach, I felt like there was a fire inside it burning me and only food could extinguish that fierce fire. As time went by, my love for food was so intense that I risked the punches and kicks of the shopkeepers and farmers just to get food. I stared at food outside semi-ruined shops for hours, until either the shopkeepers beat or cursed me away or I managed to steal it before they spotted me. I would stand in front of restaurants and stare at the people eating. I would try to look as miserable as I possibly could so that they would feel sorry for me and give me a little of their food. Sometimes they would and other times they just ignored me and ate the last bits of food from their plates. I could not think about anything else but FOOD! Everywhere I went, all I would do was look for food, like a butterfly seeking flowers.

I was not the only child in love with food. All Afghan children were.

Autumn was not a good season for Hekmat, Arif and me. There was very little in the fields for us to eat. Shopkeepers also did not have as much food in their shops as they had in the summer. We did our hardest to steal whatever we could find. Most shopkeepers knew why we stood in front of their shops; our village shopkeepers wouldn't let us close to theirs. So we walked far away and found new shops. We were mostly caught and beaten and rarely succeeded in stealing any food from a shop. Most of the time, I had to carry my empty stomach around with me and endure the pain of it until my mother gave me a piece of Naan. Every so often, when I could not bear the pain of hunger any more, I joined my sisters who always surrounded my mother with their tearful eyes and demanded food. Mother tried to keep us quiet by telling us stories, but nothing could keep us silent but food. Our mother tried all methods to keep us quiet, but if all failed her last resort was to flog every single one of us with a tree branch and then throw all of us out of the compound, locking herself in alone and crying.

One afternoon, Mother threw us out of the house after flogging us. Hekmat told me to go to the fields with him. Farmers harvested all their crops and I did not see anything that we could find to eat. Despite that, Hekmat and I walked until we reached a turnip field. But instead of one guard there were three farmers who guarded the fields from hungry children. We had no option but to wait. Wait and wait for the right time to strike. After a few hours the three farmers disappeared into their hut and we thought it was the right time to hunt as much turnip as we could. Both of us jumped into the turnip field and uprooted turnip after turnip until I spotted someone charging towards us. I screamed at Hekmat to flee. But before Hekmat knew what was happening the farmer had already grabbed him. I feared that the rest of the farmers might be around and would catch me also, so I ran towards the village with the few turnips I had with me. I sat outside the village and after a while saw Hekmat. He had several bruises on his face, his nose was bleeding and he was crying. The farmer had ruthlessly punched and kicked Hekmat. Despite the fact he was badly beaten by the farmer and tears were still falling from his eyes, the first thing he did was to snatch a turnip from me and he began eating it.

We sat beside the stream and he cleaned away his blood. But his tears kept falling. The more I looked at him the more I became enraged. At last I decided to take my revenge. I asked him to go back with me to the peasants' field and throw stones at them and hopefully we would be able to hit them. Hekmat was more than happy to do this. We walked back to the fields and the three peasants were fulfilling their afternoon prayers. It was a good opportunity for Hekmat and me to throw stones before they had finished their prayers and then chase after us. We threw loads of stones at them, but they all failed to hit them. When one peasant had finished his prayers he chased after us. Our stomachs were full and our legs were able to carry us wherever we wanted to go. He failed to catch us.

I did not like my house at all. Whenever I stepped into it, I saw my little sisters' wet faces. Their open mouths screamed for food like bird chicks in their nest when their mother returns. In the past Mother did not let us outside the house as she did not want us to be out of her sight. Now that we all cried and asked food from her she wanted us to go out of the compound and leave her alone. I was free! I could go wherever I wanted in my spare time without being punished by my parents. Sometimes, when I managed to satisfy my stomach, I went with other children to a ruined Soviet Union base where there were abandoned Soviet tanks and armoured vehicles. We each got into them and pretended we were fighting one another.

My poor father was struggling to find food for us. He went from one friend to another and from one villager to another asking them to lend him money so that he could buy food for his family. No one had money. Wherever my father went, he found people in the same condition as his. He had to ask for days and weeks and months until he found someone who had money and was willing to lend it to him. He was drowned in debt. Yet he had to borrow more money without knowing how to pay it back. Every day he woke up early in the morning with a heart filled with hope and optimism that he would find a job. Every evening, when he returned home, his heart was full of hopelessness and despair. He blamed himself for the misery and suffering of his children. He thought he had failed to carry out the responsibility of a father and a husband. He was angry, hungry, hopeless and in poor health and was confused and had no idea what to do. My mother did not complain about anything at all. When he was around, she pretended that her world was like a paradise of gardens and streams of affluence. Both, however, knew what was going on just by looking at their crying children. They could neither provide food for our stomachs nor could they provide clothes and shoes for us. We had grown out of our tattered clothes.

There were always several cuts in the soles of my feet, and the same with my other siblings (with the exception of Tariq). The winter was closing in and we had neither warm clothes nor shoes to wear. It seemed like we were all going to be imprisoned in the house throughout the winter. My sisters cried often to our father to buy shoes for them. But Father could do nothing but stare at them and wipe the tears from their faces.

Winter for the Afghans was a flood of crisis and they had nowhere to escape. Afghans had to remain quiet and pray to God for their survival. After so many years of destructive winters, everyone knew what kind of crisis the winter would bring itself. Even my parents knew that their children would demand more food in the winter than in the other seasons. All they could do was pack their children around them and watch the crisis approach. Tariq took more responsibility in the house than the rest of us. He even forced Arif and me to collect cattle dung in the late autumn as the weather was dreadfully cold. He scared Arif and me by saying, 'If you do not collect enough cattle dung our youngest brother, Tamim, will freeze to death in the winter.' It frightened us as everyone loved Tamim. Everybody wanted Tamin to play with them and, sometimes, we even fought with one another over Tamim. Nobody liked to see him crying for food. We all gave a bit of our food for him when we had it. If Arif and I hunted something special from the shops, we would secretly steal Tamim from my mother, out of the house, and take him to a quiet corner of the village and share our hunt with him. We did not want our parents to know we were stealing food. If they ever found out, it would have been catastrophic for both of us.

A four-year-old child died in our village, from some petty illness, and all the villagers mourned for her. When someone died, the children would supply water for the people who dug the grave in our vast cemetery, which was the village children's playground too. We all carried water until the time of the funeral. Throughout the funeral all villagers, even Tariq, stood behind the

Mullah and prayed. Hekmat, Arif and I, who did not know how to pray, remained quiet and when the prayers were over everyone sat and the Mullah began his speech. He spoke for a long time in the cold weather. During his speech, he said something that caught my attention:

> 'God has created everyone and without God's will nothing will move from its place, not even a tree leaf would shake without his will. He gives life and He is the only one who takes life. Everything that happens around us is God's will.'

From that moment onward, I blamed God for everything that was happening to me. Whenever I encountered a difficulty, I blamed God for it, as I thought that God had brought about all these difficulties.

Tariq, Arif and I were still in search of cattle dung when the snow began to fall. I could see in the eyes of other Afghans that they hated the snow as much the Afghan women hated the Taliban, despite knowing how important snow was for their agriculture. The snow that saved Afghans and their crops also took lives, mostly older people and children. In a matter of a few hours, the snow painted the earth white. My feet were as cold as ice as I had worn out my shoes. Arif and I cried for Tariq to let us go home as it was cold and we did not have warm clothes. Tariq was cold too, but he did not want to take three empty buckets back. After several hours it was severely difficult to find cattle dung under the snow. Arif and I refused to touch the snow any more, even when Tariq threaten to beat us. At last, Tariq was left with no choice but to take empty buckets home. We had not managed to collect enough cattle dung throughout the year for the winter, as there were other children from various villages who were as desperate to collect it as Tariq was. My mother could not afford to burn cattle dung in the day during the winter to keep the room warm. At night, when the weather descended to 15 to 18 degrees below zero, she burned cattle dung in the house not only to keep us warm but also to cook our dinner and lunch.

I felt hungrier in the winter than the other seasons. My mother brought out a big pot of *Shurwa Berenj* (rice soup, filled with water and a few grains of rice swimming beneath it like fish) at lunch times. We had to race for the rice to catch it like fisherman. Tariq, Arif and I were good rice catchers in comparison to our sisters. In only a few moments we would seize all the rice and our sisters had to fill their stomachs with the water, and soon after lunch they began crying for food again. For years we raced to eat food faster than one another, so our tongues and mouths got used to scorching food and even the hottest food did not burn us. Each time my poor mother prepared the little food we had, she would beg my siblings and me to stop eating so quickly. When our mother placed the pot before us, we would look at one another and, if one of my siblings appeared to eat faster than the others, then everyone would attempt to eat it faster and in a second the food would disappear! My sisters were the ones who suffered the most, as usual, as they were not as good as Tariq, Arif and I were. After an hour or two our stomachs would cry again for food. My siblings and I looked around the house to find anything that was edible, but nothing could be found. There was nothing in the fields that I could steal in the winter. Tamim, my youngest brother, was almost two years old and he could barely speak a few words. One day tears were falling from his innocent eyes and he, for the first time, told my mother that he was hungry. Mother wept all day long on that day.

I spent two hours in the mosque every day to learn the Quran. During this time I begged God to end our misery. I enjoyed very much the two hours that I spent there because it was very warm as the villagers had to collect money and buy firewood for the mosque each winter.

One day I told the Mullah that I didn't know how to pray. When he heard this, he became very angry and gave me several slaps on the face. 'You are a grown man and yet you don't know how to pray?' said the Mullah. He started teaching me five times prayers, as well as beating me constantly. I felt pain when he punished me. But there was something more painful than his physical punishment. He cursed me and bullied me with different, unpleasant names. Hekmat, Arif and I hated the village Mullah because he tortured us when we did not learn. So when we were outside the mosque, we would curse him and called him different names, and mock him all the time. Some of the village children would ridicule me in the mosque, as I used to wear my mother's flip-flops, because I did not have my own. As soon as we got out of the mosque I would fight and quarrel with those children who laughed at me.

Most of the day I was imprisoned in the house along with my siblings. I had no shoes to wear, and even if I had, our mother would not let us go out when it snowed. Hekmat knocked on our door for hours and called for Arif and me to come out and play *Barf-Jangi* (snowball fighting). But we couldn't play with him barefoot. One day Hekmat came up with a plan that both Arif and I would be interested in. The Mujahidin's rockets had destroyed most of the compounds in our village and they were empty. He asked us to join him and set a fire inside the ruined rooms and warm ourselves. Arif and I were party to this and did not mind walking in the snow to get to the ruined compounds.

As we walked barefoot in the snow, it took us a long time to find an empty ruined room in the village, as they were all crammed full with men and young boys who were heroin addicts. They would all gather together and stayed as long as they had heroin to smoke, and most of them smoked themselves to death. Heroin addicts looked frightening and Hekmat, Arif and I were scared of them. Most of them were too weak and their bodies seemed like they had no flesh and blood. All we could see were bones enveloped in a pale skin. In the freezing winter, the weather was unbearably cold, but their bodies began to sweat when they smoked heroin. They broke the old windows and doors to set fire to them.

We had learned from them how to set fire, so we too began breaking the old doors and windows and set fire to them, and warmed ourselves. Heroin addicts came and used our fire to smoke their heroin. Sometimes they even offered it to us. But my father's advice was in all corners of my mind – 'drugs are your most vicious enemy'.

One day, as we entered an old room, we saw a boy in his early twenties lying on the floor. We thought he might be asleep, so we set our fire, sat around it and warmed our feet and our hands. After some time, our fire died out and we left the ruined room. The next day, when we came again, still that boy was lying there and that is when we thought that there was something not right with him. Hekmat and I shook the boy, but he gave no response. We shouted at him to wake him up, still he did not react. We ran to the village leader's compound and knocked on his door. His son came out and we told him what we had seen in the ruined room. When his father and a few other elderly men went to examine what we had found, they discovered that the boy was dead.

Later, village leaders and other elders knocked on every door in our village and warned parents to protect their children against heroin. Young men became addicted to heroin because they had neither school or university to go, nor any job. When my parents found out we were going into the ruined compounds and making fires there, they were enraged, particularly my father. His face and eyes were filled with anger and fury. He flogged us with his long tree branch. Father was aware of the effects of heroin. He used to say to us, 'Once you have swallowed its smoke then you are going to be hooked on it for the rest of your life and nothing can save you from its brutal jaws. And you will kill people and steal from them in order to supply yourself with the heroin.' He would sometimes take my brothers and me to show us heroin addicts who were in appalling conditions and would tell us if we smoked it we would be in the same state as them.

The Carpet Weaver Boy

My father was anxious for his children's future. He did not want us to grow up without a proper education or skill. One snowy night he told Tariq and me to be ready in the morning, for we were going somewhere. Tariq and I had no clue as to where our father would take us.

In the morning we followed Father, still with no idea of where we were going. It was freezing cold. After a while he knocked on a door. Two gentlemen came out and greeted us and asked us to follow them. The compound yard was beautiful and there were many fruit trees. At the corner of the compound there was a big old mud hut. As we stepped into the huge room I could hear the sound of children, but it was dark and it took my eyes some time to adjust.

When I was able to see, I saw strange machines I'd never seen before. There were about fifty to sixty children, some of my age, most younger, and a few older. It looked like all those children were fastened into these strange looking machines. Every child had a device in his hand, similar to a knife. I had no idea what was going on. My father introduced us to the two men. Both were in their twenties. The older one said that his name was Naqib, but we must call him Ustad Naqib (master Naqib). The second man said his name was Halim and we must address him as Ustad Halim. My father had brought us into a carpet factory to become apprentices; Ustad Naqib and Ustad Halim were the owners. Father wanted us to learn carpet weaving for several reasons. He was really anxious that we might become the victims of heroin. He knew that we were not learning anything good in school, so he wanted us to learn a craft. Before leaving us there, he told us that we had to learn this skill in order to survive in the future.

Ustad Naqib and Ustad Halim told us their father had been killed in the Mujahidin fighting in Kabul during the factional war. If they hadn't known the carpet weaving craft then they would have starved to death alongside their mother and siblings. Ustad Naqib and Ustad Halim did not weave wool carpets like other Afghans; they wove extremely beautiful silk carpets. I had never seen such carpets in my whole life. The weaving of each carpet was as difficult as building the Great Wall of China. Ustad Naqib and his brother sold their carpets very cheaply to a Pakistani company and as soon as the carpets reached Pakistan, it was no longer an Afghan carpet. The Pakistani company sold them on to the rest of the world with a very large price in the name of Pakistani carpets. The poor Afghans could not export their carpets anywhere else but to Pakistan. Young children suffered the most, weaving the carpets with pain and sweat; the Pakistani business people gained the most.

Ustad Naqib told me to sit with a group of four children, who were younger than me, and observe how they weaved a carpet and learn from them. One boy was in charge of the carpet and two others worked under his supervision per machine. While I learned, I saw Ustad Naqib and Ustad Halim beat children who failed to work hard. Not only did they beat the children in charge of each machine but also tortured the younger children.

When the sun went down and no one could see each other. Ustad Naqib said, 'It's time to stop working and go home.' When the children heard this, it was as if they had been granted the whole world's happiness. Every child cheered. 'What is happening? Why is everyone so happy?' I asked the kid who sat beside me all day long. 'Because we are free, no more work until tomorrow morning,' he said. At that time I did not properly understand why they were so happy. Before I left, Ustad Halim, told me, 'When you arrive home, tell your mother to prepare your breakfast early in the morning. I want you and your brother to be here before sunrise, and if you can't come on time, do not bother to come at all, because there are so many other boys who want to work and learn a profession.'

On the way home I saw Hekmat sitting outside our compound. He shouted, 'Where have you been? I have been sitting here all day long asking your family where you are, but none of them told me.' I told him that I had to wake up early in the morning and come back when it is dark. He was sad to hear this. I told him that my father wanted me to be an apprentice in a carpet factory. When he heard that, he said that he too would like to become an apprentice. He said that he would ask his parents for their permission to let him become a carpet weaver. Arif wanted to join us too, but one of us had to stay in the house to collect the Taliban leftover food for the sheep and Palang, as well as clear the snow from the rooftop. Tariq and I woke up early in the morning and asked our mother to prepare breakfast for us, but there was nothing she could prepare, so we had to walk with our shrunken stomachs towards the factory. She promised she would send our lunch earlier to the carpet factory. Father told us to go straight to the mosque once we had finished carpet weaving.

The next day Hekmat came into the factory accompanied by his father. The first few days of our apprenticeship were very interesting for the three of us. However, after a few months, we came to realise that it was worse than the communists' dungeons in Afghanistan. If we did not weave faster, Ustad Naqib and Ustad Halim and then the boy who was in charge of the carpet beat us up. We complained so many times to our father that the carpet factory owners were torturing us every day, but he said that we were apprentices now, and the master sometimes punishes his apprentices when he gets upset and we must put up with it.

I was a quick learner and learned how to use the carpet pattern faster than Ustad Naqib expected. When Ustad Naqib found out that I could use the pattern, he was very pleased, but it did not mean that he and his brother stopped beating me. I frequently cut my left index finger with a *Changak* blade. A *Changak* was the device that we weaved the carpet with and it had a sharp blade for chopping the strings off. Sometimes children cut their fingers with it by accident. I went through tremendous pain every day to weave the carpet. I began to hate the dark carpet factory as much as I hated school. Ustad Naqib and Ustad Halim punished and shouted at me regularly to work faster, but how could I work faster when my stomach was empty, my head was dizzy and my hands shivered as a result of the lack of energy? They wouldn't even allow me to wipe sweat from my face. My mother was not there so I could not express my pains through my tears. In the carpet factory no one bothered to pay attention to tears. Ustad Naqib and Ustad Halim had heard the children's cries for so many years that they no longer even bothered to ask the reasons why they were crying. The only thing that was of importance to them was that carpets were being made faster and quicker so that their family could survive their own brutal hunger.

When we finished work we had to go straight to the mosque and taste the pain of the Mullah's cable and then go home. At home it was, as usual, my sisters and brothers surrounding my mother crying for food. My father spent days begging the Taliban to give him a job, and nights sitting in the corner of the room lost in his thoughts. He had no idea what to do, with all those responsibilities that lay on his shoulders. The responsibility to provide food for our stomachs. The responsibility to save us from the ferocious winter. The responsibility to provide clothes and shoes for his barefoot children. The responsibility for our safety and our education...

The carpet factory became a prison for me. I was nine years old. My heart hurt while I watched children my age playing in the village when I had to go and work in that dark room, from dawn till dusk, and endure the pain of hunger and torture.

There was a small window in the dark room that enabled light to come through. Whenever I shifted my eyes from the carpet, they refused to look anywhere else but towards that window. Each day I would look at that window hundreds of times, for only one reason – to watch for nightfall so I could get of this cruel, dark room.

Friday was the only day that I could walk in the gardens of freedom. On Thursday nights I could not sleep. I spent the night awake, looking at the stars through our window and impatiently waiting for the brightness of the morning to swallow the darkness and set me free.

When the morning arrived, nothing could stop me. The first thing I did was run to Hekmat's compound and knock on his door. Hekmat felt the same way as I did. Our village cemetery was a great playground for children and we played there all day long. I spent the whole Friday playing and I even forgot about my hunger. As time passed, there were things going through my mind that told me, 'Time is running out, play, run, talk, laugh and spend time with other children, because you are soon going back to that dark factory.' As the sun disappeared, I was overwhelmed by sadness.

When I woke up before sunrise the next day, I didn't want to go to the factory. But my parents forced me to go. On the way there, tears fell from my eyes. For almost a year I begged my parents endlessly to rid me of this carpet weaving. I wept to them almost every evening and showed them my blistered hands and the wounds I had sustained when I was tortured so that I wasn't forced to go back.

For a few hours my parents would agree for me not to go back to the carpet factory when they saw my injuries. But after another few hours they changed their minds and forced me to go back. They thought it was vital for me to learn carpet weaving to gain a useful trade and use it in the future to survive. But I wanted to be free and play.

After many months, Ustad Naqib gave us a salary. Tariq said that he would buy a pair of new shoes when he got his first salary. I did not only want to buy a pair of shoes but clothes as well, as I had grown out of mine. Ustad Naqib called me forward and handed me a 10,000 Afghani note. I was so happy that my legs forced me to run home and show it to my father. The last time, with a 10,000 Afghani note, we bought several big pomegranates, so I thought that I would be able to buy shoes and clothes and they must be cheaper than pomegranates as they are not edible.

When I left the factory, I saw the earth was buried under thick snow, but nothing could stop me from running to show my salary to my parents. As Tariq and I reached home, we showed our 10,000 Afghani notes to our parents and told our father to take us to the city and buy clothes and shoes for us. Our father smiled and said that we can't buy clothes and shoes with 10,000 Afghani, as it would cost more than 500,000 Afghani to buy them for both of us. He asked Tariq and me to give him our money so that he could buy rice for us, but we both refused. We ate our dinner, which was not enough as usual, and went to bed. That night our father swept snow off the rooftop as he was afraid we might be buried alive if the roof were to collapse. The next morning we had nothing to eat in the house, so Tariq and I refused to go to the carpet factory as we were both hungry. Our brothers and sisters did not have enough energy to cry. Our mother did not have enough energy to stand and do the house chores. Tariq became so ill-tempered that when I tried to talk with him he slapped me and told me to be silent and not to bother him. My body was shaking. I went into the yard and ate lots of snow and hoped it would satisfy my stomach, but it didn't.

That morning, we heard nothing from Palang. He did not bark for his food as he usually did, despite the fact that my mother had not fed him for some time. Tariq went to check on him. I had my youngest brother, Tamim on my lap when we all heard Tariq screaming. We all went out and saw Palang lying dead in the snow. Everyone's heart was filled with pain and grief. It was a good excuse for us to cry as much as we could, to reduce the mountains of pain and grievance that laid in our hearts.

Palang had died of hunger and went far away from this brutal world, somewhere we would never see him again. What a terrible life he'd had. He spent days and nights without food. We buried him in the corner of our yard on that snowy day.

We cried for Palang for many days. I knew that death meant the disappearance of someone for good. I stopped crying. I knew that my cries could not change anything. I wiped my sisters' tears off their faces instead. Palang was their best friend and they would not forget him. My youngest sister would go and sit beside Palang's empty den and cry, so we had to destroy Palang's den as well. I made up tales that Palang was waiting for us in heaven and we would see him in the life after death. My parents knew that we would die, just like Palang, one after another if they failed to find food for us.

My father, Tariq and I took the sheep and went to the bazaar to sell them. I wore my mother's sandals in the snowy and stormy day and walked beside my father. The chill hit my face and burned it. Kabul city was miles from where we lived and we had to walk, as we did not have money to travel in a vehicle. We walked for more than an hour. My sandals were packed with snow. I could not feel my feet, nose, ears or any other parts of my body. I could not walk any more and I could not abide the pain that the coldness had inflicted on me. I burst into tears and screamed, so did Tariq. My father looked around to find a shop, because generally shopkeepers had a fire inside to keep themselves warm. But he could not find any open. The only shops were those that were destroyed in the Mujahidin conflict. My father said that we had no choice but to walk faster and find a shop. I did not know what my poor sheep were going through, as those poor animals were voiceless and could not cry like Tariq and I could. With hungry stomachs, bodies filled with pain and tears in my eyes, I marched alongside my father and brother in the ruined and empty streets of Kabul in search of someone to buy our sheep.

We eventually arrived in the city. It was heartbreaking to see poor children encircling their mothers and begging for a loaf of bread in the freezing weather. Most people did not have anything to give. There were *Spandi* children running after cars and begging for money, or for food, in the freezing weather. We went to *Sar-e Chawk* and waited for someone to buy our sheep, but there was no one there. People were starving; no one could afford to buy sheep. We stood for over three hours as the snow fell. Children much younger than me sat alongside their mothers in the ruined and empty roads and streets of Kabul, half buried under the snow, begging from the few people who passed by.

We gave up and headed back home as we could no longer stand the cold weather. On the way a pickup truck filled with Taliban stopped beside us and asked my father if he wanted to sell his sheep. My father took the sheep close to the Taliban, who sat in their vehicle so they could have a good view. Father told them the price and, without any bargaining, the Taliban agreed to pay us. They said they didn't need our sheep's stomachs and we could have them if we travelled with them to their base where they would slay the sheep. My father was more than happy to take our sheep's stomachs home. At this time I realised that my sheep were going to be killed. We loaded them into the back of the truck and sat beside them while the Taliban drove towards their base. My sheep were taking their last breaths, so Tariq and I stroked them. I could not stop my tears from falling; those two sheep were so dear to me. I had spent years feeding them, playing with them, watching them grow.

My poor sheep were unaware that they were about to be slaughtered. We reached the Taliban base and unloaded the sheep. There were many other Taliban who came to look at them. After a while, the Taliban cook arrived with his sharp butcher's knife. Three other Taliban helped him to kill my sheep. I tried to remain strong and not show any emotions, but the tears forced themselves out. The Taliban killed my sheep and I watched the streams of blood flowing out of their throats. My sheep had bitten their tongues as they were slaughtered.

They gave us our sheep's stomachs and we walked back to Kabul to buy food for our family. My father took Tariq and me to *Manda-e* and bought shoes and jumpers for us and on the way back home my father gave some money to several beggar women. My little hungry siblings were extremely sad when they found out that our sheep had been killed. Mother cooked the sheep's stomachs for us, but I could not eat it.

One evening Simaa Khala entered our home with a happy face, and told my mother that the Taliban had given Merza Kaka a job. The next morning Merza Kaka woke up early and went to start the job. As Merza Kaka arrived, he realised that he was not the only one who would start work with the Taliban. There were several other desperate fathers who were promised a job. The Taliban put Merza Kaka beside other men in the back of their pickup trucks and drove off. After some time they stopped in Shamali plain, north of Kabul. Shamali was a marvellous place, famous for its fruit gardens, especially for its delicious grapes. The Taliban equipped Merza Kaka and the other men with saws, axes, shovels and spades and led them through the gardens and then told them to chop down every single tree in every single garden and in return they would receive money. On hearing what the Taliban said, every one of them was shocked, but every one of them was thinking of their starving families, none of them could afford to refuse the job. Merza Kaka had no choice but to chop down the trees.

Inhabitants of Shamali were mainly from the Tajik ethnicity and bitterly resisted the Taliban. They ambushed the Taliban from their gardens and devastated them over and over again. So the Taliban destroyed the gardens. Shamali was one of the places that suffered the most at the hands of the Taliban.

As each tree fell down, children surrounded it in search of old and dry fruit and that broke Merza Kaka's heart, watching vulnerable children searching for food. Merza Kaka was shocked by what he had seen in Shamali. He said that the entire Pakistani army had come into Afghanistan to fight for the Taliban. He went and told other villagers as well what he had seen. Merza Kaka was confused, it was not the entire Pakistani army, but certainly thousands of Pakistani troops came to help the Taliban. The cruel government of Pakistan has devastated Afghans so badly for its evil ambitions in Afghanistan for decades. But it's very natural that a weaker nation always attracts neighbouring and the world's powerful governments. The ancient culture, superstition, lack of education, naivety, poverty, war, lack of freedom produces Afghan men who are a perfect tool to be used by regional powers and international superpowers. For many decades empires and neighbouring countries used Afghan men to achieve their objectives in the region. The Taliban themselves were also a tool, used by powerful governments to achieve their wicked objectives in the region.

Winter was over, the snow began to melt and the valleys and mountains looked red with poppies (flower poppies, not opium poppies). Schools once again started. For half a day we had to go to school and in the latter half of the day Tariq and I were obliged to go to the carpet factory until evening and

Arif had to go and collect cattle dung. Most of the time I played truant and wandered in the streets as I did not want to be punished by the teacher.

Hekmat, Arif and I went to the Kabul stadium again in the hope of watching football and Karim-e Pijaru. We jumped through the fence into the stadium. This time there was neither football match nor an execution. This time there was a boxing match. We instantly liked it and wanted to become boxers. Again the next day we went to the Kabul stadium and watched another boxing match and later played on the stadium pitch. We found out that there was a football match in the afternoon and Karim-e Pijaru would be playing.

I could not attend the match as I had to go to the carpet factory, and if I did not Tariq would tell my parents. But I was so keen to see Karim-e Pijaru that I told Tariq about him. Tariq too was amazed by Karim-e Pijaru and he decided not to go to the carpet factory either. Instead he would go with Hekmat and me to watch the football match. We once again jumped through the fence into the stadium. Hekmat and I had no problem finding food during any season but winter. We shared the food we had collected with Tariq and waited for the match to start.

At last the footballers came onto the pitch and I searched to find Karim-e Pijaru amongst them. I asked several people around me to show me Karim-e Pijaru, until one pointed towards him and at last I saw a man with long dark hair and a thick beard. He certainly was a fast runner, but I soon reckoned that people had exaggerated that he was as fast as a Pijaru vehicle. Nevertheless, he still was my favourite player. I was amazed by the football match. We watched for some time. Suddenly the Taliban entered the stadium pitch and stopped the football. They asked everyone to perform late afternoon prayers and those who did not pray would be punished by the Taliban. Hekmat and I had to run from one corner of the stadium to the other as we did not know how to pray. Once the prayers had finished, the football resumed.

When the match came to an end, we all walked towards the exit. We noticed that the Taliban had captured several western journalists who were concealing themselves in the basement of the stadium to film the match. The Taliban put them all in the back of their pickup trucks and drove them off. It was the first time in my life I had seen westerners. Everyone thought that the Taliban would kill them all.

Hekmat, Tariq and I, and sometimes Arif too, often went to watch football in the stadium. Sometimes there was no football match, instead either the Taliban shot or hung someone, or amputated a person's hand or leg. At first it was awfully hard to watch a man being shot or hung, or to watch someone's hand or leg being chopped off. But after some time I did not mind. There were people who came from a great distance to watch the execution or amputation just because they enjoyed it.

Time and the people in Afghanistan were moving backward while everywhere else in the world was moving forward. Culture and customs and languages, society as a whole, was being spoiled day after day. This happens to every nation that is burning in the flames of war, poverty and ignorance.

Since Palang had died, I could no longer go into our yard at night as I thought there were demons hiding themselves in the dark, watching me. My father told me there were no demons in the world. He was right, there *were* no demons in the world, but they were in my mind. I was not the only one who was scared. My cousins and siblings were frightened of them too. Sometimes, when I was alone in the village, house or fields, I could feel the existence of demons. I sat amongst the village children and asked if they had ever seen any. Some said no and some said yes. I asked those who saw the demons to tell me what they looked like. Most of them made up tales. Hekmat did not believe in demons at all and when I told him I was frightened of them he laughed at me.

In the summer of 1998, news spread all over Kabul that the Taliban had massacred thousands of helpless people in the Mazaar Province, mainly from the Hazrara ethnicity. In 1997 the Taliban tried to capture the province, but had been defeated very badly, suffering heavy losses at the hands of the pro-Mujahidin fighters. When the Taliban finally captured the province as an act of revenge, they killed thousands of men, women and children, and even cattle. Those who came from Mazaar Province to Kabul told the tale of the massacre. Some said that the entire Mazaar Province stank of human blood and rotting bodies. Some said that the massacre was continuing relentlessly. No sources would tell how many thousands of people had been killed.

An Afghan man, a Tajik father of three, described to UN officials how he had:

> 'Never before witnessed such a scene of bestial violence. They were shooting without discriminating between men, women and children. Soon the streets were covered with dead bodies and blood. No one was allowed to bury the corpses for... six days. Dogs were eating human flesh and going mad and soon the smell became intolerable.'[23]

The Taliban committed similar crimes in the Bamyan Province against the Hazara ethnicity and people lived under the Taliban food blockade for some time. People ate grass in Bamyan Province, since they had nothing else to eat.[24]

Massacres of Afghans in the northern part of Afghanistan by the Taliban filled everyone's hearts with fear. The Taliban seemed invincible. Day after day their empire expanded and I could see the pride and swagger in them. By 1998 they had conquered 95 per cent of Afghanistan. My heart filled to the brim with fear as I had heard tales of their cruelties. Hekmat, Arif and I would no longer dare to follow *Amar bill Marouf* when they were punishing their rule-breakers. Every Talib I saw, after the massacre of the Afghans in Mazaar Province, I feared. They looked much more fearful to me than before. When I looked at them while they were executing, hanging and amputating people in Kabul stadium, I feared them as much as victim did. They were on the roads, streets, in villages, mosques, bazaars and cities. It seemed like there were more Taliban living in Kabul than poor civilians.

The Taliban Empire was so huge and so strong that their destruction seemed beyond impossible for poor Afghans. My parents thought they would have to spend the rest of their lifetime under this dark regime. My mother did not go outside of our compound for years. She was imprisoned within four walls. She heard about the viciousness of the *Amre Bill Marouf* from village women who were beaten by them. Sometimes, my father asked her to go out and see the outside world and he would escort her, but she was too fearful.

As we were playing truant most of the time, one day the teacher threw Hekmat, Arif and I out of class and said that he preferred not to have us. So we spent half of our day in the ruined, ugly and beggar-filled streets, roads, villages and sometimes even the city of Kabul. Most of the time we searched for food. Sometimes we were alone and sometimes we were with other scavenger children, and we searched like hyenas in every corner. Football and footballers absorbed us so much that we went to the stadium almost once a week. I watched so many football matches, but one stood out in particular. One day a Pakistani football team came to Afghanistan to play against the Afghans. The Afghan team scored six goals and the Pakistani team scored none. I was excited for months.

By now every one of us had a favourite team and a favourite player. Sometimes Tariq, Hekmat and even Arif and I argued with one another; each said that his team and player was better than the other's. We almost knew the names of every good player. My favourite team was *Sabawoun* and my favourite player was no longer Karim-e Pijaru, but Arif-e Kargar. When Hekmat, Tariq or Arif said something unpleasant about them I would defend them. Sometimes we quarrelled for hours with one another. However, Ustad Naqib and Ustad Halim were fed up with us as we did not weave carpet when the football was on.

My family were still living beneath the perilous shadows of extreme poverty. My father kept looking for a job as well as borrowing money from anyone who was willing to lend it to him. My poor mother had to cope with my tearful siblings who demanded food for their hungry stomachs. However, once again, the *Toot* season arrived and I did not have to be worry about food. My brothers and I brought plenty of *Toot* into our home and everybody ate it.

By then, I was the master of tree climbing. In a blink of an eye I would reach the top of tall trees. Sometimes, when the tree owners spotted me in their tree, they would ask me to climb down. I knew if I climbed down, they would punish me, so instead I climbed up to the top of the tree. The peasants threw rocks at me, but their rocks could not reach me. They would sit beneath the tree and wait for me to climb down. I would sit in the top of the tree and wait until the peasants got bored and left. Sometimes I gave up, climbed down and was beaten anyway.

Simaa Khala and my mother, along with other village women, gathered in our house once or twice a week and sang songs secretly. When I was free I would sit silent beside my mother and listen to the village women sharing their pain with one another. Sometimes they laughed, sometimes they cried and sometimes they sang. There was a very nice woman who had a splendid voice and sang the Taliban song each time the village women got together. Every woman loved to hear her wonderful voice, as did I, and I still remember how her beautifully sad song started:

Khuda aaurd ballaa ra; God has brought demon,

Guru-e Talbaa ra; The crowd of Taliban.

Women cried and cried during this song and even when the song was over, still their tears did not stop. Every woman's heart was wounded in the almost two decades of war. Some had lost beloved children, some husbands, some were forced into marriage, some were oppressed by their husbands, like Simaa Khala, and some had sent their children far away into alien lands. Most had no food to feed their hungry families.

There was no family in our village that was left unwounded by the decades of obnoxious war and brutality; not only in our village, but all over Afghanistan. Poor Simaa Khala sang sad songs, usually for her two sons who were far away from her love and in a land where they struggled to provide bread for their family. When Simaa Khala sang, the tears flowed from her eyes. Our village women were strange, when one cried the rest cried too. Sometimes they made me cry. But they were as equally funny. One moment I would see them bursting in tears and the next they were in gales of laughter. I really enjoyed sitting beside my mother and listening to the women until she would unexpectedly slap me hard on the back of my head and throw me away from their assembly. She would say, 'You are a boy and you are supposed to hang around with village boys. The more you sit with women, the more you will pick up their behaviour.'

Worse Comes To the Worst

The Mullah and my parents and everyone else who found out that I did not know how to pray were angry with me. I was no longer a child through their eyes. I was a grown man to them. The Mullah tried all sort of punishments to force me to learn praying, but he failed. I too tried a lot to memorise what the Mullah had taught me, but as soon as I walked out of the mosque, I forgot everything. One day the Mullah hit me on the nose and it started to bleed. Seeing my own blood frightened me and I began crying. Crying was considered an embarrassment amongst boys of my age; all of the village boys laughed at me. The Mullah told the boys in the mosque that they should not call me Laiq, instead they should call me Tanbal. The Mullah's physical torture was not as painful as when someone called me Tanbal. When the boys called me Tanbal, I started to fight them. Fortunately, I always won the fight, as Hekmat, Tariq and Arif were on my side. Most children did not even dare to call me Tanbal after that, as there were too many of us.

One day we were walking in a village with our shrunken stomachs and we noticed a wedding ceremony and decided to get a free lunch there. There were two angry guards who stood outside the compound door and they chased any strangers away. We had to pass the guards if we were to get our free lunch. The three of us were dreadfully hungry and needed food. We sat a few yards away from the compound and waited for an opportunity to get inside. Regrettably, we were not the only unwelcomed guests. Beggar men, women and children came from miles away with pots and plates in their hands in the hope they too could get some food from the wedding ceremony. We could do nothing but wait. The smells that arose from the food stirred my appetite and filled my dry mouth with saliva. We decided to get into the house and ignore the guards. We all asked one another to go first. At last Arif dared to walk first towards the guards. By now there were four of them outside the door. People usually wear new attire, or if not, at least clean attire at a wedding ceremony. Ours were neither new nor clean and we would easily be spotted.

As Arif reached the guards, they instantly saw that he was neither a relative nor did he live in the village. Without saying a word one of the guards slapped him in the face and pushed him away. Luckily, an elderly man witnessed the guard slapping Arif. He shouted at the guard not to beat Arif and he took the tearful Arif inside the compound with him. Hekmat and I too followed. The guards did not attempt to stop us.

The groom was a Talib who already had a wife back in his own village and his new wife was from Kabul. We ate plenty of rice and meat. Hekmat said that he did not remember the last time he had eaten meat. The food was incredibly tasty and we ate and took our empty plates to the cook over and over again, and he filled it for us with rice and meatballs and spinach and chips. At last we were full to the brim, but still we wanted more. When Hekmat took the plate to the cook, the cook chased him away. The wedding was over right after the lunch. As it was a Talib wedding, there was no music.

Some Taliban chose to marry urban girls. Most urban people were landless and they suffered a lot under the Taliban, who did not like educated and moderate urban people at all, since they considered that urban people were weak on their faith. Many urban parents forced their daughters into marriage with the Taliban in order to survive. So many of the Taliban married young girls from Kabul and other urban areas and took them to the rural parts of the country, and some parents never saw their daughters again.

Hekmat, Arif and I and even Tariq used to go miles away into different villages in search of weddings. Finding a wedding was hard, but eating such delicious and healthy food for free was worth the hardship. We not only filled our own stomachs up with food, we even took away plastic bags of food for our sisters and brother and mother. After a while, we knew which sort of wedding to attend. If it was a Talib's wedding there was always ample food and not too difficult for us to get. But if it was a non-Talib wedding we either couldn't get into the wedding ceremony or, if we did, there was not enough food for us. Consequently, we tried to avoid non-Talib weddings.

In 1998 the summer drought hit Afghanistan and took the lives of people as well as their cattle and crops. The water disappeared from the wells of our village. Villagers dug deeper wells but there was no sign of water. Poor Afghans were not only searching for food, now they had to search for water, too. There were a few compounds outside our village that still had water in their wells, but they refused to let anyone use it as they were afraid their wells might dry up. Village children woke early in the morning and went in search of water miles away. My brothers and I had to go into a village that was more than an hour's walk from ours to fill our buckets with muddy water from a mosque's well. It was extremely difficult to carry two buckets of water for each of us when our stomachs constantly demanded food under a sun that poured invisible flames upon us from the heavens.

I got diarrhoea after drinking impure water at a time when my family could do nothing but watch me suffer. After a few days I lost so much weight that I did not have enough energy to stand on my own two feet; someone had to carry me around. My parents thought I was going to be wasted in that summer and there was nothing they could do, just like a wounded deer against a jungle predator. But, to everyone's surprise, I survived yet again!

School exams were close and yet we were still wandered the streets. We did not tell anyone in our family that our teacher had thrown us out of school. Our parents were lost in the deserts of poverty, misery and despair and barely remembered to ask how we were doing in school. Hekmat, Arif and I had to do something before we missed the school exam. One day we all walked into the class and when the teacher saw us, he charged towards us and whipped us with his cable, but we had to bear the pain and hoped that he would still let us attend the class. The pain was grave and the three of us began crying, which we weren't supposed to do. We begged the teacher to let us attend the class otherwise our parents would kill us if they found out we were no longer students. But the teacher was adamant – and we were adamant not to leave at any cost.

The teacher threw as out of the class one after the other. Hekmat and Arif decided to leave, but I refused, as I knew that if I did not sit the exam it would have serious repercussions. I refused to go with them. They too changed their minds and sat with me outside and hoped the teacher would take pity on us and allow us to attend class. We sat outside the classroom until the lesson had finished and then we walked among the other students back home. Hekmat and Arif wanted to tell the truth to our parents, but I warned them not to. The three of us went again the next day and begged our teacher to let us attend. We were the first to enter the class and waited for the teacher so we could see what his reaction would be. The students entered our classroom one after the other. At last the teacher arrived and was surprised to see the three of us sitting in the back row.

He walked straight to Hekmat and asked, 'Who allowed you to enter my class?' Hekmat had no reply to the teacher's question. The teacher slapped Hekmat really hard in the face and the sound of it shocked everyone. He dragged Hekmat out of the class. Hekmat did not cry, despite receiving such a hard slap. The teacher returned and then it was my turn. He asked the very same question of me. But I didn't remain silent like Hekmat. I begged the teacher to allow me stay in the class otherwise my parents would kill me if they found out that I was no longer a student, He hit me with his cable on my arm. But before he could drag me out of the class, Arif fled as he knew that he would be the next. The teacher was determined that he would not allow us in his classroom. We spent another half a day outside, hoping he would let us in. But he did not. The next day we did not go to school. Instead we went to a big apple orchard and stole apples and went straight to the Kabul stadium with our pockets filled. Inside the stadium we met a group of boys who were selling chewing gum, biscuits and cigarettes. They had a ball, so we played football. We gave them one apple each and they were really happy. I could not concentrate on the ball when I reached the part of the pitch where the Taliban executed men. Without warning, five Taliban surrounded us. First they took our ball and then gave each one of us a slap without us knowing the reason. (We later found out that we were not allowed to play football in the stadium.) They refused to hand our ball back.

I was encrusted with fear that my parents would find out that I was no longer a student in school; my mother would beat me to death if she found out, as in her dreams my brothers and I would become doctors and engineers. I told Hekmat and Arif to beg the teacher until he let us back into his classroom. We kept attending the class before anybody else turned up and the teacher kept beating and throwing us out of his classroom. One day, as the three of us were sitting outside the classroom, one of our classmates came out and said, 'The teacher has asked for the three of you to come in.' We entered the classroom and the teacher asked us to stand before the class, so we did.

I remember vividly those few words our teacher said to us, 'You are not cheating your parents. You are cheating yourselves.' Then he let us attend the class.

Exams began. But there was nothing in our heads that we could write down onto the exam papers; we did not even know how to read and write. We tried to copy from our classmates' exam papers, but the teacher warned everyone not to let us do that. He forced us to sit alone, where we were unable to copy from anyone. The teacher wrote the exam questions on the broken blackboard that we had in our class. I copied the questions from the broken blackboard, but handed the exam papers in without answering a single question. At the end of the year, when I received my school results, I failed in all subjects. All the way home I trembled, for I was fearful of my parents' punishment. Arif and I handed our school report to our mother as we knew she couldn't read. If Tariq was home, she would take them to him to read for her. As soon as Tariq told her that we had failed in all subjects, she charged towards us. But, before she could catch us, we fled outside the compound where she could not come, since she still feared *Amr Bil marouf*.

Severe punishment was still imminent. Our mother refused to feed us as well as not allow us to enter the compound. All I could do was not to go to the carpet factory and mosque and wander about until night-time when my father would come home and punish us.

Hekmat could not hand his exam result to his mother as she was an educated woman and could read. So he handed his school exam result to his sister and fled the compound. We spent the rest of the day stealing turnips from the fields. As the sun went down, fear arose inside us. Gradually our chit-chat disappeared in thoughts of the predestined punishment.

At the end of the day we went home. First my father punished us verbally, which was much more painful than any physical punishment. However, our school results gave my parents far greater punishment than the one they were giving to Arif and me. The pain that our parent's punishment inflicted upon us faded away after some moments, but our exam result pain remained in my parents' hearts for months. My father was annoyed at us for failing to learn reading and writing in so many years.

Mother told Arif and me, 'I have repeatedly told you two to study for the sake of your future. However, you keep refusing. When you grow up uneducated and suffer in your lives, do not blame me. I would rather be buried under the tons of earth yet keep my words alive in your minds that I did tell you to study not once, or twice, but to a limit that my tongue got tired.'

Hekmat, Arif and I failed each time in our exams but it did not mean we had to study the same grade again. In the winter the teacher called us to re-take the exam. During that exam we could not answer a single question either. But the teachers passed us. Sometimes I really tried hard to study, but my mind refused to learn and I blamed God. I really thought God had created me unintelligent.

Ramadan arrived, but this time my parents were not the only ones who had to keep fast. In 1998, Tariq was ten and I was nine years old. My parents said that we were of a legitimate age to keep fast. I could not believe that I would survive if I did not drink or eat all day long. Mother woke Tariq and me up at two in the morning to eat. The next morning, as I woke up, I went straight to Hekmat's house and told him that I was fasting. Hekmat's parents did not force him to fast, but I scared Hekmat that God would burn him in the hell in the world after life if he didn't fast.

It was around eleven o'clock in the morning and I was weaving a carpet. My head was bursting with pain and there was no energy to move my hands. My stomach was utterly empty and there was a dim curtain before my eyes. Everything seemed so dark and so gloomy around me in the bright sunny day. At midday, I thought that I was going to die. I asked Ustad Naqib to let me go home and eat some food before I died. But he not only refused to allow me, he shouted at me not to dare break my fast. He too said that I am a grown man and I have to endure the pain of hunger.

I had to get out of the carpet factory. We were not allowed to go to the toilet without Ustad Naqib or Ustad Halim's approval. I asked Ustad Naqib to permit me to go to the toilet. But instead of the toilet, I fled home. I forced my legs to carry me to home. When I asked my mother to give me food to eat, she not only didn't give me any food but tore at my hair too for trying to break my fast. I left our house with my stomach filled with hunger and my heart and mind with wrath towards my mother.

It was turnip season so I had stolen several huge turnips and filled my stomach with them. However, Tariq managed to fast all day long. Tariq's characteristics were the opposite of mine. He was good in school lessons. My parents were proud of him and he never stole anything regardless of how hungry he was. Teachers in school and Ustad Naqib and Ustad Halim too were admirers of Tariq. They were not the only ones. The whole of the village – men, women and children – were impressed by Tariq's ethics. Everyone told Arif and me that we could not be Tariq's brothers, because we were the total opposite of him.

The next day I returned to the carpet factory. Ustad Naqib was mad at me. He said I was the first apprentice who had walked out of the carpet factory without permission. He gave me a severe punishment for it.

My mother had very firm faith in God and in Islam and when I told her that I was not able to keep the fast she warned me to keep the fast or she would not feed me at all. I had to pretend that I was holding the fast to my parents even though I was not. My mother was always sceptical about my fasting and would always inspect my mouth.

It was midway through Ramadan when, one day, my father came home and said that the Taliban had given him a job in their fuel depot. Paperwork was much too complicated for the Taliban and they did not like it, so they chose my father to do it for them. However, they did not tell him how much they would pay him and he did not mind whatever the amount was so long as it was more than nothing. He started his new job. His working place was several miles away from our house, so he had to wake up before the sun rose and walk all the way there. He went much earlier than the Taliban would have expected him to as he feared he might lose the job. A whole month elapsed, but the Taliban did not pay him a single penny and he dared not ask as he was afraid of losing his job.

By the end of 1998 the Mujahidin factions had lost almost all control of the bigger cities to the Taliban and were left with very little space to move. The Taliban kept pushing them towards the north of Afghanistan. Countless young Afghans were dying each day, some for the Mujahidin leaders and some for the Taliban. Almost all regional governments were arming and financing the Taliban or the Mujahidin factions. Pakistan and Saudi Arabia were funding and arming the Taliban Empire. Central Asian countries alongside Russia supported the Mujahidin, since they feared that if the Taliban were to dominate the entire of Afghanistan, they would export religious extremism into Central Asian republics. Iran too supported anti-Taliban factions because of the Taliban's anti-Shia Muslim feelings and the killing of Iranian diplomats in Afghanistan. All regional governments armed and financed these brainless factions for their own interest. But it was young, uninformed Afghans who sent each other to their deaths. It was tormented and hungry Afghans who suffered. It was their homes, gardens and cities that were being ravaged again and again.

A nation that refuses to march with time will definitely remain backward, reactionary and will be exploited by other nations. 'A people who are weak and who are left behind in the march of time invite trouble and ultimately have only themselves to blame', says Jawaharlal Nehru, the first prime minister of India. Any nation that clings to the old practices, cultures, beliefs, and way of life and refuses to adapt to the new ideas and change is doomed. Unfortunately, Afghans have refused to let go of their old practices, ideas and way of life. They have refused to adapt to changes and the new way of life and are paying a terrible price for it. Every powerful country overruns them, kills them, humiliates them, destroys their livelihoods and uses them for their own advantage. Afghans must not only blame the foreigners for their misery, they themselves are equally responsible for it.

From the early 1990s until almost the fall of the Taliban in 2001, there was fierce competition between the BRIDAS and UNOCAL oil companies for the vast and untapped gas reserves of Turkmenistan. UNOCAL was a powerful American oil company and BRIDAS belonged to an Argentinean man. These two companies had big ambitions. They both wanted to run a gas pipeline from Turkmenistan via Afghanistan to Pakistan. Due to the fierce war and lawlessness in Afghanistan, neither of these two companies completed the project. A lot of theories appeared after the domination of Afghanistan by the US, that the US invaded Afghanistan in order to run this pipeline through the country and exploit the vast amount of gas that lies in Central Asia, in particular in the Caspian Sea. These theories do not show the full picture of domination of Afghanistan by the US. The US and its allies certainly are in Afghanistan to exploit Central Asia's gas reserves, but that is not the only reason behind the occupation by them. The US have a long-standing geostrategic ambition in Central Asia and for this reason the US and other western governments and their intelligence services worked secretly for decades to have a foothold Central Asia. The famous British Political Geographer, Halford John Mackinder, as far back as early twentieth century described Central Asia as the 'geographical pivot of history'.[25]

Afghanistan is a great geostrategic advantage for the United States and its allies against the rapidly rising Asian countries surrounding it. The United States and its allies want to use this crucial part of the world as a military base for their imperialistic adventures in the region. The ultimate objective of the United States and NATO in Afghanistan is an enduring military base and a puppet regime.

Zbigniew Brzezinski, the former US National Security Adviser, had stated as far back as 1997 that for the United States, control of Central Eurasia – the region encompassing Afghanistan and Pakistan and their neighbours in the states of the former Soviet Union – was a prime goal of post-Cold War US military and foreign policy. He stated, 'Whoever either controls or dominates access to the region is the one most likely to win the geopolitical and economic prize.'[26]

Economist and author William F. Engdahl explained in his book *Full Spectrum Dominance: Totalitarian Democracy in the New World Order*, how the US government uses every means to dominate the globe and, in particular Eurasia. Since the beginning of the twenty-first century the US has aggressively accelerated its struggle for the domination of Eurasia. No other person explained so fantastically the importance of Eurasia for the primacy of the US Empire than the former US National Security Adviser Zbigniew Brzezinski in his book *The Grand Chestboard: American Primacy and its Geostrategic Imperatives*.

The winter snow was about to start and my siblings and I had to endure the pain of hunger as well as bitter coldness of the winter yet again. Food did not exist in our home and if there was any, my mother concealed it and rationed it. We needed something to burn, Arif did not collect enough cattle dung and we already burned most of it during the summer when cooking. My mother asked my father to demand his wage from the Taliban. But Father said that we should wait for a few more days and hopefully the Taliban would pay him. The weather was already unbearably cold. The carpet factory was extremely cold. My feet began to swell up as a result of the cold weather. I did not understand at the time what caused them to swell up. They would not fit in my shoes. I was obliged to walk barefoot from home to the carpet factory and from the carpet factory back home. Day after day, my feet expanded and looked hideous. My mother covered my feet in warm cloths at night and hoped they would shrink. Everywhere there was misery and suffering in my life.

Tariq and I learned to weave carpets without Ustad Naqib and Ustad Halim's supervision. We let our father know about it and as soon as he found out that we had become masters of carpet-weaving, he went to speak with Ustad Naqib. 'It is time for my sons to weave carpets for you, in return for more money,' said my father. First Ustad Naqib refused to let us work for ourselves. He still wanted us to work for him almost for free. My father said he wouldn't let us work for Ustad Naqib any more if he did not pay a decent wage for the two of us. So Ustad Naqib was left with no choice but to let us weave his carpets by ourselves in return for more money, but he had given us a three months ultimatum to weave one carpet. It was not possible for Tariq and me to make a marvellous silk carpet in three months. Anyway, we brought a carpet device from the carpet factory into our compound and installed it into our room.

Soon Tariq dragged poor Arif too into this terrible craft. It was time for Arif to be dispossessed from the very little childhood freedom he had. War took childhood freedom from all Afghan children and my brothers and I were amongst them. Arif was just a little boy when he became a carpet weaver. It was gravely dull for him to sit all day long and weave carpets while he could hear the little children's voices who played in the village. He cried a lot at the first few months not to work. He wanted to play with other children in the village, but no one was there to listen to him. My parents could do nothing but close their eyes and shut their ears when they looked at Arif. Arif struggled to set himself free from the prison of carpet weaving. Each time he tried, he was beaten by Tariq and forced to sit and weave carpet. Carpet weaving by hand is extremely difficult and tiresome.

It was now the school holidays and Tariq wanted to use it as an opportunity to make the carpet within three months. Tariq forced Arif and I to wake up at dawn and weave until late evening when it was dark and we were not able to see. I wanted to go out and play with the other village children. So I tried to stop work before the evening and go out, but Tariq did not want me to leave work early. We began to fight each other every day. Tariq was much stronger than I and each time we fought, I was the one who got hurt. One time Tariq grabbed my right hand and sank his teeth into my thumb; I thought he was going to bite it off. I screamed very loudly for help. Arif tried to free my thumb out of Tariq's sharp teeth, but Tariq refused to let it go. My mother came and forced my thumb out of Tariq's mouth. My thumb was in grave pain for several weeks.

Each time I attempted to abandon carpet weaving and play with the children in the village, Tariq would stop me and eventually it ended up in fighting and my poor mother would burst into tears watching us hurting each other. One day Ustad Naqib came to inspect his carpet. My father was there. Ustad Naqib complained to my father that we were not weaving the carpet quickly enough. I was standing beside my father, when he suddenly slapped me in the face and blamed me for not weaving the carpet late into the evening. Tariq, Arif and I had only one day off work in the whole week and that was a Friday. I impatiently waited for Friday to come and give me my freedom. But Tariq told us that we had to sacrifice our one day of freedom as we needed to weave the carpet. Arif and I disapproved. But our disapproval could not give us our one day of freedom back. So, we began to weave the carpet on the Fridays too.

The winter snow began to fall. Now we had to weave the carpet as well as scrape the snow from the rooftop. My mother forced my father to demand his salary from the Taliban before her children died in the harsh winter. At last he dared and, luckily, they gave it to him. His wage was much less than what he had expected. We had the choice of buying food or firewood. Each was as important as the other. If we did not eat, we would be wasted and if we did not keep ourselves warm, we would be still wasted. My father came up with an idea. He bought rice with one half of his money and coal with the other half.

Sometimes, when the weather was very cold, we could not weave the carpet as our hands froze and we could not move them. Tariq had no choice but to set us free. I forced my swollen feet into my shoes and ran outside. Despite the terribly cold weather and painful feet I played with the village children in the snow. I built a huge snowball or played snowball fighting or went with children to the ruined compounds and sit by the fire to warm ourselves up. Sometimes, children who had food in their houses stole a potato and we cooked it in on the fire and shared it with everyone. The mosque was the only refuge and I sat beside the warm *Bukhari* (stove) and did not leave until the Mullah whipped me out. The Mullah was mad at me all the time as I always failed to memorise his lessons. One day the Mullah said that I was only coming into the mosque to warm myself and not to learn. So he threw me aside from the warm *Bukhari* and let a boy who was good in his lessons take my place. The Mullah hated me as much as my school teacher did, and I hated them equally in return.

Every day news came from the north of the country that the Taliban were defeating the Mujahidin in every city, village and valley. This war was as much an ethnic war as it was a factional war. Tajik, Hazara and Uzbek ethnics were on one side and the Pashtun on the other. The effect of this madness could be seen all over Afghanistan. Tajik, Uzbak and Hazara could feel fear in the areas under the Taliban influence and Pashtuns had the same feelings in the areas under the Mujahidin influence. Even children felt this fear. Most children, who were from Tajick, Hazara and Uzbak ethnic groups, feared Pashtun children in our village.

My father earned money that was not enough to feed us but was much better than nothing. He fed us with debt for several years. Some began to demand their money back. The debt hurt my parents very badly. They were always anxious about how to pay back their debts. My father decided to give a portion of his wage to his lenders each month. It meant that we had to make up for the portion that my father took away from his wage by eating less. Sometimes he got confused as to which lender to give the money first, since many of them demanded it at the same time. When Tariq saw my father's position he put more pressure upon Arif and me to weave the carpet so as to earn more money and help our father with his debts.

My mother sat beside her best friend, Simaa Khala, and shared all her pains with her. The sisters had to cope with their hungry and unclothed children, who encircled them all the time and demanded food. For years Simaa Khala and my mother did not walk outside their compounds. They spent most of their lives inside, ignorant of what was happening in the world. Simaa Khala had far more pain than my mother. She was living with an abusive husband and her two sons were far away in Pakistan.

The winter circle began to leave Afghans alone, though it filled its greedy stomach with the lives of countless Afghans, mainly children. Nature sent beautiful flowers out to decorate the fields, hills, valleys and mountains, gorgeous birds emerged from nowhere and began singing, and trees burst into flowers. Nature sent all this exquisiteness just to welcome the spring, but our eyes were blinded by misery and poverty. War and poverty forced the joy and happiness out of Afghanistan. Death and danger had hidden themselves even in the beauty of the superb flowers in the valleys, hills and mountains of Afghanistan, as they were filled with mines and unexploded devices.

Our First Significant Wage

We failed to weave a carpet in the three months ultimatum that Ustad Naqib had given us. Ustad Naqib began moaned to my father and each time he moaned Tariq put more pressure on Arif and me to work harder. By now, school had started and we could only weave the carpet for half a day. Hekmat, Arif and I once again began playing truant. We got out of the house in the name of school, but usually went straight to the stadium to watch executions, amputations, football and boxing. We could manage to find enough food to feed our stomachs before they began to cry. Shopkeepers around our village and on the way to school all knew us. As soon as they saw us they chased us away, sometimes by slapping and whipping us with a tree branch and sometimes with their offensive language. My father did not want us to fail at school again, so he forced Arif and me to sit with him and learn how to read and write at night. But he too shouted at us and even tore at our hair when we failed. Every night he spent two hours with us, teaching us. Whatever the teacher, the Mullah, and my father were teaching me, my brain refused to learn it. I could do nothing but accept their punishment.

The more I grew the more the verbal punishment hurt me in comparison to any physical punishment. One day I failed to answer the teacher's question. He threw an old broken metal chair at me, which hit me in the stomach. At first I thought that the chair had ripped it apart, there was severe pain in my belly. Although it was already very painful, I dramatised it further by rolling on the floor, holding my belly and screaming at the top of my voice. The teacher and students panicked and Hekmat and Arif became frightened. With a lot of difficulty I managed to walk back home. I showed my belly to my mother, which terrified her.

When my father found out that the teacher had struck me with a broken metal chair, he complained to the headmaster of the school. He found the address of the headmaster's home and took me there. By now the pain in my belly had faded away but the wound looked much worse than before. He showed the headmaster and he too condemned the teacher. But that did not mean the teacher stopped beating me. He stopped punishing me for a week or so, and then he punished me with his cable, two and sometimes three times a day as usual.

At last we weaved a carpet. It had taken us five months. Ustad Naqib was not very happy that it had taken so long, but we received money for it and that was important. My father bought a 45kg bag of wheat flour with some of the money and saved the rest. Our clothes were severely ragged and each one of us had grown out of them. We did not have a proper turban either and students made fun of us at school and in the mosque. My father took the three of us to Kabul city. It was terrifying as usual watching mothers with their children begging people. The number of beggars rose day after day. More and more poor and hungry men, women and children left their houses and went into the city, villages, roads and streets begging. Children clung to people's legs and begged.

'Brother I am a helpless widow, my children have not eaten food for two days and they will die if I don't feed them,' said one woman to my father. Four children, with worn out clothes, cracked faces and filthy and sticky hair lay scattered around the beggar woman. My father gave her a 1,000 Afghani note. As we walked towards *Manda-e* more women and more children begged with their tearful eyes, but he could not afford to give money to all of them. It seemed there were more Taliban in the Kabul than civilians, all of them there to hassle tormented Afghans. The misogynist Taliban forced women under the burqa so that they burned in the flames of poverty, oppression and hunger silently and nobody could even see them. Wherever Afghan women went, they were caged; in the house by four muddy walls and outside under the burqa. Urban women's lives under the Taliban regime were as bitter as ever before. I had seen how brutally they were whipped by heartless Taliban. Those women were free of all guilt but one – being born female in Afghanistan.

My father bought some clothes and a turban for each of us and we headed back home for afternoon prayers. Taliban pickup trucks drove through the streets of Kabul city as usual, looking for those who attempted to evade prayers, they brutally forced Afghans to pray. I do not know what they were trying to achieve by forcing Afghans to pray, but I certainly know that they had reached the mountain top of ignorance.

My father and Tariq went to pray in the mosque and Arif and I stood in a corner waiting for them to finish and then go home. Both of us were terrified that the *Amr Bil Marouf* might torture us if they saw that we were not praying, but luckily that did not happen. I was so excited with my new clothes and turban that I wore them instantly and went out and displayed them to all the children, but rather haughtily. Most children did not have a second pair of clothes or shoes. They would wear one pair of clothes for months and even years.

One day a neighbour who lived a few compounds away from ours forced their young daughter, who wasn't older than thirteen, to marry a Talib whose age was certainly far greater than my father's, for one simple reason – just so the rest of her children would not die from starvation. The Talib paid 50,000 Pakistani rupees to her parents as a dowry. The wedding was not an Afghan traditional one; there was no engagement ceremony. The Talib directly held the ceremony and wanted it to be a quick one. During the ceremony the Taliban cooked ample food and invited everyone from our village to eat for free. Hundreds of people came from very far away villages to eat.

When the wedding was over and it was time for the little girl to leave her parents' house, she refused to go and cried and begged her family not to send her away. When I saw her, I was astonished to see that she was almost the same age as Tariq and was tiny in size in comparison to the groom. She did not want to leave her parents' house, so several women had to drag her outside. Her wedding clothes were covered in dirt; she screamed like a child who was being taken away from her mother. Women who attended the wedding ceremony cried as they observed the little girl weeping for her parents not to send her away with that old man. Her mother fainted. Her father cried as well. My mother, along with several other women, wanted to help. Her mother cried and blamed herself. Village women tried to tell her that it was not her fault. Soon after that another family did the very same thing with their daughter.

It was evening when Simaa Khala ran into our room and embraced my mother and said something that we did not understand. When she lifted her head, her eyes and face were covered in tears, but her lips were wide with a smile. I thought Simaa Khala had gone insane. 'Tomorrow my children are coming from Pakistan,' said Simaa Khala. She was so happy. The next day Akmal and Ajmal came back from Pakistan and as they walked into the compound Simaa Khala ran towards them. As she was running the tears fell from her eyes like cherry blossom falling in the wind. She embraced Akmal and kissed his face continuously then embraced Ajmal. Simaa Khala cried for some time. I was confused and did not understand why she was crying when her sons were back. I did not realise that they were happy tears.

Akmal and Ajmal had been separated from Simaa Khala for some time. She burst into tears every now and then when she remembered and went through the pain of separation from her little children. How grave the pain must be for a helpless mother when she gathers the remains of her children after the fall of nasty bombs and rockets upon them. I wish Americans and other westerners who let their predatory governments invade helpless people in the so-called Third World could see their war through the eyes of helpless Afghan mothers whose children are being crushed by bombs and rockets that they paid for.

Akmal and Ajmal told how they were being forced by the owner of the carpet factory to wake up before sunrise and work until midnight, and if they refused they would be beaten and not fed. Hearing this, Simaa Khala shed bitter tears. Akmal told us that life in Pakistan was much worse than in Afghanistan. There were so many millions of Afghans in refugee camps. They lived in places where ordinary people refused to live. Corrupt Pakistani police treated them inhumanely. Most of the Afghans were illegal and when the Pakistani police caught them, they demanded money. If they did not give them money they would beat and imprison them. Poor Afghans were being treated like sub-humans inside and outside of their land.

Sometimes I doubted that there were other countries outside Afghanistan. I thought people were making it up. I asked so many different questions about Pakistan to make sure it truly existed. Akmal and Ajmal stayed for a few weeks with their parents and then had to go back to Pakistan again. It seemed as though time gone by as fast as the speed of light for Simaa Khala. She hadn't seen enough of her sons. But it was time for them to go again. Ajmal did not want to go back to Pakistan and carry on working day and night under the oppression of the carpet factory owner. But he had no choice. Yet again he left Afghanistan for Pakistan with tearful eyes.

The Taliban still did not pay my father an appropriate salary in return for his hard work. One month they would pay him and for several months they did not and Father would dare not argue with them as he knew that if he lost his job he would never find another. The Taliban did not like my father as they knew he was in the army during the communist regime. Though my father dressed like them and wore a turban, still they were not on good terms. They looked down on him with very little respect. There was nothing he could do but continue with his work. He needed money to feed his hungry family. He was drowning in debt. Lenders demanded their money continuously, some even quarrelled with him. Still we were crying for food, in particular my little sisters. My mother could do very little to keep us silent. Most of the time she told us to endure it like a tree in the drought, but we were tired of enduring. I hated the word *Awsayla* (endurance). Whenever I heard it, it stung me like a scorpion.

Arif and I were still not good at our lessons. We attended school for one day and did not for several other days. The teacher punished us harshly every time we went back to school. Still we kept stealing food from the fields and ruined gardens and from shops. One day we attended school and on the way home were so hungry we could hardly walk. We reached a field and pulled out carrots, unaware that the peasant had seen us. He stealthily moved towards us and yet we were ignorant of him. We began biting our delicious carrots when the peasant grabbed us.

He asked Arif, 'Why do you steal my carrots?' Arif's mouth was filled with carrots and yet he said he did not steal his carrots. The peasant asked him, 'What is in your mouth then?'

Arif replied, 'Carrots.' Before Arif could say another word the peasant slapped him so harshly that all the chewed carrots burst out of his mouth and flew in all directions. The peasant kept on slapping and punching poor little Arif over and over again with his sturdy hands. When the peasant was done with Arif, it was Hekmat's turn. He slapped and punched Hekmat and tore at his hair. Before he had finished, I ran. Running with an empty stomach was a terrible punishment, but I chose to run rather than be beaten by the peasant. The peasant saw me run, so he left Hekmat and chased after me, but he failed to catch me. I was lucky and got away.

One time I failed to escape the wrath of a peasant. It was afternoon and we were hungry as usual. I jumped into a cornfield and Hekmat and Arif were supposed to watch out for peasants. One farmer spotted me from his hut and caught me, but Hekmat and Arif escaped. The farmer took me out of his cornfield, grabbed my head and smashed it against his mud hut's wall very hard. It felt like my head had burst open. He punched and kicked me all over. Then he lifted me high into the sky with his strong hands and threw me to the earth, and I thought all the bones had broken in my body. I thought the farmer was going to kill me. He grabbed my head again and crushed it against the wall. I was not able to cry any more. My ears could not pick up any sound and my body could not feel the pain, only my eyes could see what was happening. I saw the rough hands and feet of the farmer battering me violently. I watched as the peasant hammered and punched me until he saw that I was no longer able to react. Then he left me lying on the earth.

I remained on the ground for some time. Later on, when I tried to stand up, I was unable to. I touched my face and it was full of lumps. Hekmat and Arif came to check what had happened to me. They were shocked when they saw me covered with dirt and blood. They picked me up. I was unable to walk and was very worried what my parents might say. There were lumps all over my head and body. I hoped that the lumps would be gone by the time we reached home. Our stomachs were hungry and the three of us cursed the peasant all the way home. I later realised why the peasant had punished me so violently. He had spent days under the scorching sun, as well as the nights, guarding his crops from scavengers who were hungry like us, who stole them and when it came to harvest time there would be very little left for the peasant and his family.

Again the summer disaster fell upon Afghanistan. The drought hit once more. The south of Afghanistan suffered the most. Crops and cattle died everywhere. The Kuchi are a nomadic tribe and heavily dependent on their cattle. Most of them lost animals in the drought and were left with nothing. Some people were lucky and managed to kill their cattle before they died of hunger and thirst. Convoys of slaughtered cattle came from all over Afghanistan into Kabul. The meat price fell dramatically, but most Afghans could not afford to buy even the cheapest meat. Afghans did not receive much help from international aid organisations as the savage empire of the Taliban had forced most of them out of Afghanistan.

Once more we stopped going to school and weaving carpets. All we had to do was provide water for our family. My mother grew spinach in our yard in the hope we could eat it, but it had all died before it grew properly. Children perished in large numbers due to unsafe drinking water. Afghanistan was full of hungry monsters and Afghans had to feed them. Tens of thousands of Afghans were dying from war, famine, disease, drugs, mines, and the harsh climate.

One day my father did not return home from work at his usual time. Mother began to worry, so she sent Tariq and me out to go and look for him. We followed the path that he took every day early in the morning to do his duty. We failed to find any trace of him. We returned home and could do nothing but sit and pray for the safety of my father. Coming home late from work might not be a big deal in the rest of the world but in Afghanistan it had several terrifying meanings and consequences and each was as frightening as the other. My siblings cried that the demons had eaten our father. Our mother attempted to convince us that demons didn't exist but she failed, because the seed had already been planted in our minds by herself.

At last we heard the sound of a car engine in the village. It was Father, but in a terrible state. The driver helped him out of the car. We called Mother to come and help Father as he was not able to walk. He sat on the ground and told her to bring all the money she had saved. He gave the money to the driver. The driver was not happy with the amount, but he decided to leave anyway. My mother and Tariq took our father inside. He first told us that he had been run over by a car. However he secretly told my mother what had really happened to him. The Taliban had accused my father of stealing fuel from their depot. They had mercilessly tortured him to confess. Not even the most courageous thieves dared to steal from ordinary people since everyone feared amputation. Stealing fuel from the Taliban fuel depot was far beyond my father's imagination. He could not even dare to ask for his salary as he feared he might lose his job, let alone steal their fuel. Now he was accused by the Taliban and he had been punished severely, but did not confess. He spent the whole night praying, reading the Quran and asking for help from God.

The next morning the Taliban who had accused my father of stealing had to prove it to their commander. He was not able to walk properly so Tariq accompanied him. Mother spent the whole day crying. We regularly saw in the stadium what the Taliban did to thieves. Arif and I too cried and prayed to God to save our father. Terrible thoughts floated in my mind, seeing our father's hand being amputated before the eyes of thousands of people. The sorrowful day elapsed and the darkness of the night appeared. At last Tariq and our father arrived home. The Taliban who had accused him of stealing fuel failed to prove it to their top commander, so all charges had been dropped. Father told every one of us to thank God for helping us.

My mother begged my father to leave his job and look for a new one. Finding a new job in Afghanistan was like finding a phoenix. He refused to leave his risky job. He had not even been paid yet. There was no food in our house and neither did we weave a carpet. My little brother Tamim got sick repeatedly and there was no money to take him to hospital. My mother told Tariq to ask Ustad Naqib to give us an advance on our salaries. Tariq and I did not think Ustad Naqib would give it to us but Tariq asked and, surprisingly, he did not refuse and gave us 500,000 Afghani. With that amount of money we could buy 35kg of wheat flour. That money saved us from starvation. As we were supplying the house with water during the day, Tariq asked Arif and me to weave the carpet at night.

By now our food had changed from rice soup to *Naan-e chai*. We were eating *Naan-e Chai* in the morning, in the afternoon and in the evening. Still we were the most privileged people amongst most Afghans to have *Naan-e Chai* in our house. Others were cooking grass for their children in order to survive. One of our neighbours had a grapevine in their compound. First they had eaten all of the grapes and then they ate its leaves.

It was Friday afternoon and Simaa Khala was washing clothes. I had supplied her with the water. I sat down to chat with her. She was talking about her children, Akmal and Ajmal, 'When my sons come back from Pakistan this time, I won't let them go again,' she said. 'I would rather die from hunger than send my children all the way into an alien land to earn food for me.'

Merza Kaka stepped out of the room and said to Simaa Khala, 'Go and boil water and make tea.'

Simaa Khala said, 'OK, I will. But let me wash these clothes with this warm water before it gets cold.' Merza Kaka said nothing and stepped back into the room. My mother came to join us in conversation and as a result of this Simaa Khala forgot what Merza Kaka had said to her. An hour elapsed.

Suddenly, Merza Kaka walked out of the room and charged towards Simaa Khala, as well as cursing her on the way.

When he reached Simaa Khala he said, 'Didn't I tell you to make tea?' Before Simaa Khala could answer he began punching, slapping and kicking her in the face, back, shoulders and head. Simaa Khala ran towards the end of the compound in order to escape his ruthless strikes. As she was running away he threw rocks at her, which hit her on the back. Simaa Khala reached the end of the compound and there was nowhere else to run. Merza Kaka trapped her. He pounded Simaa Khala as much as he could. My mother could do nothing but remain silent, and her tears fell from her eyes onto the ground. Simaa Khala remained there while Merza Kaka went back inside. My mother sat beside Simaa Khala. She wiped her sister's tears and allowed her own tears to flow. Simaa Khala had been beaten atrociously just because she forgot to make the tea while she was washing the clothes, and Merza Kaka did not bother to make his own tea as he was lying down in the room and doing nothing. I heard all the time that Merza Kaka was beating Simaa Khala regularly, but this was the first time I had witnessed it. I was so infuriated and wished I was strong enough to stop him. Unfortunately, Merza Kaka was not the only man who physically and verbally tortured his wife. Very few Afghan women were immune from torture, abuse and insults.

In the summer of 1999, the Taliban's dream was turning into a reality. Not very much of Afghanistan was left outside of their control. They seized province after province from the Mujahidin. They pushed the Mujahidin deeper towards the north and it seemed like the Mujahidin were going to be trapped there. More and more people were killed in their brutal war. Afghanistan produced children and the two vicious faction groups pushed them towards the jaws of death.

At the peak of the summer no one had water in the village and the only place we could find any was a place that was miles away. Hundreds of people lined up there under the burning sun waiting to take a bucket of water home. Tariq, Arif and I had to wait for several hours in the queue before we filled our buckets with water. Sometimes people did not line up; instead they fought one another and hurt each other badly. Tariq was worried about missing school. But Arif and I didn't mind. We wished that water would never appear in our well again so that we could keep missing school. We would wake up far before the arrival of the new dawn, in the darkness of the night, and begin getting water before hundreds of other people stormed the well. People travelled for miles to get this water.

Tamim was growing and he too knew, like my sisters, to whom he should cry when he was hungry. My poor mother had to listen to unpleasant cries of my two little sisters as well as him. Sometimes, during mealtimes, my siblings and I fought and beat each other over a small piece of Naan. As usual, Tariq was the strongest amongst us and he usually got the food. Mother could no longer punish Tariq and me, because we were no longer kids. When she beat me, I knew what to do to make her regret it. I went outside and threw rocks at our home and as my mother was so fearful of the *Amr Bil Maaruf* she dare not come outside and stop me. All she could do was to take my sisters and brother and take refuge somewhere before the rocks that I threw hurt them. Soon my cousins copied me when Simaa Khala beat them.

One day Zakia, Simaa Khala's only daughter, entered our room, eyes filled with tears, and said, 'My mother is looking to find fuel to burn herself.' All of us ran towards Simaa Khala's house and when we saw her, she was sat by the fire in the kitchen and was busy cooking food.

Mother asked her, 'What is going on?' She laughed and said she was joking with Zakia.

My mother was anxious about Simaa Khala and feared that her sister may not continue this endless journey of anguish, misery and hardship. Simaa Khala was suffering with her abusive husband who mistreated and tortured her frequently as she was stuck into the bond of marriage with him. She was in severe pain watching her children tailing her with their tearful eyes and demanding food. Afghan women who could not live in the world of pain, humiliation and misery set fire to themselves. Women's self-immolation was nothing new in Afghanistan; it was as old as the Afghanistan tradition itself. However, it had increased since the arrival of the US and the Soviet Union's Cold War in Afghanistan. It reached its peak during the Mujahidin and Taliban eras. Both were hardliners and women-haters and made the women's lives as miserable and difficult as it never had been before. And both had been created by the people whose slogan was the idealistic words of democracy, freedom and human rights.

My mother knew she had to keep an eye on her sister. She spent more time with Simaa Khala, trying to cheer her that there was an end to this journey of pain and misery and we must carry on for now. Yet she herself could not see the end of the dark journey. The future of Afghanistan looked as dark as a moonless and starless night. Everywhere one looked there was the Taliban wandering arrogantly and harassing poor and helpless Afghans. Women had no freedom under the regime, and it seemed like poor women would remain under the oppression of the Taliban forever as the empire seemed invincible.

A rocket crashed not far from our village. It certainly shook our village and then the dark cloud rose. I was grown enough to be amongst the first to run to where the rocket had fallen. People were struggling to excavate the victims out of the ruins. I took a spade that someone had brought and began searching for people who may be buried under the ruins. Some managed to dig out a boy of my own age perhaps. He was already dead, so people put him aside and looked for those who were still living. Many people were dug out, but only a few were alive.

This rocket was fired by the Mujahidin. The Mujahidin had left Kabul and most parts of Afghanistan but their rockets did not. They regularly fired long-range rockets at Kabul. Their victims were no one else but the poor civilian men, women and children. Regularly their rockets pounded different parts of Kabul. Nobody knew which of those rockets would fall upon them. Afghans did not know when they would be crushed under the Taliban and the Mujahidin's feet. Some cheered in Kabul that the Taliban would soon defeat the Mujahidin and the bloodshed would be over. But they were unaware that far more barbarous and mighty powers were sharpening their teeth for their throats.

My life went on. I was unsuccessful in both school and the mosque. The teacher told the smart students to help Hekmat, Arif and I with our lessons, but that too got us nowhere. Our school was a war-torn apartment block built a long time before the wars broke out and it had three storeys. The teacher warned me that he would throw me down from the third floor if I didn't learn his lessons. He frightened me and I tried to learn. I sat with Tariq and my father and they helped me to learn, but I failed. One day the teacher selected four healthy and strong students and told them to throw me off the third floor. The students thought the teacher was joking so they did not do what he had said, until the teacher flogged them with his cable. The teacher opened the broken window for them and shouted at them to pick me up and throw me out of the window.

The others had no choice but to do what they were told as our teacher was a high official in the Taliban regime. As my strong classmates lifted me up and walked towards the window, I began crying and flapping. I grabbed hold of the broken window as they were struggling to push me out of it. Hekmat and Arif were frightened and begged the teacher not to let the students throw me out of the window. But he was determined that I would be thrown out. As I was struggling, I unintentionally kicked one of my classmates in the nose, and it began to bleed. Now there were three of them left and they could not force me out of the window easily. After a while, with both me and them struggling, the teacher got bored and told the students to sit back in their places. He then called me to him and gave me the most brutal punishment that I had ever received from any teacher. He hit me on the palms of my hands until I could no longer feel them. For several days the pain remained and I was unable to weave carpet for some time.

Again, at the end of the year, I brought home my school results, which tremendously disappointed my parents and, as usual, I received severe punishment. In the mosque the Mullah kept punishing me every evening for not learning his lessons. Life was severely bitter for me. Everyone and everything hurt me. Sometimes I took refuge in the world of imagination far away from this cruel world. I flew high into the sky and far away into a wonderful world where I could see neither a ruined school, nor a brutal teacher, nor my classmates who always bullied me, nor the vicious Mullah, nor the dark carpet factory and boring carpet weaving, nor peasants and shopkeepers. I remained in that wonderful world until someone disturbed me and, in less than a second, brought me back down to earth and all the way back to my war-torn village.

This marvellous world of imagination is very kind, not only to the poor, hungry and oppressed, but to everyone, even the rich and powerful. In a world of imagination a person can become anyone or anything they want to be. The world of imagination is far more kind and beautiful than this cruel and stingy world of ours. The poor can become rich, the slave can become free, dreams turn into reality, the old can become young again, and the rich can become richer. The world of imagination is a perfect world, yet it does not belong to us. Our world is full of brutality, exploitation, hunger, misery, trouble, hatred, intolerance, ignorance, division. I often wished that this troublesome world of ours were like the world of imagination where every wish and every dream came true.

Merza Kaka brought his sons back home from Pakistan as they were being maltreated by the carpet factory owner. The day they arrived home, Simaa Khala was the happiest mother in the whole world. Her tormented heart was cheerful for months after the return of her sons.

In 2000, the Taliban decided to ban the poppy cultivation in Afghanistan. They preached all across Afghanistan to the peasants that God had forbidden it. Afghans knew what the Taliban meant by prohibition. Almost everyone stopped poppy cultivation in all parts of Afghanistan that were under Taliban control. Those farmers who cultivated opium were severely punished and imprisoned, as they were breaking Taliban law. Afghanistan was no longer a country that took the lives of untold humans around the world with its opium. In 2001, Afghanistan produced less than 10 per cent of the world's opium. Some argued that the reason the Taliban banned poppy cultivation was because they wanted to increase the price of opium. It is an absurd argument. Poppy cultivation undermined the Taliban regime amongst Afghans. And the other reason behind the prohibition of the poppy cultivation by the Taliban was that they were seeking international legitimacy for their regime. Some Afghans still believe that the prohibition of poppy cultivation by the Taliban had a religious basis.

Naturally, empires become violent and arrogant when their end is near. The Taliban's brutality and violence and arrogance were touching the sky in those days.

In 2001, the Taliban destroyed the *But-Hai-Bamyan* (Bamyan Statues). The Bamyan Statues were the last spot of beauty on the face of ruined Afghanistan. Two giant statues had been carved into a cliff in the sixth century. They were the biggest statues of Buddha in the world. These giant statues had been in Bamyan for over 1,500 years and had seen mighty empires appear and disappear in Afghanistan. They were the pride of Afghanistan, the symbol of Afghanistan to the world. Local people who witnessed the two magnificent statues being destroyed said that Arab and Pakistani engineers helped the Taliban in the demolition. Who really was behind the destruction of those two majestic statues? Surely, it was not the Taliban who planned it, since the Taliban themselves were puppets of Pakistan and the fundamentalist Saudi monarchy. Most in Afghanistan blamed the Pakistani government. Those two statues were not the only cultural heritage that had been destroyed by the Taliban. They had destroyed most of the remains of the rich and ancient civilisations that once inhabited Afghanistan. The Taliban blindly obeyed and followed their leaders and did what their leaders told them to do without using their own minds; and their leaders danced to the tune of the Pakistani government and the fundamentalist Saudi monarchy. The problem with an ignorant man is that anyone can ride him, like a horse, towards his own ambition.

He who blindly conforms, obeys and follows a leader is a dangerous person. It is not something that I am quoting from scholars, it is a fact that I have seen through my own eyes. Anyone who blindly obeys leaders and follows them is as dangerous as the soldiers. If we are to obey and follow leaders then why do we have super-intelligent minds? If we don't doubt and question and find out for ourselves then how can we find reality or truth? Throughout history man has blindly obeyed and followed leaders, like a sheep that follows the butcher and walks towards the abattoir. Most people around the world think that leaders know more than them and therefore guide them to somewhere, but they got them to nowhere. Still mankind is as brutal, aggressive, intolerant, divided and superstitious as he was thousands of years ago. Look at the wars, chaos, exploitation and division all across the globe that leaders have caused.

I wonder if you have ever watched a shepherd. A shepherd does not look after the sheep for the benefit of the sheep; he does it for the benefit of himself. Power hungry leaders divide humanity by encouraging them to be nationalistic and ready to shed human blood in the name of their country and their flag. They control education and information to keep humanity ignorant. They squander an enormous amount of wealth of humanity on destructive weapons and the military. They turn millions of young people into soldiers and teach them war, destruction, hatred and violence. He who cannot lead himself follows others and there is no lack of people like Adolf Hitler to lead them.

A wise man always tries to free himself from the curse of authority and leader, but an ignorant man in the contrary always gives himself to the authority and leader. Where there is authority and leader there is exploitation and oppression.

In 2001, the United States ran out of patience and attacked its prey. The execution of the agenda of the 'Project for the New American Century' or (PNAC) began. PNAC was a Think Tank based in Washington. Its fanatic members known as neoconservatives were in highly influential positions in

George W Bush Jr's administration. This Think Tank plainly called for the domination of the world by the United States. Regime change in Iraq was their dream, which took the lives of more than a million helpless Iraqis and shattered their entire basic infrastructure. 'Rebuilding America's Defence' is a document published by the PNAC in 2000. In this document they have explained how to dominate the world. In order to implement their agenda they were hoping, in their own words, for a 'catastrophic and catalysing event – like a new Pearl Harbor' to occur in the United States that would mobilise the public and allow them to implement their agenda. September 11 was exactly what they were wishing for.

Until the end of the twentieth century, the US government could disguise it's imperialism in the threat of communism, democracy, freedom and human rights. Ever since the beginning of the twenty first century it embarked on a path of naked imperialism. It illegally invades hungry and defenceless countries, bombs their livelihoods, kills them in large numbers and terrorises them all. The US government kills and tortures prisoners. It sends Drones into the countries of those who can't defend themselves and murders people without trial. The path that the US government has embarked on is the path of oppression and exploitation, demonisation and de-humanisation of the hungry and defenceless; it is the path of hypocricy, lie and dishonesty. It is the path of racism. By embarking on this path, the US isolates itself and makes itself hated around the world just like all the past imperialists.

The US's naked, arrogant and racist imperialism reminds me of what the Medieval Greek historian Herodotus said over two thousand years ago. He said that a nation's history has three stages: Success; then as a consequence of success, arrogance and injustice; and then as a result of these, downfall.[27] Invasion, oppression, terrorisation, demonisation and dehumanisation of poor and defenceless people around the world by the US are signs of the downfall of the US imperialism. Injustice has a short life. It cannot go on forever.

It Cannot be a Coincidence

The twentieth century came to an end. The most violent, destructive and horrible century in human history. The poor and the defenceless considered that imperialism and imperialists had vanished alongside the destruction of millions of human beings. They thought that the Cold War too had ended and there would be no more demonisation, killing, subjugation and exploitation of the defenceless people by the empires. They thought that the age of conquering, massacring and exploiting the poor had gone. But the poor people were unaware that the predatory Imperialists now united like wolves in invading, conquering and exploiting the poor and defenceless. They were oblivious that imperialism had reached its most advanced stage.

I wonder if anyone has noticed the resemblance between the imperialists and wild predators. If one noticed it, one might be surprised that there is very little difference between them. They both prey on the weak and the defenceless. Imperialists never invade those who can retaliate; their prey of choice is defenceless. The wars of the ugly imperialists have always been with the weak. Had Afghanistan been a strong country, the British, nor the Tsar, nor the Soviet Union, nor the US would dare to come near it. But Afghanistan was weak, backward, divided and always has been a geostratigically important place. Since the late modern history of Afghanistan, empires had already attempted to dominate the country, but almost all of them were forced to drink from the cup of shameful defeat. Now it was the United States and its gang's turn to try their luck. Very cleverly and with lots of intrigues and trickeries they built a case for themselves to justify the domination of Afghanistan.

In September 2001, two aircraft were flown into two New York skyscrapers one after another and a third hit the Pentagon. The whole world watched these horrific events. Most Americans, who never had experienced war in their lives, saw the horror of it in their own country. People jumped from the tall buildings one after another to their deaths. Soon the buildings were reduced to dust, almost as if a huge monster had torn them down with powerful claws. And miraculously the third building, or building 7, collapsed by itself, as if an invisible plane flew into it.

Almost 3,000 innocent people perished in the terrorist attack. It horrified a great number of people around the world, in particular in the west, and it really was a terrifying moment for them as almost all of them were unfamiliar with war and its horrors. The fearmonger politicians and media frightened them of the evil enemy who hated their freedom. Tales of the evil enemy were virtually identical to the tales that my mother told me about the evil demons who loved to eat children. When Government deliberately denies public political and historical knowledge, they believe in these sorts of tales. Did these terrorists really hate the Americans' freedom and way of life? Did the Americans know the history of their government's policies towards the so-called Third World, in particular towards Arab countries?

Nevertheless, hours after the 9/11 horrific attacks, the government of the United States and its allies accused the Islamic terrorist group Al Qaeda and their leader Osama Bin Laden, who once upon a time was brought by the United States of America into Afghanistan and he fought for them against her enemy, the Soviet Union. Most Afghans did not know this man at all before 9/11 and still masses of Afghans who live under US and NATO bombs have never heard his name. He was neither the leader of Afghanistan nor was he from Afghanistan. None of the nineteen hijackers were from Afghanistan, nor did ever a single Afghan carry out terrorist acts against any country in the West. But the empire of America and its allies began bombing Afghan men, women and children, their villages and cities, day and night, endlessly and indiscriminately for over a decade in this so-called War on Terror. Al Qaeda had several other bases in other countries as well as Afghanistan, but the United States chose to attack the dreamland of the empires. Whoever Osama Bin Laden was, he turned the long dream of the United States into a reality. As early as the beginning of the Cold War, US elites imagined controlling the dreamland of the empires and now it was almost time for their dreams to come true. The Taliban were willing to hand Osama Bin Laden to the United States government, if they could prove to them that Osama Bin Laden was the mastermind behind the 9/11 attacks. But the US ignored their proposition and went on with the bombing and domination of a shattered country and a starving people.

Before the 9/11 attacks, the world knew very little or nothing about this tormented and helpless nation. The history of Afghanistan began after 9/11 for the masses around the world and in particular for Americans and other western nations. Very few people knew about the pre-9/11 Afghanistan. Many around the world were ignorant of what this oppressed nation went through. They did not know that empire after empire had overran these poor and unguarded people's houses, villages, gardens, fields, cities and country over and over again. Empire marched into Afghanistan with its horrible weapons and destructive troops and massacred Afghans, burned their houses, villages and whole livelihoods until it had exhausted itself, and then left. And soon the next one filled its place and buried Afghanistan under the blood and tears of the poor Afghans. This process dragged on until the day when it was the turn for the US to come after this nation, who had been more than oppressed already, with its destructive military and hideous weapons. Now the United States associated the name of helpless Afghans with Islamic terrorism.

For decades the United States had set fire to Afghanistan and defenceless Afghans were burned in this fire. The United States government made a deadly trap out of Afghanistan for its greatest enemy – the Soviet Union – and successfully entrapped it. The United States government pushed millions of defenceless peasants to fight its enemy. The United States has armed the entire population of Afghanistan to the teeth and untold numbers of people have been murdered with these weapons. It empowered the very religious fundamentalists with whom it's at war now. The United States government handed the fate of tormented Afghans into the hands of religious fundamentalists and the savage government of Pakistan and the Saudi monarchy. Today it uses the terrible state of Afghan women as a pretext to legitimise its domination of Afghanistan. But, it was the very empire of the

United States who handed the fate of exploited Afghan women to the religious fundamentalists who hated women. Today the empire of the United States is butchering Afghans in their thousands each year in a war with the people that they themselves created and empowered. They claim that they are modernising Afghanistan, but it was they who sent Afghanistan back to the dark age in the 1980s.

Who really perpetrated 9/11? Unfortunately, powerful governments tried the 9/11 method frequently throughout history, as a pretext to invade the poor and helpless nations around the world. Throughout history the callous rich and powerful demonised the poor and the defenceless people in order to steal from them. The fascist Adolf Hitler demonised Jewish people in Europe to achieve his nasty ambitions. Today western governments have demonised Muslims in order to achieve their evil objectives. It's extremely dangerous to divide nations and civilisations, but these neurotic men who are running our world are doing this again and again. An average human being is historically and politically so under-informed to see the true motives behind the demonisation and division of people and civilisations. The enemy and exploiter of humanity always divides ordinary people, turns them against each other and fills their hearts with hatred for each other so that they could carry on with their exploitation. George W. Bush and Barack Obama do not hate the fundamentalist king of Saudi Arabia who denies freedom to the Saudis and exports fundamentalism throughout the Muslim world. The Western politicians rub shoulder with him while turning ordinary Westerners and Muslims against each other. An empire always needs an enemy to scare its subjects into control, to distract them from internal problems, to exploit defenceless human beings and to keep itself alive. An empire cannot survive in peacetime. History demonstrates that empires weaken and die during peacetime. The US Empire knows that it won't survive in today's world without a fake enemy. It does not invent enemies for itself for fun; it invents an enemy for its very survival. Ever since the end of the World War II the US government has been at war with the enemy who is trying to destroy America. First it was communism and now it is Islamic terrorism. After the end of the Cold War in 1991, US elites were very uneasy about running out of enemies.

The United States former Secretary of State, Colin Powell, very nicely expressed his anxiety after the disintegration of the Soviet Union in an interview in 1991, 'Think hard about it. I'm running out of demons. I'm running out of villains. I'm down to Castro and Kim II Sung.'[28] Would Americans allow their elites to squander hundreds of billions of dollars on military each year if they were not frightened of the 'evil enemy' who hates them and threatens their way of life? Would Americans allow their elites to build innumerable military bases in every corner of the globe and squander enormous amount of US taxpayer's money, if they were not frightened of the enemy who is trying to attack them? Would the Americans allowed their government to wage aggressive wars, from which the Military Industrial Complex profits enormously, only against those nations who can't defend themselves, if they were not frightened of the enemy who hates their freedom?

George Orwell in his famous novel, *Nineteen Eighty-Four*, portrays a society ruled by a totalitarian party. In order to control and exploit people, amongst other things, the party is perpetually at war with other countries. The media is strictly controlled by the party and it always spreads fear and glorifies the party. People are being watched all the time through surveillance. Thinking is a crime. Anyone who thinks is being punished and killed. The party distorts history so that the historical record always supports the party line.

George Orwell wrote 'The war is not meant to be won, it's meant to be continuous. Hierarchical society is only possible on the basis of poverty and ignorance. This new version is the past and no different past can ever have existed. In principle the war effort is always planned to keep society on the brink of starvation. The war is waged by the ruling group against its own subjects and its object is not the victory over either Eurasia or East Asia, but to keep the very structure of the society intact.

I wonder if America has headed in the direction of the society that George Orwell had depicted in his novel.

The US government is perpetually at war and continuously frightens its subjects of the 'evil enemy' who's destined to destroy them. The 'War on Terror' is a permanent war. On 16 May 2013 Assistant Defence Secretary Michael A. Sheehan told the US senate that the War on Terror was going to last 'at least for another 10 to 20 years.'[29]The media only radiates fear, hatred, racism and lies. The government is spying on people. The government is filled with secrecy. Cities are under total surveillance. An average American is under-informed or mis-informed about other nations, cultures, religions, races and civilisations. Economically America is one of the most unequal countries in the world. One per cent of the population owns 35 to 40 per cent of nation's wealth.

There are scholars around the world screaming that 9/11 was an inside job and only an intelligence service was able to carry out such complex operation. There are a great number of books arguing that the US government was behind the attacks. David Ray Griffin, a retired professor of philosophy, has written a very well-researched book called *The New Pearl Harbor: Disturbing Question about the Bush Administration and 9/11.* He poses some serious questions about the US government's involvement in the event. There are large crowds of Americans who are accusing their own government of the atrocity. A great number of journalists state that 9/11 was a false flag operation carried out by the US government.

Imperialistic powers had tried 9/11 style methods several times in Asia and elsewhere in the seventeenth, eighteenth, nineteenth and twentieth centuries. In 1933, Adolf Hitler burned the Reichstag, the German Parliament, and used it as a pretext to destroy the communist party in Germany. In 1939, SS troops disguised in Polish military uniform attacked a German radio station, and Hitler used that as a pretext to invade Poland. Japan's army carried out a false flag operation in 1931 by blowing up a railway in China owned by Japan, accused Chinese dissidents, used it as a pretext and then dominated Manchuria.[30] The US government has carried out false flag operations repeatedly in order to invade the poor people's land like that of the Gulf of Tonkin incident, which never happened, to escalate a full scale occupation of

Vietnam where millions of innocent people died. *Operation Northwood* was similar to that of 9/11. In 1962, a bunch of elites within the US government drafted a plan to carry out a series of terrorist attacks in the United States and use it as a pretext to invade Cuba, but was rejected by the Kennedy Administration.[31] Doubting and questioning is not idiocy; not doubting and questioning is idiocy.

I don't know who really was behind the attacks: the US government or Islamic terrorists, the former ally of the US government. But if I consider the War on Terror as a just war then it would be disrespectful to the lives of countless Afghans who have been slaughtered and still are being slaughtered by the destructive troops of NATO and the US. How can I believe that the invasion of Afghanistan is a coincidence? There are two hundred countries around the world and each time a murderous empire emerges it invades Afghanistan. In the last three centuries, first came the British and the Russian Tsar and then came the brutal Soviet Union and the United States. How can it be a coincidence? The US plotted for decades against the long-oppressed nation of Afghanistan in order to pave the ground for the occupation of Central Asia. Truth is like the sun, which cannot be veiled forever. The true motives of the War on Terror have already begun to unveil.

Is the war of the United States of America and its allies genuinely with the Islamic terrorists or someone else? The US and its allies' war is with these rising nations of Asia, not with the terrorists. The East is rising at an unprecedented speed. Many eastern nations are catching up with the west economically, militarily, scientifically and technologically. The rising of developing nations means that the United States and its allies have to share the power and prestige in the future, and that is what they are unwilling to do. The United States and its allies are using every means to keep their dominance over the world. In the name of War on Terror they have disguised their real ojective; the domination of the world's natural resources and geostratigically crucial parts of the world, from where they threaten these rising nations. There is already an intense competition between the United States and its allies and the new rising nations for the world's natural resources. The US and its allies know that there will be fighting for every spec of natural resources in the next few decades between the industrialised nations. The United States has invented this vague and ludicrous term 'War on Terror' to dominate natural resources-rich Asian and African countries. Any wise man who's a little politically and historically aware knows that the US war is not with terrorism, because US creates terrorism for itself. If by pouring fuel on fire one can extinguish fire, than the US can defeat terrorism by invading and occupying defenceless people's countries and bombing their houses, killing their children and women, and terrorising them all. Of course there are Islamic terrorists in many Muslim countries. They are brutal and destructive with medieval mindsets and they are parasites only cause harm to their countries. But they are being used by the Western Governments to achieve their Economic, political and Geopolitical goals in Asia and Africa. Afghanistan, Syria and Libya are perfect examples of this where the Western Governments have funded, armed and supported Islamic fundamentalism to achieve their economic, political and geopolitical objectives. In Afghanistan, Pakistan, Yemen, Mali…the Western governments are supposedly at war with the Islamic terrorists, but in Syria and Libya they are beind supported, funded and armed by them.

The United States government has behaved many times more violently for over half a century in Asia, Africa Latin America and elsewhere around the world, than those terrorists who killed almost 3,000 innocent human beings. No empire has ever dropped as many bombs upon defenceless people as the United States has. Since the end of World War II it has perpetually bombed defenceless nations and slaughtered millions. Yet it claims to be the champion of human rights, democracy, freedom and justice.

Still the clouds of bombs, rockets, missiles and bullets of the Soviet Union and the US did not sit in the mountains, valleys, cities, villages, roads and streets of Afghanistan. Yet again Afghanistan was about to be torn apart by US and NATO bombs alongside countless poor men, women and children who had seen nothing throughout their lifetimes but war, hunger and suffering. Still the earth did not suck the blood and tears of those Afghans who had became the victims of the Soviet aggression and the United States proxies, yet they were about to become the victim of another superpower. Still millions of Afghan refugees who lived in the brutal refugee camps of Pakistan under the blistering sun for decades did not return home and yet more Afghans had to be displaced by the United States and its allies' aggression. History witnesses that it was not the Afghans who chose to be ruled by religious fanatics and turn their country into a safe haven for Al Qaeda. History remembers that it was the United States and its allies who empowered religious fanatics in Afghanistan then handed the fate of the shattered Afghans to them and turned their country into a safe haven for the terrorists. If anyone were to be blamed for the nurturing of the terrorism in Afghanistan, it is the United States government itself. The shattered nation of Afghanistan did not deserve to be slaughtered because they had gone through all of this already.

War-torn Afghanistan was about to be bombed by the world's most powerful nations on earth and many Afghans were unaware of it. Very few people knew about the invasion, as nobody told them. Especially in the rural areas, almost everyone was unaware until the bombs fell upon them. We were living in Kabul and we were the lucky ones. We found out about the US invasion through the radio before the bombs crushed Kabul but we did not know that sick men filled the hearts of most Americans and other westerners with hatred for us. We were in class one day when our teacher said that America was going to attack Afghanistan if the Taliban did not hand over Osama Bin Laden to them. This was the first time in my life I had heard 'America', as well as 'Osama Bin Laden'. We began to question one another; some asked 'who is Osama Bin Laden?' And others asked 'what is America?'

The headmaster gathered all the students together and said, 'America is the strongest country on the planet and it has so much power that it can destroy Afghanistan in moments. America has innumerable *Bam-e Atom* (atomic bomb) and the most sophisticated weapons and technology on earth with a very strong military.'

All the students talked about the United States. The *Bam-e Atom* or atomic bomb interested me a lot. I asked my classmates; 'What is *Bam-e Atom*?' but none knew about it. I kept it in my mind and paid attention to the headmaster's speech and the students' questions.

Students asked the headmaster, 'Who is Osama Bin Laden?'

He said, 'I do not know who Osama Bin Laden is.'

No one knew the person. Those Afghans who found out about the US promised invasion were panicking, because they knew that this new war was going to be different from the domestic ones and the memory of the Soviet invasion was still fresh in many minds.

Only thirteen years before the Soviet troops were busy massacring men, women and children of Afghanistan. Untold Afghans lost their lives as a result of their lunacy. A quarter of the total population of Afghanistan fled their country; some went to live in the burning refugee camps of Pakistan, some went to start a life of humiliation in Iran. Innumerable people were displaced inside Afghanistan. Cities, factories, hospitals, schools, bridges, villages and intellectuals vanished altogether because of Soviet and US madness. The Mujahidin first and the Taliban later turned Afghanistan into hell for Afghans for a decade. The United States were about to start the bombing of Afghanistan while several million Afghans were at the risk of starvation. Aid organisations warned the US government that its invasion would disrupt aid to needy Afghans. Ruud Lubbers, the UN High Commissioner for Refugees (UNHCR), travelled to Washington DC to inform the State Department that millions of Afghans already faced starvation and homelessness, and that US attacks might hit many more.[32] But the US government not only ignored them, it did everything it could do to hide the horror, barbarism and the terror of its invasion of Afghanistan.

As author and journalist Jonathan Steele observed in his book, *Ghosts of Afghanistan*:

'In the days after 9/11 the United States specifically asked Pakistan to close its frontiers to Afghan refugees. Since Pakistan had hosted millions of Afghans who fled Soviet bombs in the 1980s and stayed for years before deciding to go home, it was happy to agree. The Bush Administration was apparently anxious about the way people in the West would react to TV footage of huge flows of refugees. Better to have them wandering around out of sight inside Afghanistan than be filmed day after day arriving in Pakistan into the care of the UN High Commissioner for Refugees or the Islamic Red Crescent.'

Afghans were tired of perpetual war, bloodshed, brutality, oppression, hunger, crimes, lawlessness, grief, suffering and hardship and they were not ready to stand against another superpower's obnoxious weapons. Afghans and Afghanistan could not deal with another superpower. The United States, the world's greatest military power, brought tens of other strong militaries with her to devastate the Afghans. Afghan houses, villages, gardens, cities and country were already destroyed and burned, but the United States of America and her gang came to destroy that which had already been destroyed. They came to oppress already oppressed people, to turn Afghanistan into a battleground that already was an enduring battleground, to paint Afghanistan red with the blood of Afghans, but it is already drowned in the blood of millions of Afghans.

They came to terrorise Afghans, but they have been everlastingly terrorised. They came to fill Afghanistan with graves, although it was already filled with graves. They came to force people out of their country, but millions of them were already living in burning refugee. They came to take fathers from children, but Afghanistan is already filled with fatherless children. They came to take husbands from wives, but Afghanistan is already filled with widows who are begging in the streets and villages. There was nothing left in Afghanistan for the destructive US and NATO troops to destroy.

Hekmat, Arif and I came back to the village. It was a very exciting time for us. The world's most powerful countries were invading the world's most poor and defenceless country in the world. We saw almost all of our village men, including the elders, packed into one place. Normally village men came together only when someone died. They had found a tiny old radio and were listening to the BBC Pashtu news, and luckily it was all about the man that Afghans were desperate to know about – Osama Bin Laden. We heard a voice speaking in an unfamiliar language, but soon found out that the voice was from the president of the United States, George W Bush, but our villagers called him *Mister* Bush. He was demanding Osama Bin Laden and other Taliban leaders, or if not the US military would invade soon.

This new invasion reminded elderly people of the brutal invasion by the Soviet army and they were fearful that the same thing was going to happen again. All day long men who had undergone the brutality of the Soviet Union told tales of the destructive troops' crimes. Everybody was filled with fear everywhere. I came home and asked my father to tell me about *Bam-e Atom*. I was shocked when he told me about it. For over a month I was anxious that the United States government might drop *Bam-e Atom* on us. We forgot our hunger and began talking about what we could do to survive the invasion.

We went to school and it was the last day of the ultimatum that the United States had given for the Taliban to hand Osama Bin Laden over. Our headmaster himself was a Talib and he called all students to stand in the schoolyard. All students came out and lined up outside. The headmaster said not to fear the United States since it will not attack Afghanistan. There was a Taliban flag hanging on the school rooftop. Some teachers said to bring it down in case the United States attacked. They may think this was a Taliban base and bomb us. But the headmaster strongly disapproved. He firmly believed that the United States was not about to assault Afghanistan. He said that if the United States invaded Afghanistan the Taliban would do the same as they had done to the Russians.

Back home my father was very anxious about the coming invasion. For the first time he made up his mind to leave Afghanistan. He went to his friends and asked them to lend him some money to flee Kabul to Pakistani refugee camps before the invasion began. However, none had any money to lend him. He desperately ran up and down and begged everyone he knew to lend him some money in order to flee Afghanistan. Those who had money evacuated Afghanistan and headed towards Pakistani refugee camps and Iran, and those who did not have anything stayed behind and looked for sanctuary from the bombs and rockets which were about to fall upon them.

Back at school most students did not attend as they feared the United States invasion. Our teacher disappeared as well, so Hekmat, Arif and I were extremely happy. We were free and we could play all day long. My father warned us not to wander about in the villages and streets. Nobody knew when the US military would start the invasion. It could have been any time. My helpless father failed to find money to take us far away, so he and my brothers and I started digging hiding holes again. We started in the morning until late evening and dug a hole in a zigzag shape. It was deep and big enough for us to hide in. The hole was ready and all we had to do was wait with our empty stomachs for Uncle Sam's savage military to begin its invasion. My parents kept praying to God to save them and their children. They told us to pray to God. Mother asked Tamim, my little brother, to pray to God to save us; but he was crying for food.

The United States government told Americans and the world that they were going to liberate Afghans, in particular Afghan women, from the oppression of the Taliban, and destroy the terrorists who killed almost 3,000 innocent people in 9/11. They promised that they would bring democracy to Afghanistan. But how could the US government liberate Afghans from the oppression of the Taliban and bring democracy to Afghanistan, when it had only a handful of Special Forces and CIA operatives on the ground? The US government asked its former proxy, the Mujahidin or the so-called Northern Alliance, who killed over 60,000 innocent Afghans between 1992 and 1996, raped countless women and children, destroyed over 90 per cent of beautiful

Kabul, tortured human beings in the most barbaric fashions, kidnapped women, looted and plundered all over Afghanistan...

The US government paid millions of dollars to the Mujahidin, whom ordinary Afghans loathed, to help them to topple the Taliban.

Tell the Sky, Stars and Moon...

The United States military was busy fastening bombs around their destructive aircrafts. The heart of the ordinary American soldier had been filled with hatred for Afghans and revenge. Propaganda machines introduced Afghan-looking men who had long beards, baggy clothes and turbans as terrorists. Large numbers of young Americans joined the army to teach a lesson to the terrorists who invaded their country from Afghanistan, without knowing anything about Afghans or Afghanistan.

Days passed, but the promised invasion did not come, so we got out of the holes and carried on living as normal. The next day it was around two or perhaps three o'clock in the afternoon when we heard the first explosion, not on the ground, but in the sky. I instantly recognised that it was the Taliban's anti-aircraft gunfire as I had been hearing it since the day I was born. My parents took all of us into the holes and hid us there. Everybody thought the invasion had begun. We heard a lot of anti-aircraft fire, but did not hear any of the US aircraft's scary sound or bomb blasts. The gunfire lasted for over two hours then faded away. The Kabul sky was filled with the clouds of the Taliban's gunfire. The night arrived and we ate the little food that my mother had cooked. My younger siblings were crying as their empty stomachs demanded more food. People could not sleep as they feared that the US aircraft may come back. We spent the night with our hearts filled with terror. The next day we heard a deafening explosion. It felt like the sky and the earth had bumped into one another. It shook the whole of Kabul. It was far greater than any explosion any Afghan had ever heard before. A dark and ugly cloud rose from over tens of miles away. This was the promised invasion's blast. My little siblings were terrorised and were all screaming. Our parents struggled to keep them quiet.

The invasion began when Afghans were devastated by hunger and more than two decades of atrocities, killings and destruction. The Taliban wasted their heavy weapons as they fired them towards the sky with no knowledge of where the US aircraft were. For the first time the Taliban experienced the power of US sophisticated weapons and their old weapons could do nothing against them. The US Special Forces and CIA, along with the Mujahidin or Northern Allies, and with the help of the US Air Force pushed the Taliban from the north of Afghanistan. Now was the opportunity for the Mujahidin to hit back at their bitter enemy. The Mujahidin did not meet much resistance as the US aircraft destroyed their opposition from above. The Mujahidin were angry. Some had lost fathers, brothers, other relatives, friends and some their property in the war with the Taliban, and wanted to take revenge on them. They captured, tortured and killed thousands of Taliban. In Kabul, US aircraft bombed day and night. My parents soon realised that it was futile to hide in the holes as the bombs were too powerful. If they fell upon us nothing could protect us. My father told us to get out of the holes and carry on life as usual.

With the drop of each bomb, ruined Afghanistan and its inhabitants shivered. No one knew which one would fall on them. There was nobody to do a body count as the lives of Afghans were cheap in comparison to the lives of Americans. Mountains, valleys, cities, villages, roads and streets were already crammed with Soviet mines and took many lives every day. It was not enough that the United States Air Force dropped cluster bombs and some of them remained unexploded and later took the lives of Afghans. The US and NATO bombardment of Afghanistan was not free from civilian causalities. Innocent Afghan civilians' lives were not that important to them. There was no one to report to the media about the deaths of Afghans that the United States and NATO bombs had caused. It's doubtful any news of the murdered Afghans reached Americans and Europeans. According to Professor Marc Herold of the University of New Hampshire, between 3,000 and 3,400 were killed in Afghanistan between 7 October and 7 December 2011 – more than the number of people who lost their lives in 9/11.[33] Indeed the US invasion of Afghanistan took many more thousands of lives indirectly. Yes, 9/11 was a horrific terrorist attack; but so was the American response to it, only on a much larger scale.

The masters of war and occupation knew how to hide the horrors of their war. They made sure no footage reached Americans. The chairman of Cable News Network (CNN) advised the news staff that it 'seems perverse to focus too much on the casualities or hardship in Afghanistan'.[34] When the Al Jazeera TV channel attempted to show the civilan casuality of the US bombardment, the US bombed it.[35] Masters of war and occupation even distorted language to hide the ugly face of their invasion by calling the massacre of civilians and the destruction of their livelihoods 'collateral damage', and calling torture 'enhanced interrogation techniques'.

Nevertheless, Afghans kept living under the US bombs and rockets and nobody knew when would be their last day. As aircraft roared above the Afghans' heads, they terrified little children, women and men. Terror was raining upon Afghanistan and its inhabitants. Each time a hateful bomb shook Kabul, my siblings screamed and took refuge in our mother's arms. At night we sat quiet and listened to the explosions that shook the earth beneath us. Tamim screamed each time a bomb shook Kabul or when he heard the frightful sound of the US aircraft. He was frightened that the bombs would fall upon our house. Everyone tried to persuade him that nothing was going to fall upon us, but he would trust no one.

My mother said to him, 'Ask the sky, stars and moon not to let the bombs fall upon us.'

Poor Tamim would put his head out of the window and scream, 'Sky, stars and moon let not the bombs fall upon us!' I guess the sky, stars and moon did listen to him, as they did not let the US bombs fall upon us.

Aircraft bombed the villages and houses where the Taliban concealed themselves, day and night. I remember each time the aircraft roared in the sky, hungry and unclothed children were terrified and hid themselves into the arms of their mothers. Fear and terror poured upon Afghanistan like sunlight. Despairing and hungry Afghans did not know what to do or where to seek asylum. However, after a few days I started to enjoy watching the dark clouds rising everywhere. It was as if powerful volcanoes were erupting all across

Kabul. Hekmat, Arif and I climbed onto the rooftop and observed the city from there and cheered when the bombs hit Kabul and shook us. *Mister* Bush said that US aircrafts would drop food and medicines for Afghans. But, when I looked at those aircraft that dropped destructive bombs and terrorised helpless Afghans, I could not believe they would also drop food and medicines. I did not know what sort of cruel game *Mister* Bush was playing with us. Nevertheless, we climbed on the rooftops and watched the sky for many days, but the aircraft dropped nothing but bombs.

The Taliban expected that they would fight the US in the same way that they fought the Mujahidin, but they were almost defeated by their enemy without ever seeing them. Sometimes the impossible becomes the possible. No one in Afghanistan thought that the Taliban would ever be defeated in their lifetime, but they were about to be vanquished before their eyes. Kabul residents watched their oppressors being oppressed! Hekmat, Arif and I watched the Taliban who came beside the stream and covered their new pickup trucks with mud so as to camouflage them and survive the US bombs. People were surprised that the Taliban was melting away so rapidly.

In a matter of weeks the world's strongest military wiped out the Taliban from the face of Afghanistan. It was morning when Hekmat knocked on the door and told me that all the Taliban had vanished from Kabul. It was beyond my imagination; it was beyond everyone's imagination. The Taliban seemed undefeatable. I ran to my parents to announce the news to them. My mother, father, brothers and sisters were so happy. Our village boys again marched in the streets like they did last time when the Taliban came into Kabul. But, this time they did not chant *Zinda Baad Taliba* (long live the Taliban) instead they were chanting *Murda Baad Talibn* (death to the Taliban). I also joined the village boys and marched in the streets and chanted this slogan all day long. The seed of hope once again began to grow in the hearts of Afghans. I had never seen Simaa Khala and my mother so happy. Hekmat and I went far away from our compounds to Kabul city in search of booty. There were lots of Afghans looking for Taliban valuables. People broke into a building that was once occupied by the Taliban. Hekmat and I entered the building, too.

Some grabbed food, some grabbed furniture, but by the time we reached there everything was taken by others. There was a small hut in the corner of the yard and its door was locked. Hekmat and I broke down the door and found several Kalashnikovs. I told Hekmat not to touch them and leave the room, but he told me that I was crazy. 'Do you know how much each one of these Kalashnikovs cost? You can buy anything by selling one of these.' said Hekmat. I refused to pick any of the Kalashnikovs up. I knew that if I took those weapons into my compound my parents would kill me. Hekmat took two Kalashnikovs. Before we left the compound, Hekmat let other looters know about the other Kalashnikovs. People rushed towards the room and took all the weapons. On the way back home we found a bag and concealed the guns inside it. I was expecting that Hekmat would be punished by his parents for what he had brought home. But, ironically, his father was very excited when he saw the weapons.

As people enjoyed the disappearance of the Taliban, simultaneously there was fear growing in each one's heart in Kabul. Everybody knew who was going to replace them. There was no way for an ordinary Afghan to forget those days when the Mujahidin turned Kabul and the rest of Afghanistan into hell, killing tens of thousands of innocent Afghans with their rockets and bullets, and yet they were about to come back. It was the United States who gave our fate into their hands the first time, and it was the United States who brought them yet again. Who would provide justice for those countless families who had lost their loved ones in the Mujahidin's ruthless war? Who would provide justice for those women who had been brutally and sexually abused? Who would provide justice for those tens of thousands of Afghans who lost their lives without even knowing their wrongdoing? In one part of the world one who committed crimes against humanity is condemned to death, like Hussain or Gaddafi, but in Afghanistan they were given rewards and power by the US and NATO. The western politicians during the campaign for the Iraq war called Sadam Hussain 'homicidal', and yet they rewarded Mujahidin leaders who filled the rivers with innocent Afghan blood.

Kabul was free of rulers once the Taliban had left. The Mujahidin did not arrive on the first day. In the village older people told stories about the Mujahidin atrocities such as burying people alive, massacres, beheading, hammering nails into people's heads, cutting off women's breasts, raping, marrying daughters by force, taking money and property, and so forth. I'd sit beside the elders as they discussed the days when the Mujahidin destroyed Kabul and I could see the fear in their hearts awakening. Men in the village and women in the house spent hours talking about those terrible days.

At last the Mujahidin entered Kabul. Hekmat, Tariq, Arif and I went to see the Mujahidin. Once again, they entered Kabul with their old tanks, RPGs and guns exactly the same way as they had marched the first time when the communist regime fell apart. What could poor Afghans do but silently watch as they entered ruined Kabul? Most parts of Afghanistan sank back into lawlessness after the Taliban was defeated. The warlords began to control many parts of Afghanistan once again.

Despite this it was such a great time at the end of the bombardment and and disappearance of the Taliban. For the first time in several years those Afghans who had a radio heard the sound of music through a Kabul radio station and a female was singing. I knew very little about music and it was enjoyable listening to it. Music took men and women back to a golden era when peace flowed in Afghanistan; to an era when Kabul was crammed with cinemas, restaurants, hotels, stunning scenery, magnificent buildings, beautiful people and electricity.

Old Afghan music took my parents back to the days of peace when concerts were held in gardens all the time; to an Afghanistan I have only ever known through their tales. They said that before the coming of the savage empires of the Soviet Union and the US, Afghanistan was a paradise. But the Afghanistan that I had always seen was crushed by bombs and rockets like wheat in a mill. I was lucky that I had not seen the peaceful Afghanistan and had no memory of it to trouble me.

My Afghanistan was the very same Afghanistan when I opened my eyes for the first time. Nothing was new or changed. My eyes always noticed ruins, endless cemeteries around me. Tears and blood were everywhere like snow in the winter. I observed mothers screaming and tearing at their hair over the dead bodies of their children. I have watched cruel men wandering about all around me with obnoxious weapons in their hands and on their shoulders as they terrorised people. I watched the sick men's aircrafts dropping bombs over people and their brainless soldiers marching into Afghanistan shedding blood. My Afghanistan was filled with death-traps. From the day I opened my eyes death roared at me like a hungry predator.

Soon men shaved their long and bushy beards, but poor women did not dare to throw their burqas away as the old custom was still there and the US bombs failed to kill it. Nevertheless, it seemed to us that we truly were liberated by the US and NATO. All of the people in urban parts saw the US and NATO as their liberators. Certainly they were my liberators and if people said anything unpleasant about them in our village, I did not like it. The US and NATO brought so much excitement into my war-weary life. The sound of bombs faded away and the dark clouds of explosions settled down. Those innocent civilians who had lost children, parents or siblings buried them and time was there to heal their wounded hearts. And the lucky ones who were not crushed enjoyed the freedom. Old stereos emerged out of the blue and Afghan music could be heard everywhere.

Most were grateful for what NATO and the US did, but only in Kabul and in the centre and north of Afghanistan and, to some extent, in the west. For Pashtuns it was a disaster. Those thousands of Taliban who perished were all Pashtun, apart from a few thousand foreign fighters who were mostly Pakistanis and Arabs. While people celebrated the end of Taliban tyranny in Kabul, others mourned the death of family members who were Taliban fighters.

The Afghan civil war was not as pale as the western media and politicians portrayed it to the world. It was an uncontaminated ethnic war between

Afghanistan's largest and other ethnic groups. The United States government and its allies were so excited for the domination of Afghanistan that they forgot about the consequences of interfering in an ethnic war of a highly complicated nation. The US and NATO destructive and angry troops poured into Afghanistan in their thousands every day. The US and British governments were fully aware of the repercussions of sending in their troops , for they knew of Afghanistan's history perhaps more than the Afghans knew themselves, and yet they decided to send their military. They needed a long-term military presence in central Asia in order to hassle the rising neighbours of Afghanistan such as China, India, Russia… in the future. The US and NATO needed an enemy in Afghanistan in order to justify their long-term presence. There would not be a need for the US and NATO in a peaceful Afghanistan. They did not come to give peace, they came to have a long-lasting presence there. The war in Afghanistan is a war that the US wanted in order to legitimise its endless presence in Central Asia. So long as there is war and chaos, they can justify their presence.

Once the US and NATO troops entered Afghanistan, they began bombing and slaughtering people and reduced their houses and villages to rubble. They raided people's houses at night and killed men, women and little children when they were asleep or dragged men out of their houses and threw them into their torture chambers. Many people had weapons because the United States supplied them in the 1980s, and now angry NATO and US troops were killing and imprisoning them for having them. In each house where they found a weapon they threw the poor men into their inhumane prisons in the name of the Taliban and Al Qaeda. Ordinary NATO and US troops did not know about the Afghan way of life, so they kept affronting people. They came into Afghanistan under the banner of assistance but harmed Afghans, just like the Soviets came in the name of helping Afghans but they did completely the opposite.

One morning fifteen Taliban pickup trucks entered our village. First we were frightened and thought the Taliban had come back. But soon we realised they were Mujahidin fighters who had captured Taliban vehicles. They looked just the way I had seen them many years ago; long hair, military trousers with military jackets that mismatched, and weapons on their shoulders. Their commander was a tall, aggressive man who smoked cannabis and later became a powerful thief when there was nothing for him to do. All the village children surrounded their vehicles including Hekmat, Tariq, Arif and I. The backs of their trucks were painted with blood and covered with bullet holes.

The commander and his soldiers had been shooting every single Talib on their way to Kabul and took their goods. The commander ordered his fighters to search every single compound in the village for weapons. When Hekmat heard this, he ran towards his compound and let his parents know. The Mujahidin searched house to house. They entered our compound, threw our clothes everywhere, found nothing but caused a great mess for my mother to clean up. I worried that they would find Kalashnikovs in Hekmat's house but, surprisingly, the Mujahidin came out of their compound empty-handed. They failed to find anything in our village despite that there were several rifles that people had looted to sell on. The commander accused a man who was from Kandahar and spoke Pashtu of being a Talib. He dragged the poor man out of the village and took him away. The commander had built his own prison and put his prisoners there.

The Mujahidin harassed many people and accused them of being Taliban in the first few days all over Kabul and other provinces. The US and NATO ground troops were being deployed into Afghanistan every day but most Afghans did not think that the US would send its soldiers. Unaware that the United States government had dreamed of a long-term military presence in Afghanistan, thousands of angry US and NATO troops arrived with their hearts filled with hatred for the Afghans.

A man transformed a ruined compound into a cinema in our village. He somehow managed to find a CD player and an old black and white Russian TV. Villagers had to pay to watch Bollywood films, but I had no money and was impatient to see what a movie looked like. I let Hekmat know about the cinema in our village, he too was very excited to see it. So we both went and as the owner of the cinema began collecting the money from each row, Hekmat and I jumped from one row to another and luckily we managed to do away with paying. He turned on the little TV and played the film. The film was very violent and so many men were killed.

People of my generation who watched the movie thought that whatever was happening in the film was real. There was something that surprised Hekmat and me, and that was the women in the film. They were all bare headed and even some did not cover their legs properly. I wondered why their husbands, fathers and brothers didn't stop them. Once we had seen the film, Hekmat and I talked about it for days. We both told the film tale to our siblings and other children in the village. It really was an exciting era for us. Afghanistan was a peculiar place indeed in those days. Some were enjoying music, beard-shaving and all other things that they could not do under the Taliban regime, and some were mourning the death of their family members.

Walking in the Footprints of the Soviets

I was on the way to the mosque when I saw big vehicles arrive in our village. Strange people, just like their vehicles, jumped out of them. They were fearsome and they wore a different type of clothes, which had so many styles. They had long rifles with many magazines. Each had a bayonet and it was similar to that of the Russian one that my father kept in the house in case thieves broke in. They had strange hats on their heads similar to that of the Soviet troops. They had strange jackets, tight to their body, which I later found out they called body armour. Village boys shouted, 'Run, they are Russians.'

All the children disappeared in the blink of an eye. Soviet troops had left Afghanistan fourteen years ago, but their fear still lived in the heart of every Afghan. People locked themselves inside their houses and waited to see what would happen. I told my mother that I had seen strange looking people in the village. She warned me not to step outside the compound. I was impatient to know who these fearsome people were and what they wanted. I went back outside and saw some village children were already talking with the strangers. I ran towards them and saw that they were not as scary as I thought. Some even smiled at the children. No one knew their weird language in our village. I was amazed by their vehicles. There was a huge gun on the top of each vehicle, with big bullets. I wondered what would happen to the person who got shot by those bullets.

There was one soldier on the top of each vehicle who was responsible for each big gun, and they could see inside the village compounds from their position, which aroused the fury of the elders. All elders went to the mosque and decided to stop these people entering our village again as the gunners could see females inside the compounds. The elders told everyone that they were *Americkaya* (Americans), and they were not going to allow them to enter our village next time and watch our honour (females) inside our compounds.

After some days the same people came to our village, but this time they did not have their vehicles with them. Elders came out to stop them before they came any further, but as the elders tried to approach the American soldiers they began shouting in their peculiar language and pointed their guns at them. They did not allow the elderly men to get close to them. It was then that I realised that elders are not as respected by others as much as they are by Afghans, and certainly not by American soldiers.

The elders soon realised that they could do nothing but let the soldiers enter our village. However, the village children welcomed them as American troops were a great entertainment for them. It seemed the troops liked the children more than they liked the elders. Whenever Hekmat, Tariq, Arif and I saw them, we spent hours chasing them and talking with them in Dari, but they did not understand. We asked them to give us chocolate and biscuits. The village children tried to steal their weapons. Sometimes children cursed them for fun and the troops said nothing. Sometimes they did not want us to chase them, so they chased us away.

While the children were having fun with the US soldiers, there were other troops who raided people's houses in the night, mainly in the southern and eastern parts of Afghanistan, and captured or killed alleged Taliban and Al Qaeda members. The Mujahidin and militias began to loot ordinary people on a daily basis, just as they had done before the arrival of the Taliban. Lawlessness increased all over Afghanistan. When Pashtuns experienced instability and lawlessness in their villages, they realised that life under the Taliban regime was far more secure and safe than under the bombs of the US and NATO troops. There are several factors involved in the re-evolution of the Taliban, such as US and NATO killing of the Civilians, support and protection of the Taliban by the Pakistan, lawlessness and corruption in government and the security forces.

In the winter we suffered tremendously like all other Afghans but our hearts were filled with hope and optimism. This time we could see the end of this appalling war, violence, poverty and misery. The US brought the world's most powerful countries into Afghanistan and it seemed they would put an end to our misery. In December 2001 world leaders gathered in Bonn, Germany, and established a new government in Afghanistan. Hamid Karzay was selected as the leader of the transitional government of the Islamic republic of Afghanistan. The day he came to power, Afghanistan's national TV showed his arrival live. There was only one man who had a TV in our village, which was powered by a small Chinese generator. He allowed everyone into his house to watch the new leader of Afghanistan. They were talking on the TV before Karzay's arrival and everyone waited impatiently to see the new leader, who Afghans had not elected but the United States had, like the Soviet and the British empires who brought their puppets from outside.

After a long wait there he was, Karzay's aircraft arrived and he disembarked with his bodyguards. Karzay stood amongst a group of people who were very well known to the Afghan nation. They were Mujahidin leaders and all members of Karzay's cabinet. Watching Karzay stand amongst the leaders of the Mujahidin, suddenly a great agitation ruptured out amongst our village elders.

Elders deserted the compound and some cursed those leaders of the Mujahidin who they had seen on TV. I was with my father when the village leader said to him, 'Don't they have honour? Don't they have shame? Don't they have a conscience? How could they stand before the Afghan nation once again? What have they done to Afghanistan and Afghans? Don't they remember it for one moment?'

The United States government and its allies did not just support the Mujahidin who committed horrible crimes against Afghanistan, they also placed the Afghan nation's destiny into their hands yet again, despite what the Mujahidin leaders had done before, of which they were fully aware.

Mujahidin leaders had no intention of serving hungry Afghans, they just wanted money and power.

The US brought 'democracy' into Afghanistan. I have seen US democracy in Afghanistan and it is disgusting. What the United States and its allies call democracy in Afghanistan, in reality is kleptocracy. Today Afghanistan is being ruled by thieves, war criminals, human rights abusers, drug mafia and warlords.

What the United States government and its allies are doing in Afghanistan is comparable to what the British Empire had done during the first Anglo-Afghan War of 1839. The British Empire unjustifiably invaded Afghanistan and ousted the Emir of Afghanistan, Dost Mohammed Khan, and established their own puppet, the infamous Shah Shujah, on the Afghan throne. That turned more and more people against the British and eventually resulted in a disastrous defeat of the British Empire in the first Anglo-Afghan War.

It has been twelve years since US and NATO set up this corrupt government over Afghans, but according to the Transparency International's Corruption Perceptions Index 2012, Afghanistan is amongst the top three countries with the highest level of public sector corruption. It is the billions of dollars that come from American and other Wester countries that enable this corrupt government run. It is the billions of dollars that has united the very warlords and war criminals who were at each others throats in the past. If the flow of these billions of dollars stops, the government will fall apart like house of cards and the warlords will be at each other's throat once again.

The winter was over and spring arrived, accompanied by the beauties of nature. Our ruined school re-opened, but this time there were little girls running towards the same school alongside the boys. A handful of female teachers came to school to teach us. Gradually the Taliban textbooks alongside the old US propaganda textbooks that taught about holy warriors, holy war, martyrs or infidels disappeared and the very same US government sent new books, much better than the ones it had sent two decades earlier. There were no pictures of weapons in the new textbooks' pages. They did not talk about *Jihad*, *Mujahid* or *Shahid*, and so on. Mathematics books were clean;

there was no such problem that had been illustrated with bullets and infidels and guns and knives.

In 2002, there was relative peace in many parts of Afghanistan, in particular in Kabul. Many urban parents started to send their young daughters to school. My parents decided to send my sisters. When Tariq, Arif and I found out we were alarmed. My brothers and I condemned our parents' decision. Most boys did not like their sisters to attend school because they were embarrassed that strangers might see their sisters' faces. My brothers and I were severely unhappy with my parents for sending our sisters to school.

We argued for many days. Father did not say much, but Mother was adamant that they should go. She said, 'I do not want my daughters to be helpless and dependent on men like I am. I want them to study and support themselves and not be a burden on their husbands.' We found out that Simaa Khala had decided to send her only daughter to school, too, which aroused our cousins' anger. And Hekmat's parents had also decided to send his sister to school. I soon found out that many parents in our village were determined to send their daughters to school and boys had argued with their parents just like my brothers and I did. I did my best to stop my sisters from attending, but Mother remained firm. Simaa Khala and my mother had unbearable pain in their hearts for being dependent on men and not having authority over their own lives, for being prisoners all of their lifetime and having no respect in society. They did not want their daughters to go through the same pain that they went through every day.

Simaa Khala and my mother took their daughters into school and enrolled them, as did so many other parents. Hekmat and I sat in our village cemetery in our spare time and were both furious at our parents' decisions and were anxious that the boys who saw our sisters on the way to school would bully us. However, our village boys did not bully us, as their sisters attended school, too.

I was willing to do anything I could to stop mine from going. One night, before I went to sleep I concealed my sisters' books, notebooks and tattered shoes in the back of our compound yard. In the morning, my sisters were looking for them. It was late and both were wailing to our mother to help them, but it was only me who knew where they were. 'The teacher will punish me if I miss the class,' my youngest sister said. They looked for a very long time and by the time they found them it was too late.

Mother found out that I had hidden their things and she punished me very harshly for it. Once my sisters started school, I started to hate both of them. I looked for excuses to beat them up and had Tariq and Arif to back me up. I constantly bullied them. So, my sisters began to hate me. They refused to talk to me and always tried to avoid me. Gone was the good bond of friendship between us. Now we were bitter enemies. Surprisingly my sisters learned to read and write in the first few months at school, which Arif and I had failed to do in eight years. Arif and I became more envious of them. In the half term school exams, they both achieved top scores and Arif and I failed as usual.

People who lived in the Pakistani refugee camps and in Iran heard that their country was peaceful again. Thousands of Afghans flocked back every day in the hope of starting a new life. For some the future looked very promising. The sound of rockets, bombs and bullets disappeared in most parts of Afghanistan. Once again Afghans began to rebuild their ruined houses. The transitional government of Afghanistan announced that they would recruit all former military officers to form a new army for Afghanistan. Former military officers were those officers who had been trained by the Soviet advisers almost one-and-a-half decades back. It really was great news for my father and Merza Kaka, since both were desperate to find sustainable work. Poor and exploited Afghans could visibly notice a bright future and thought this time it wouldn't be a mirage.

Afghans usually celebrated their weddings with gunfire. Our village leader knocked on doors and warned people not to celebrate weddings with gunfire, as the US bombed a wedding and killed one to two hundred innocent people just because they had fired into the sky. This was the first terrifying news that came into our village since the arrival of the troops. More news spread in our village every day that US troops were raiding people's houses, killing and dragging people out of them and scaring the families with their dogs. That is what the Soviet military did to Afghans and now it was the US and NATO's turn. The Taliban leaders looked for opportunities on the other side of the border to come back. They watched what the US and NATO were doing. Day after day anger grew, hearing from people and watching in the news their fellow compatriots being murdered by non Muslims.

We had to leave school temporarily in order to work faster to weave our carpet to feed our family. My cousins, brothers and I did not see sunshine for months as we worked from early in the morning until late at night. Akmal and Tariq put pressure on us to work faster and if we could not work faster, they would beat us. It was shameful for boys to cry so when I fell asleep on the floor I cried quietly in the darkness of the night. I cried for not being free and playing in the village with other boys, for spending the day and half of the night working in a dark room and being slapped by Tariq many times a day. One day Tariq battered Arif because he failed to weave the carpet fast enough, so Arif fled and hid himself behind my mother. But our mother beat him too.

Arif stood before her and screamed, 'God I wish I were to die, to get rid of all these hardships!' Arif made my mother cry. He was only eleven but already tired of his life. All the children of Afghanistan were victims and did hard jobs for very little money or food. Our carpet weaving skill was an unfruitful craft. We worked day and night on empty stomachs for months, but in the end we could not earn enough to feed ourselves for only weeks. My father was looking forward to the government giving him a job in the new army.

At this time the owner of our houses returned from Iran. They first appreciated us for keeping their houses safe in wartime, and then they demanded rent, which we could not pay. Simaa Khala and Merza Kaka decided to leave the house and go to the ruined house that my father and Merza Kaka had once bought before the civil war started. Our compound's owner let us live with them for some time. Once again Simaa Khala and my mother were to be separated from one another. My mother did not have anyone apart from Simaa Khala to drink tea with, to sing, cry, share her pain and sometimes even laugh with. They both cried before Simaa Khala moved out. I have not seen such a concrete bond of friendship in my miserable lifetime such as the one of Simaa Khala and my mother. They were more than sisters, they were friends and companions, they were everything to each other, yet this cruel world tore them apart time and again. Merza Kaka and Simaa Khala and their children began to reconstruct their war-ragged house and started a new life.

I rarely had time to play with Hekmat as I was working day and night. My heart was wounded and only freedom could cure it. But freedom was too expensive for a poor person like me and if I stopped carpet weaving, my family and I would starve to death.

At the end of 2002, my mother gave birth to my fourth brother. Everyone was greatly pleased, as he was a boy not a girl. However, Tariq and I were grown up and understood that more mouths needed more food, so we argued with my parents not to produce more siblings for us.

It was the last days of school when a teacher who came from Kabul city told us *Shagerda* (students), 'Two explosions took place not far from where I was, in Kabul city, and killed so many civilians including little children and injured so many others.' This was the very beginning of the new war, more deadly, more destructive and more devastating than the war between the Taliban and the Mujahidin. Ramadan arrived and I was now old enough to participate as I did not want to go to hell and, besides that, boys laughed at me if I did not keep the fast. It was extremely hard for me to fast as well as weave the carpet with an empty stomach. Throughout Ramadan I had headaches, felt dizzy, ill-tempered and a dark and gloomy curtain was before my eyes. We usually did not celebrate Eid as we had nothing to celebrate with.

On the first day of Eid, my siblings and I were playing in the room with my father while my mother was cooking tea for us, when she screamed from the kitchen. A sharp pain emerged in my mother's back and she was unable to walk. We thought it might be a momentary pain and would soon fade away. The pain was so grave that my mother spent three days of Eid wailing. My siblings and I were really anxious and cried along with her. She was unable to walk and our father had to carry her around. There was no money in our house for her treatment so my poor mother remained at home. My father ran from one friend to another to borrow money for her treatment, but he failed to get any. I again blamed God for my mother's suffering. Tariq knew how to pray so he decided to perform five times prayers and pray to God to heal our mother. Months elapsed but she remained in excruciating pain. My new brother was a few months old and she was unable to look after him. Our sisters were too young to look after him, so he ended up crying all the time. In the winter we managed to take our mother to the hospital. The doctor said she had hurt her backbone, and he gave her lots of expensive drugs. She used up all the medicine throughout the winter but we noticed no improvement in her health.

At the beginning of 2003, we came home from the carpet factory and our father told us that a man loaded with explosives had blown himself up in a crowd and killed and injured dozens. I was shocked on hearing this. I had seen Afghans fight and kill each other, but this was the first time I had heard of an Afghan who loaded himself with explosives and blew himself up amongst a crowd of hungry people. Who was he? Where did he come from? And why did he blow himself up in a crowd of innocent people? These questions were in everyone's minds.

Countless Afghan children who lived in Pakistan had been trained in the Madrasas to fasten explosives around themselves and come back to harm the government and the US and NATO troops; but instead it was civilians who were the main victims. Some young boys, Pakistani and Afghans, were sent to kill Afghan civilians and some had been told that Afghans were not Muslims, if one kills them one would go to paradise. From one side the Afghans were getting killed by the US and NATO bombs and angry soldiers in the name of terrorism and insurgents, and from the other side they were getting killed by suicide attacks in the name of infidels. The war escalated in southern Afghanistan. Suicide bombers blew themselves up everywhere. NATO and US bombs fell upon Afghans. Again Afghanistan was engulfed in another war. All hope of Afghans died yet again! Again the journey of war, poverty and violence seemed endless.

One day Hekmat told me that they were leaving Afghanistan to start a new life in Iran. I first thought he was joking, but soon found out that he was not. His father was fed up with life in Afghanistan. He hoped Afghanistan would get better one day, but Afghanistan seemed like it never would. It seemed like the broken ship of Afghans was sailing in an ocean of war, poverty and misery that had no shores. Hekmat's father knew that Afghanistan was about to be engulfed in a new war, so he decided to leave before it was too late.

They chased a trail they believed would lead them to a life free of war, bloodshed, poverty and suffering. They tried to go to Iran illegally, which most Afghans did and are still doing. Many have lost their lives as they tried to enter Iran. So many had died or been maimed under Iran's border force's torture. Iran's inhumane prisons are filled with poor Afghans. Each year the Iranian government beats and ejects thousands of Afghans from its country and forces them back to their own country to live in the warzones.

Hekmat was extremely happy to go to Iran. He promised me that once he grew up he would help me to go and live there too. He said Iran was a much better country than Afghanistan. 'You won't see a single ruined house, you won't hear the sound of bombs in Iran. There are many jobs for everyone.' I wished my family too would go with Hekmat's family to Iran to live but that was not possible.

Before the farewell, I called Tariq and Arif to see Hekmat for the last time before he left for good. The four of us sat in our village cemetery until late into the evening talking, and then it was time to say goodbye forever. In the first few months after Hekmat went, I really missed him, but my life did not stop without him.

The owner of our house respectfully asked my father to leave, so we had to go and live in our own ruined house. My mother was happy because she would be with her sister once more. When we reached our old village it was shocking. All the houses were reduced to ruins by the Mujahidin fighting. Most of the village was empty. In our house there was only one room and that had been crushed by rockets. Our water well was completely ruined and there was not a single drop of water in it. Several rockets landed in our compound yard and left huge holes, and still there were several unexploded rockets. The village was filled with unexploded munitions.

Simaa Khala was shocked on seeing that Mother couldn't walk. But there was nothing she could do. My father, Tariq, Arif and I spent weeks repairing the room. Now we were a big family and it was difficult for us to fit into one room, but we had to. We dug a new well, and we set a tent up and began weaving carpets in our yard. My brothers enrolled into a new school just outside our village, which was a ruined compound with very few students. The teachers were as cruel as the ones in the former school. More and more people moved into our village. Afghan refugees returned from Pakistan and Iran in tens of thousands; they believed that the US and NATO forces would provide security in Afghanistan. Over a million Afghans had returned since the US invasion. However, countless others were escaping the NATO and US bombs as well as the Taliban violence, to Pakistan and Iran. Those who returned began building compounds with the money they had earned in exile. Fields vanished and compounds were erected in their place; most of the fields outside our village turned into houses. Those Afghans who returned from abroad and did not have money to buy land and build a house lived in tents and hoped the government would give them a piece of land, that they might find a job one day, and that they would be able to build a new house. All the people who came back from Pakistan and Iran soon realised that they had made a terrible mistake. There were neither jobs nor peace. Whatever money they had earned in exile had been used and they were left exposed to starvation, war, harsh climate and disease.

One day someone knocked on the door. I opened it. It was a group of men, women and children with lots of bags. One of the women's faces was familiar but I could not remember who she was. She hugged and kissed me and said, 'My son, don't you remember me? I am *Surya Khala.*' Then I realised that she was my mother's youngest sister who had left Afghanistan several years ago while I was only a few years old, and those men were my maternal uncles who also lived in Iran. I ran towards the compound and told both Simaa Khala and my mother. My mother was still unable to walk. However, she dragged herself outside the room to welcome her siblings, whom she had not seen for so long. It was an extraordinary moment for them to see their younger brothers and sister.

Nobody dared move or do anything, everyone stiffened, watching each other. Tears fell from everyone's eyes. Such were the catastrophes of war that divided families for decades. Each one of my uncles had married and had two or three children. Their children were much cleaner and healthier than us. My aunt and uncles had been ousted from Iran by the government, their livelihoods left behind. But they were not that disheartened for the delusion of peace kept them going. They were so happy and thought Afghanistan would be like the old Afghanistan once more, before the coming of the savage empire of the Soviet Union and America. My aunt and uncles began a new life in Afghanistan unaware of the expanding war in the south and in the east. More NATO and US troops poured into Afghanistan day after day. Military bases appeared in all corners and their helicopters and aircraft frightend people continuously.

By now there were a few media channels that brought news from outside. In those days, elders sat together and spoke about Iraq's invasion by the United States. I did not know anything about Iraq at the time but have read about it since. The Iraqi tale is also a very sad one, like the Afghans'. They too have walked the same path as Afghans for decades. They too were the victims of imperialist powers and dictators. The US government shattered Iraq so mercilessly for its oil. It took the lives of more than a million Iraqis through sanction, many of whom were little children. Later it overran Iraq and devastated Iraqis in the most barbaric fashion.

Today the world's most powerful nations' leaders behave extraordinarily violently and barbarically against those nations who can't defend themselves. Had Iraq had weapons of mass destruction, countless Iraqi men, women and children wouldn't have been killed and Iraq's entire infrastructure wouldn't be ravaged. Throughout history the weak and defenceless were the victims.

I Became a Rock-Carrier

Our work did not bring adequate money to feed my family. We looked for another job so that we could earn sufficient bread. Refugees returning to Afghanistan were buying land and building houses in our village and they needed labourers. We managed to buy a wheelbarrow to do extra work. Lorries could not bring rocks to the construction site in our village as they were too big for the streets. So they shed the rocks far away and had to pay workers to carry the rocks to the construction site. Unexpectedly, this time Tariq refused to work as a rock-carrier and decided to only weave the carpet and concentrate on his school lessons. Arif and I spoke with the owner of the land who wanted to build a compound: he promised that he would pay us the normal wage of an adult labourer if we were to carry two lorry loads of rocks from outside the village to the construction site each day.

We woke up before dawn. It was completely dark, but we had to work at that time because the weather was burning during the day. First, we carried all the small rocks we could find but the problem was that most of the rocks were too heavy for us to lift up and put in the wheelbarrow. Rocks were piled up on the top of each other like a mountain. I tried to pull out a rock from the bottom, when suddenly all the rocks slipped down and caught my right hand. My hand was trapped under the colossal rocks. Arif was unable to remove rocks and release my hand. I screamed for help but there was no one around. Arif ran and knocked on a nearby door. By the time the people answered, other villagers had heard my cries and they all came out of their compounds. The pain was unbearable. At last the villagers removed the rocks. My hand was squashed and I could not feel it. The man I was working for took me to the hospital, where the doctor bandaged it and gave me a drug. Gradually the pain grew in my hand. At home my family and parents worried about my hand, but were more anxious that I would be unable to weave the carpet. Tariq and Arif were alone and could not weave the carpet faster.

My father woke up every morning, walked for several miles to the Ministry of Defence and hoped he could start the promised job soon. Our life was as bitter as it had ever been before. My mother was in grave pain and we could do nothing but watch the tears from her eyes fell down on her face.

Simaa Khala and my mother did not want their siblings who returned from Iran to know about their misery. My mother said, 'I don't want help from my siblings, since they have spent all their lives in foreign lands and earned little money with great difficulty.' However, it was extremely hard for them to hide their miserable living conditions. Our clothes, mattresses, pillows, blankets and all other furniture were old. My younger siblings cried for food in our uncles' and aunt's presence. However, my wounded hand gave me an opportunity to spend time with the boys in our ruined village. I spent most of the day playing football. There were some rich children in our village who had returned from Iran; their stomachs were not as hungry as mine. They looked much healthier than me and their clothes were much cleaner than mine. I spent a lot of time comparing myself with these fortunate children and sometimes wished to be one of them. But when I looked at the other village boys I realised that I was not the only deprived boy. It seemed that almost all of the children in Afghanistan were in the same circumstance as I was.

The village children and I walked through the local bazaar to the football ground. Unexpectedly a thunderous explosion deafened our ears. I jumped into the nearby ditch, which was filled with stagnant water, so did everyone else. We remained there for a few minutes and then got out to see what had happened. As we ran towards the explosion site, we saw four men lying down on the ground each covered in blood. Two were trembling and two others seemed dead. A man who was approximately 30 metres away from where I was had the back of his head open, just as if someone had hit him hard with a big mallet and burst all of his brains out. As I went deeper into the explosion area I looked around and realised that I was surrounded by dead and injured humans, bodies lay all around.

After a few moments people who were unharmed rushed to pick up the people who were covered in blood. Still my ears could not pick out a sound. I thought I had lost my hearing. It was a suicide bomber who had targeted the Afghan national army officer's bus. Almost all of the army officers were dead and their bodies were in a terrible condition. There was blood and gore everywhere. I saw a woman whose face was concealed under a barque lying dead alongside her daughter, who was no older than my youngest sister, and they looked like they were both asleep. There was another man who was dying. His turban was still on his head. He had a large injury to his chest and was surrounded with his blood and the potatoes he'd wanted to take home for his family. There was another man in his late twenties who had fatal injuries all over, holding his stomach with one hand while the other was covered with blood, begging people for help. People came from everywhere and loaded cars with the dead and injured and drove to the hospital. People were frightened of what they had seen. Those who helped the casualties in the car were covered in blood. Later police and the International Security Assistance Force (ISAF) came and sealed off the explosion site.

What a big difference there is between the ignorant man and the man of knowledge. There is a huge dissimilarity even in the way they are fighting for a cause. The ignorant man tightened explosives around himself and detonated it in public and decorated the earth with innocent people's blood and flesh. Mohandas Karamchand Ghandhi too fought for a purpose. And he showed the poor and defenceless people how to gain their freedom.

In 2003, the Taliban began fighting in the southern part of Afghanistan with NATO, US and Afghan forces as well as detonating themselves. The war expanded as it started in the south and headed towards the east and west. Large numbers of people were killed by the US and NATO air and ground forces as well as by the Taliban, IEDs and suicide attacks. The Taliban planted IEDs and their main victims were civilians. Many people did not dare go to the city because of the suicide attackers and US and NATO troops. Nobody knew whether they would live for another day or not. Nobody knew which bomb, which IED or which bullet would take their lives. Afghans are in a dilemma, if they stay in the house they will die by hunger or by a bomb or bullet, and if they go out they may be killed by a suicide bomber, or by a huge merciless bomb that comes from the sky like an eagle upon its prey. Most of these horrors take place in the southern part of Afghanistan.

My hand recovered and it was time for me to start work, carrying rocks and mud bricks in the morning and weaving carpets in the afternoon until late at night. At the end I had no energy left to even sit with my family and talk. Instead, I went straight to bed. People who did not know my name in the village called me *Lagharak* (skinny) as I worked hard and did not receive sufficient food. My mother had to endure her pain as well as spend most of her time trying to keep Khyber, my new born brother, silent, who was crying for not receiving enough milk. Neighbours who could not tolerate the pain of hunger sent their children to our house to ask if we had spare food to lend them and the answer was always no. There was constant knocking on the door to our compound. As one beggar was told we didn't have any food, another would come knocking on the door. Sometimes when they came knocking everyone refused to answer. The time came when one of my siblings would guard the compound door and chase the poor beggars away. Everywhere was full of beggars and they persisted for food or money.

A man with his family came back from Iran after more than a decade. He built a house in our village and started a new life. One night a group of burglars raided his house. It was around one o'clock in the morning when we heard gunshots and then women's and children's cries. Everyone in the village woke up and ran towards the compound to help the newly-arrived man, so did I alongside my father and brothers. The man and his wife resisted the burglars and refused to give up their lifetime earnings to them. The burglars shot the man and his wife along with other members of their family. The elders called the police and the next day when the police arrived, they looked around and then left and we did not see them again. After a week, the burglars broke into another villager's house. The poor villager had nothing, just like us. The burglars tortured the family to tell where they had hidden their wealth, and beat them until dawn. Luckily, they did not shoot them as they had the other family. In the morning we found out that the burglars even tortured the children. After the fall of the Taliban, crime increased again all over Afghanistan. In some cases the police and government officials themselves were the killers and the thieves. Some people began to prefer the Taliban regime than the corrupt government and US and NATO's bombs and night raids. Day after day lawlessness increased all over the country.

Ramadan arrived and Simaa Khala and my mother were happy because it was an excuse for them to force us to keep fast and not demand food. My sisters were under ten years old. They cried that they did not have the ability of holding the fast, but our mother scared them by saying that if they did not keep the fast, God would throw them into the fierce fire of hell in the life after death. And if they kept the fast, God would allow them to enter paradise where there would be every kind of fruit, apple, pomegranate, fig, date, everything they could want. Gardens, trees full of fruits, streams flowing beneath them. The weather would be neither burning hot nor freezing cold. There would be pretty animals who were not scared of humans that would come and play with them. If they wanted to go to Paradise they had to keep the fast. Listening to what my mother said to my sisters, I became determined to keep the fast despite the hunger that tortured me all day long. My younger siblings wanted to go to Paradise, but there was a problem – they could only fast for a few hours. Carrying rocks and bricks during the day as well as weaving carpet at night, I thought I might die by the end of Ramadan. My hands and legs shuddered, my head burst with pain, and the bright and sunny world looked as dark as a moonless and starless night.

Ramadan finished and it was Eid. Traditionally the average Afghan family did certain things in Eid, the females tidied the house and if they could afford it they would buy new furniture. They bought dried nuts and sweets for the guests who came to congratulate them. Family members treated themselves to new clothes, especially their children. However, few children at that Eid dressed in new clothes; most of the children wandered about with the same pair of worn out shoes or sandals and shredded clothes. Some children even grew out of their clothes as they had worn them for several years, just like me.

Again, like other Eids, we neither bought new furniture nor sweets or dried nuts, nor treated ourselves to new clothes or shoes. Instead, we were anxious about what to offer the people who would come to congratulate us. Being poor for all our lifetime and having experienced so many Eids without food and money, we knew how to evade any guests. Our parents locked us inside the compound and warned us not to make a noise. Guests knocked on the door and when they thought that we were not at home they went to visit someone else. We certainly had relatives, but not the taxi fare to visit them. Eid is a time of happiness, but for my siblings and me it meant hiding in the compound and not making a noise. When Eid was over, we went and apologised to our friends and lied to them that we had gone to our relatives' houses during the three days.

One of the countless suicide attackers had blown himself up in front of the University of Kabul and killed several students. Amongst them was a genteel boy from our village whose body was torn into pieces. Everyone in our village mourned the death of that young man. It was the villagers' responsibility to help the family. So, we did not work, instead we dug his grave. My brothers and I dug the grave along with other villagers and carried the body of the boy from the house to the graveyard. When we picked the coffin up, the young boy's mother and sisters clung to our legs. His mother screamed, 'God stop them, they have taken my son from me!' His mother and sisters screamed for hours. Their cries shook the entire village just like US bombs. At the funeral ceremony my cousins, brothers and I went to help. We helped the chef with the cooking and then it was lunchtime. I sat in a room full of elderly people. I always enjoyed the elderly men's discussion. They talked about the brutally chaotic situation of Afghanistan. There was an elderly man speaking to others in the room. I still remember a piece of his speech:

> *Some murder us in the name of terrorism. Some murder us in the name of insurgents. Some murder us in the name of the Taliban. Some murder us in the name of freedom. Some murder us in the name of helping. What is happening to this ill-fated nation?*

We had made our last carpet. The day Ustad Naqib handed us our money he said that he was going to close down his factory because thieves, police and other government authorities looted each time he delivered his carpets to Pakistan. Before we stopped carpet weaving, my parents knew that they had not chosen a lucrative profession. It was problematic and we could not make sufficient money to feed ourselves. Simaa Khala and Merza Kaka also regretted choosing carpet weaving for their children. After seven years of hard work, we gave it up to do hard labour jobs, such as rock and brick carrying. I was no longer a *Qalin Baaf* (carpet weaver). I had at last broken out of the cage.

There was a boy in our village whose father was a bricklayer. They were relatively less poor in comparison to the other villagers. I started cheating this village boy by building kites in my spare time and selling them to him at higher than the market value. Sometimes, the village boy did not have money to pay, but he promised he would pay in the immediate future. His father knew that I was cheating his son. I used to go and knock on the boy's door and demand my money and the bricklayer would pay me. I would satisfy my stomach with that money. This game of kite-selling lasted for months.

One time the bricklayer ran out of patience and when I knocked on his door, instead of giving me my money he pounded me with punches. I cursed him, and that enraged him more. He grabbed me by my hair, picked me off the ground and then dropped me back. He punched me in the face until my mouth and nose were bleeding. I tried to hit the bricklayer back, but my punches and kicks did not hurt him. What really hurt the man were my curses and for that he kept beating me. Village children watched me get pounded by the man and they thought he was going to beat me to death, so they rushed to my house and informed my father. My father and brothers rushed towards the bricklayer's house. As my father arrived, he saw the man still beating me despite the fact that I was covered in blood. Soon my father clashed with the bricklayer. More close relatives of his arrived to defend him. Merza Kaka arrived to defend my father, but they were outnumbered and beaten and humiliated in the village. My cousins, brothers and I attempted to help Merza

Kaka and our father in the fight, but we had been beaten too. They broke my father's arm and Merza Kaka was badly injured in the eye. Village men finally arrived and put an end to the fighting. Merza Kaka and my father had been beaten badly and humiliated because of me. For months my father was in grave pain and I abhorred myself when I watched him. Everyone was upset and refused to talk to me in the house. I wished that I would melt away like the snow rather than live any more.

When Death Becomes Freedom

A rich landlord wanted to build a huge compound. He did not want to buy mud-bricks, as it would cost him dearly, so he decided to hire workers to make mud-bricks for him out of his own land's soil. Everyone was jobless and everyone wanted the job. Arif and I decided to apply. The landlord first refused to hire us, for he believed we were too young. My father could not lift heavy weights after the doctor advised him against. The landlord recruited some strong adult labourers to do the job for him. But he felt sorry for Arif and me and decided to employ us too, but for a probation period. Arif and I had to prove that we were able to make bricks properly. This new job was far more difficult than rock-carrying. On the first day we started in the afternoon, when the weather was extremely hot. We worked until ten o'clock at night to prepare the mud then we went home. We had to wake up before dawn to turn all the mud we had prepared into bricks before sunrise, and then head to school. Arif could not work as fast as I could, so we sometimes quarrelled and fought. By the time we turned mud into bricks, both Arif and I were shattered. My legs were unable to carry me and my hands were full of blisters and when I went to school, I could not concentrate and fell asleep in class. When teachers caught me sleeping, they would punish me.

Making bricks was the hardest job I had ever done in my young life. Village elders advised me against the harm that I would sustain in the future if I carried on making bricks. They said we were too young and that this work would harm most parts of our body, in particular the spine. There was nothing I could do, for I had to provide food for the family. After some time, we proved that we could make bricks. So, we carried on doing the hard job for months. My poor mother was still in agonising pain and money could help her, but we did not have any. It was difficult for me to watch my mother in pain all the time and my little siblings hungry. I was annoyed with God and sometimes argued with Him in my mind. But one day I thought God was not helping my family because I was not praying. Therefore, I decided to learn how to pray. It was odd, Mullah failed to teach me five times prayers for years, despite punishing me every day, but I managed to learn five times prayers in a week from a generous elderly man in the mosque. Therefore, I began five times prayers and asked for God's mercy.

The US and NATO troops increased the shooting of innocent Afghans in the city, roads, streets and villages as the threat of suicide attacks increased. The bombing of Afghan villages and houses as well as night raids increased too. The Taliban were very weak in the direct fighting with the troops. As soon as the Taliban fired at the troops from their village, US and NATO aircraft quickly came and dropped a huge bomb on them. The bomb destroyed the Taliban as well as the civilians who lived there. The US and NATO troops cheered that they had destroyed their enemy. But they were ignorant of the fact that while they may have killed three or four Taliban, they had also turned an entire village against them. Those civilians who lost family members in the bombing took weapons and sought revenge. So, the US and NATO troops were not vanquishing their enemy; they were creating more enemies. The war was spreading from the south and many Afghans realised that there was no difference between the US and NATO troops and the Soviet troops. All of them came to kill and shed blood and humiliate.

In late 2004, Simaa Khala gave birth to her last child and it was another girl. Merza Kaka did not stop mistreating, despite the fact they had seven children together. My mother was there to wipe the tears from her sister's eyes and encourage her to endure the pains of this miserable life. After Simaa Khala gave birth to her lovely little daughter her behaviour changed. She was a completely different person. She always was nice and kind to everyone, but from that time onwards, she became extra nice. She spent every free moment of her time with every one of us. Living was bitter for everyone in our family, but Simaa Khala poured sweetness in with her nice words and made everyone laugh with her jokes and stories. In the evenings, she prepared tea and invited everyone to drink, joke and laugh. The way she stared at everyone was as if she was seeing us for the last time in her life. My mother no longer had to encourage Simaa Khala, since she now encouraged my mother to endure the bitterness of living and gave hope for the sweetness of it. She left her own chores and came to help with ours, as our mother was unable to do them. Merza Kaka had never been nice to Simaa Khala, but she began to be nice to him. She looked for every opportunity to keep him happy. She read the Quran every day for hours. She did not miss her prayers and encouraged everyone else to pray. When she woke early in the morning for the morning prayers, she woke everyone else too.

One afternoon I was sitting in the sunshine when Simaa Khala came and sat beside me and advised me to study my school lessons, so as to have a nice job in the future. 'My heart hurts,' Simaa Khala said, 'watching you, your brothers and cousins doing back-breaking labour since your childhood.' She truly was like my own mother and never treated my siblings and me any different from her own children. She loved all of us equally, but sometimes she said jokingly, 'Laiq is my favourite nephew.'

She spent more and more time with my mother. Sometimes both disappeared in the memories of their past for hours and then appeared back in the true world of pain and suffering. Sometimes they laughed and sometimes they cried. Sometimes they talked and sometimes they sung for one another. One evening, Simaa Khala made everyone laugh with her interesting jokes. After some time, all the children dispersed and Simaa Khala spent a little bit more time with my mother. She told her, 'I ask God to heal your illness each time I pray.' She stared at my mother for a while and a few teardrops fell from her eyes, then she left my mother alone. We ate the very little food that my sisters cooked that night, and we played for some time with one another before everyone slept.

It was around one o'clock in the morning when something woke me. I looked at our yard and saw flames rising from our old ruined water well. Father also woke up and went to check and I followed him. The old well was two metres deep and was wide. We threw all the garbage inside it. It was not possible to see what was burning inside the well, as it was filled with flames. However, the smoke smelled revolting. My father said the rubbish might have caught fire.

We both went back to the room and fell asleep. Approximately one hour later when everyone was asleep again, we heard someone screaming. Screams were coming from the very same well that the fire was rising from. We all ran towards it. Still the fire was rising from the well. When I reached the well I saw Merza Kaka was fighting with the fire. Everyone thought Merza Kaka had caught fire. Tariq thought that burglars had broken into our compound, so he ran and fetched the Russian military bayonet that we had in the house. My father brought a blanket and gave it to Merza Kaka to kill the fire. As Merza Kaka killed the fire with the blanket, we saw a dark, chunk lying at the bottom. It was too dark to know what that it was until my uncle yelled, 'My life is ruined! My wife burned herself to death!' I could not stay in this nasty dream any more and tried to wake myself up. I struggled to wake up but realised I was not dreaming.

When my mother heard, she fainted. I felt as though someone had stabbed me in the heart. I screamed so loud that it shook the entire village. Everyone screamed, tearing at their hair and hitting and scratching themselves. Merza Kaka extinguished the remaining fire, but Simaa Khala was burned. There was nothing left of her body. We removed the body from the well and hoped to take her to the hospital that she might survive. Her body was dark and the flesh fell from her like leaves falling from trees in the autumn.

I had seen so many dead humans in my life. I had seen headless, legless, handless men, women and children who had been blown up by Mujahidin's rockets, Soviets mines, US and NATO bombs and Taliban suicide bombers; but not one was as terrorising as Simaa Khala's burned body. When I looked at her I could not stop screaming. I screamed at the top of my voice and wanted to tear the earth and the sky with my cries and put an end to everything. Her beautiful hair had vanished, all that was left was her dark skull. There was no skin or flesh on that beautiful face. She looked far more frightful than the demons I had visualised. My little cousins, brothers and sisters, my uncle and my father all screamed and hurting themselves. The neighbours and villagers heard our screams and thought burglars had broken into our house. They came one after another from all over the village to fight.

But there was no burglar they could fight with, it was Simaa Khala's horrific body laid on the floor. Her body looked so fearsome that every neighbour screamed when they saw her face.

My father ran up and down in the village to find a vehicle to take Simaa Khala's body to the hospital but it was too late, Simaa Khala did not want to go to hospital. That was why she jumped into the well. We covered her remains with a blanket and took them inside. Merza Kaka beat himself and screamed over and over again. Simaa Khala's children and my siblings surrounded her body, they screamed and their tears fell on Simaa Khala. Najiba, Simaa Khala's last child, was only three months old and crying for her mother. They gave her to me to look after. Najiba did not stop crying. She was hungry but her mother had abandoned her in this cruel world. At that terrible night, I looked at the sky and searched for God. I wanted to ask him why he did this. Each time I looked at Najiba's tearful innocent face I felt my heart would burst. Najiba was the world's most unlucky child who lost the love of her mother during the very first days of her life. Why should she be punished at the very beginning of her life, without any wrongdoing? I screamed until I was unable to scream any more. I fell to the floor and remained there until I had enough energy to stand on my feet again. After a few hours my mother returned to this terrifying world. She could not believe that her best companion had left her. My mother had spent her entire life alongside Simaa Khala and suddenly her sister was gone.

My mother screamed and cursed Simaa Khala, 'My stupid sister, you left me alone! What do I do without you? Oh, my ignorant sister what have you done to yourself? To whom did you leave me? You have devastated me. Oh, my ignorant sister!' My mother screamed, tore at her hair, hit herself, hurt herself like everyone else. Simaa Khala took her life in such an extremely horrible manner that even her children were frightened to look at her. We surrounded her body and mourned until morning. More villagers arrived the next day and offered help.

Throughout my life, I had watched other families screaming for the death of their children, parents or relatives, but now it was my turn to weep for the death of beloved Simaa Khala and people watched me. I believed death did not harm us, it just wanted to play with my family and me, but I was wrong. Death did not even feel sorry for Simaa Khala's hungry children. Later in the morning, my maternal uncles and aunts arrived. They too were shaken seeing their sister's body. They too screamed, tore at their hair, hit themselves. We did not have money for the coffin and funeral. Poor villagers collected money for the coffin and funeral. We spent the day grieving over her body until it was time for her burial. By late afternoon, her grave was ready. Village men carried her coffin to the cemetery and I watched Simaa Khala being buried under tonnes of earth.

I came back from the ceremony, jumped into the old well, picked up the burned bits of flesh that had fallen from Simaa Khala's body, and went and buried them. I jumped back into the well and sat there and wailed as much as I could. My head was bursting with pain. I fell asleep and did not wish to wake up ever again. Unfaithful Simaa Khala left everyone behind in this world of cruelty. She let no one know that she had made up her mind not to carry on this endless and meaningless journey any more. But she did not care for those who accompanied her in this never-ending journey for so long. She treacherously betrayed all of them and abandoned them in the middle of this cruel journey. My heart, mind, blood and everything refused to acknowledge the death of Simaa Khala. In every person I sought Simaa Khala. In every face I sought Semaa Khala's face. I wanted to find a path to take me to Simaa Khala, but she took shelter from the poverty, pain, war, mistreatment to a pathless place. Gone was my kind aunt.

On that fateful night, Simaa Khala had spent a lot of time playing with her children. She kissed and hugged them one by one. She made them all laugh and told them the most fascinating *Qesa* (tale). Later, everyone went to bed. She too took Najiba and went to her bed. Simaa Khala was playing with the baby when Merza Kaka told her to sleep. Then Merza Kaka and Najiba fell asleep. Simaa Khala remained awake, took one last look at her children and then took the lamp and left. She poured the lamp's fuel on herself. She feared that she might get caught; so as she set fire to herself, she jumped into our old well so that nobody would see her.

Simaa Khala left memories everywhere to punish us for the rest of our lives. Her face and voice came from every corner of our compound. She was in the room, yard, walls, in the faces of her children. She was everywhere. She had turned our bitter lives to hell. She turned the suffering and miserable life of my mother into a nightmare. My father was worried for his wife because she spent day and night grieving. When she talked, she only talked about Simaa Khala. She said, 'I am going to die. My eyes do not stop searching for my ignorant sister and my mind does not stop thinking of her for one moment.' She was so lonely without Simaa Khala.

My mother could not look after my little cousins, as she still was in severe pain. So, my cousins suffered even more without their mother. I wish she had considered her children's lives before she set herself on fire. She was the backbone of our family. She was our smiles and laughter, our courage and motivation. I was drowning in a bitter river of grief and it seemed there was no way out of it. Our house was hell for me. The flames of Simaa Khala's absence burned me from one side and the flames of my little cousins' misery and suffering and cries burned me from the other side. I wanted to run where I could not hear the cries of my little hungry cousins and where Simaa Khala's memories could not reach me. And where I could not see the teardrops falling from the eyes of my mother onto the ground all the time, which was as painful as flames searing upon my heart. But a poor man is like a wounded bird with broken wings and cannot fly. There was nowhere to give me refuge. I was caught in a trap of sorrow and grief. For years Simaa Khala's memories and the cries of her children tortured me. For years my heart cried and there was nothing I could do about it.

We hoped time would heal the wounds of our mother. But, time too failed to cure her broken heart. Sometimes she sat on her own in the same place she'd sat with Simaa Khala, and she talked to herself, lost in her memories. She did not know how to carry on living without Simaa Khala. She did not know from where to start a new life. Everyone was lost in grief and sorrow. Everyone, children and adults, spent days crying. Rafi, Simaa Khala's last son, was a very young boy and did not wholly understand what death meant. Sometimes he came to my mother with his tearful eyes and asked, 'When will my mother come back?' Each time he asked this question, he reduced everyone to tears. Sometimes, he cried for his mother. I could not just sit and cry. I had to cry and simultaneously carry rocks, make bricks and do other back-breaking labour. I had to carry on this hefty life that was filled with sorrow, grief and misery.

My mother gave birth to my youngest sister. By now the government had finally given my father a job in the new Afghan National Army. But he had to leave his mourning family and go to a dangerous province in the east of Afghanistan called Paktia, where the Taliban had power over most of it, and work there. The route from Kabul to Paktia was extremely dangerous. The Taliban ambushed US and NATO troops as well as Afghan police and the army each time they passed through. When my mother heard the news, she cried again and said, 'I just lost my sister and now you are trying to put yourself into death's mouth. If we are going to die, let everyone die together.'

However, nothing could stop him. This was the only opportunity for him to earn bread for us. He decided to take this huge risk and go to Paktia and fight with the Taliban in order to feed us. In return he would receive enough money to satisfy our stomachs. An Afghan Army convoy took him to Paktia. He remained in Paktia Province for several months before he could return to Kabul. He was extremely sad throughout these months, watching young Afghan soldiers killed by the Taliban every day, and people's lives, houses and villages destroyed in the ugly war. The Afghan national army were under-equipped and ill-disciplined. US and NATO personnel trained them for a short period of time and then sent them to fight to their death.

There were no jobs for poor young Afghans and each one had a family to feed. The only job they could get was with the Afghan Army or police. Both jobs put their lives and the lives of their families at great risk. Many were killed by the Taliban because of their jobs, and their family members had been harmed by the Taliban, but they had no choice if they wanted to feed their hungry families. After several months my father returned home with his earnings. Arif and I hoped that we would not have to do back-breaking toils any more. However, we soon found out that most of our father's salary was spent on our mother's treatment. He took her to the hospital and had to buy very costly medicines that doctors prescribed, yet none of those expensive medicines rid my mother from the dreadful illness. The pain gradually expanded from her back to her legs and her health deteriorated day after day. We sometimes did not know whether she cried for Simaa Khala or because she could not bear the pain. But eventually she learned how to live without her sister.

As soon as my father received his salary, he sent it home for Mother's treatment. Arif and I kept working to feed our younger siblings. Tariq concentrated on his lessons. He joined an English class and did very well. He stayed awake until late at night and studied. Arif and I still had no interest in school and books. We much preferred our back-breaking labour to studying. Our sisters were much better in school than Arif and I. They could fluently read and write, but we could do neither. By now we had all had been transferred to a bigger school. In fact we had transferred to the most famous school in Afghanistan, Habibia High School. The school produced so many well known people – king, presidents, ministers, artists. When I first stepped inside Habibia High School, it was nothing more than a ruin. Its walls had been destroyed by the rockets, missiles and bullets. Its doors and windows had been stolen. Luckily, India had already started fixing it for the children of Afghanistan. They even provided chairs and tables for students. It was a nice place for studying, but Arif and I still did not like it.

I was sixteen years old and my dream was to work and earn money to help the family and see our mother healthy once again. Winter came and all the people stopped house construction. Therefore, there was no job for Arif and me to do. So I took my wheelbarrow to Kabul city and carried people's luggage from one corner of the city to another. Sometimes the luggage was too heavy and it fell to the ground, so the owners would either beat or verbally abuse me, or just not pay. One time a man asked me to carry two big bags of wheat flour. They were too heavy and I lost my balance, so both bags of flour fell in the wet ground. He beat me badly and tried to take my wheelbarrow away from me in return for the damage I caused him. I cried and begged the man not to take my wheelbarrow. Several other men gathered around us to find out why I was crying. They all asked the man to take pity on me and pardon me. After that incident I no longer wanted to carry people's luggage in the streets of Kabul. I opened a business in the city. Arif and I bought shoes from big shops and sold them in the streets. It was a very dangerous business; nobody knew when a suicide attacker would blow himself up. Suicide attackers frequently blew themselves up and killed dozens of innocent people, but that was not the only hazard; the angry and conceited US and NATO troops were as dangerous. They shot people if they considered them as a threat. Not all of them were just angry at poor and exploited Afghans for the 9/11 atrocities, which Afghans had nothing to do with. There were some soldiers amongst the US and NATO troops who were highly sick in the mind and loved shooting poor, oppressed and defenceless people. Many times they opened fire at civilians and sent them to their deaths.

More recently on 11 March 2012, a US soldier walked out of his base at night in Kandahar province, went into villages and slaughtered nine children, some poor women and some men while they were asleep, and then he piled their bodies up and set them on fire. A little girl, who was barely five or six years old and had been shot in the leg by this US soldier, said to a journalist, 'He was shooting. He shot my father's dog first and then shot my father in the foot and then he dragged my mother by the hair, my mother was screaming and he held a gun to her. And my father said, 'leave her alone', and then he shot him right here (pointing at her chest).' The little girl said that there were several soldiers who carried out this massacre. Other people whose family members had been brutally murdered said the same thing, that more than one soldier slaughtered their family.[36] On the 12 February 2010 US Special Forces raided a house killing three innocent women, of whom two were pregnant, and two men. To cover up their barbaric crime, they dug up the bullets out of the bodies of their victims and washed their wounds with alcohol.[37]

Nevertheless, we started our risky business in Kabul city's streets unaware of police and traffic officers. Every five minutes an officer came and demanded a bribe. If we did not give one, they confiscated our shoes. I sold a few pairs of shoes, but police and traffic officers took most of the money from me. For almost two months Arif and I stood in the bitterly cold weather, but it seemed like our business was headed towards failure. Arif and I lost the very little money we had invested. I was so despondent that I took refuge in sleep for several days. Arif and the rest of my family were disheartened as well. My ill mother tried a lot to hearten me, but I was badly hurt. Police and traffic officers were thugs. They were not there to help hungry Afghans. They were there to fill their pockets with the money that hungry Afghans were earning with such difficulty. Police and traffic officers were not the only ones who were corrupt. From top to bottom everyone in the Afghan government and Parliament was extremely corrupt. Those Mujahidin leaders who killed tens of thousands of Afghans in the Mujahidin's factional war and now dominated government had built unprecedentedly beautiful buildings in the best parts of Kabul for themselves. They had invested money in Dubai and elsewhere around the world. They had sent their families into western countries to enjoy much better lives. Where did they get that money from? It was the money of those Afghans who went hungry every day. The United States and its allies kept the warlords, mass-murderers and drug dealers in power at the expense of the miserable Afghans. Top ministers were involved in the drug trafficking and other immoral businesses.

Anyway, Arif and I lost all of our money. So, we remained jobless throughout the winter. I hated sitting in the house all day long. It was very difficult for me to watch my cousins cry for their dead mother. My own poor mother's health deteriorated day after day and I could do nothing but watch her cry. When Father sent his salary, Tariq and I would to take our mother to those doctors who were supposed to be professionals. They all gave long prescriptions, which were very pricey. Sometimes we couldn't afford to buy all the medicines the doctors recommended, so we bought half of them and waited for our father to send money to buy the other half. By now I was a grown man and my mother had faith in me to send me to Kabul city to buy food. However, she was extremely worried that I might get killed by suicide bombers or US and NATO troops who indiscriminately fired at people. She often warned me to stay away from crowded areas, as suicide attackers usually blew themselves up in crowds. She warned me to stay away from US and NATO vehicles as well. She said that if I saw them I was to walk away, otherwise they might think I was a suicide attacker and shoot me. That was true, so many innocent Afghans had been shot dead by US and NATO troops who had mistaken them for suicide attackers. So, when I saw a US or NATO convoy in the city or roads I left the vicinity. When I walked in the ruined Kabul city area I was very vigilant and as soon as I bought the food I would head home without any hesitation.

In the summer of 2005, a doctor warned my father that my mother's health was getting worse and he had to take her outside Afghanistan to a specialist. The doctor recommended he take her to Pakistan, as there were modern private hospitals with more professional doctors and better equipment. He gave the address of one hospital and said it would cost us at least $1,000. When my father heard this he shuddered. He had never had $1,000 in his lifetime. That amount of money was not easy for a poor man to earn in Afghanistan. Father had to do something, because Mother was in a terrible state. None of the Afghan doctors knew the true cause of the pain in my mother's back and legs. Some said that she had hurt her spine and that caused the pain. Some said she had given birth to too many children. Others gave different reasons. My father asked his friends to lend him money. The problem was that he had not returned the money he had borrowed a long time before. He still asked. Few loaned him some more money but most didn't. He then asked his comrades in the army, but they were as poor as we were. After some time he managed to save enough money, but with great difficulty.

He could not take my mother to Pakistan, because he had to go back to Paktia and carry on his perilous job. Tariq was lost in his school lessons as well as learning English, so my father chose me to take her. We went to get passports for my mother and me, but there were thousands of Afghans also waiting to get passports. Some of those millions of Afghans who lived as refugees in Iran and Pakistan had returned to Afghanistan since the fall of the Taliban, and now they wanted to escape back to the refugee camps of Pakistan and Iran. At first they also thought that the US and NATO would bring peace to Afghanistan. They also considered the NATO and US troops as liberators of Afghanistan. They soon realised that it had been their liberators who dropped destructive bombs upon them; it was the liberators who raided their houses at midnight, who shot them in the roads and who humiliated them on a daily basis. And the 'honest and democratic' government was nothing more than a bunch of warlords, war criminals and drug traffickers who killed countless Afghans and destroyed Kabul.

Those who returned from abroad saw the horror of the so-called War on Terror, which in reality is a war of terror, began to flee their country yet again, towards Pakistani refugee camps and Iran, which did not want Afghans in their country any more. Poor Afghans were homeless in their own country as well as others'. Poor Afghans were in despair. If they stayed in their own country they would be hunted by the US and NATO, or by the Taliban suicide attacks or IEDs. And if they fled their country and lived in refugee camp they would have miserable lives.

As we reached the entrance gate of the passport department, a police soldier standing in the gate with his Kalashnikov in hand boldly demanded a bribe from my father to allow us in. My father knew he had no choice. Then we went further and another soldier who guided people towards the department with his Kalashnikov in hand also demanded money before he let us go to the department. There were three men working in the entire department, and they were supposed to issue passports for thousands of people. They told my father that it would take at least three or four months before they could deal with our case. However, if we give them $300 as a bribe then they would give us passports in less than a week. Father threatened the three officers by saying that he would complain to their chain of command. That did not scare them at all because the money they demanded was not only for those three officers, it was being shared between all of their chain of command. My father had no choice but to leave their office and go back home. He decided to send us to Pakistan without any legal documentation.

Despite my cousins going to Pakistan to work sometimes, I was still sceptical of the existence of another world outside. In school our geography teacher had a large globe map. I looked to see where Pakistan was. There were dark lines that divided Afghanistan from Pakistan. These dark lines also divided other countries from each other all across the globe. I believed that these black lines were hollows that separated one country from another.

My mother and I sat in a vehicle alongside others who wanted to flee the Afghan war and poverty. The beauty of the high mountains, green valleys, long tunnels through the high mountains and angry rivers of Afghanistan amazed me all the way. Afghanistan had been destroyed so badly throughout her history, but terrible wars had failed to steal her beauty from her. When I looked at her mountains, rivers, valleys and hills I thought that war had never occurred in this beautiful land. However, when the vehicle passed through cities and villages, all I could see were hungry people, ruined houses, schools, factories, hospitals and dead Soviet tanks everywhere, and the sky was filled with NATO and US helicopters and aircraft. My mother was very uncomfortable all the way to Pakistan due to the pain.

At last we reached the Khyber Pass, a vital route for centuries that connected central Asia with south Asia, and a vital part of the silk route. Through this pass NATO and US troops received their supplies. The driver asked us to get off at the border. We found the hospital that the Afghan doctor recommended. The doctors took an X-ray of my mother's back. They gave her another long prescription and told my mother to use all the medicine that they had recommended and if she did not recover then they would carry out an operation. Pakistani doctors said the operation would cost $2,000. So, my mother and I had to return home and pray for God to help with the medicine that the doctors had given her.

I was walking in Kabul city with a bag of flour on my back when someone hit me on the head with a bottle filled with water. I was hit so hard that everywhere went dark for a few seconds. When I looked up I saw a US soldier pointing his huge gun right at me,ready to fire if I did not stop. I looked like a suicide bomber, since most suicide bombers were young boys like me. Perhaps the soldier thought my bag was full of explosives. Other Afghans who watched were furious at me for being reckless. An elderly man shouted at me to be watchful because the foreign troops were there looking for excuses to shoot. There were rumours amongst people that US and NATO troops were shooting Afghans because they hated Muslims. I could do nothing but pick up the bottle of water and drink it. Although I was very careful to avoid crowds and NATO and US convoys, I became even more cautious after that incident. Day after day, hatred grew in the hearts of Afghans towards the troops. Birds disappeared from the sky once the jet aircrafts and helicopters had taken their place. Afghans loathed US and NATO troops walking in their roads, streets, villages and farms, arrogantly harassing and humiliating them. Very few people believed that the US and NATO were in Afghanistan to fight the Taliban or Al Qaeda, because all Afghans knew that the roots of the Taliban and Al Qaeda was in Pakistan, which was the United States ally.

My mother consumed all the medicines that the Pakistani doctors recommended, but pain refused to leave her. My father was very confused about what to do. His wife was in a terrible condition and he was drowning in debt and unable to pay. Most of his salary had been spent buying medicines and very little money remained. However, this year Tariq had a great surprise for everyone. He became a teacher in a prominent English academy. My mother was extremely happy and even ordered my sisters to bake one extra Naan and give it out for other hungry people. After some time, Tariq became a very well-known teacher and his students were everywhere. So many village children went to Tariq to learn English.

Arif and I were in eleventh grades in school and yet could not read and write, which most students mocked us for. I had no choice but to learn reading and writing. It was during this year that I at last managed it. When Arif noticed he also asked Tariq to help him to learn. Amazingly, Arif's handwriting was the most beautiful handwriting in our class. Sometimes, students and teachers asked him to write their letters. His handwriting also stunned my father and his friends.

However, the holes that Simaa Khala's death had drilled into our hearts had not healed yet. Still tears fell from everyone's eyes in memory of her. When we all gathered nobody talked about anyone else but Simaa Khala. Simaa Khala left her children to be drowned in the sea of pain, torment, sadness and hunger. A family shatters without its mother and that is what happened with my poor cousins. They became so miserable without their mother. They were lost without her.

My Aunt and the Beast

Anger, poverty and all sorts of difficulties that surrounded me in life made me a tough boy. By now people trusted me with all sorts of back-breaking toils. My rugged and blistered hands were able to do all types of work. Sometimes people came from miles away and asked me to work for them. Brick-making was a far more difficult job, but after a while I became a very well-known brick-maker. Arif and I produced three or sometimes even four thousand bricks in four or five hours, which impressed our employer. Life went on accompanied by war, poverty, suffering and despair. The future looked as dark as ever. Year after year war expanded into the most remote parts of Afghanistan. Year after year civilian casualties increased. Countless Afghans were crushed under US and NATO bombs, bullets and Taliban IEDs and suicide attacks. Poor Afghans were surrounded by troops and the corrupt Afghanistan government from one side, and by the savage Taliban from the other. Each claimed they were there to help Afghan people. Poor and exploited Afghans did not experience anything but killing and harm from all sides. Hamid Karzay, the incompetent president of Afghanistan, who knew that US and NATO bombs and the killings of civilians put his throne of power at great risk, begged and even cried for NATO and American leaders to stop bombing children and women. But US and NATO troops turned their deaf ear and blind eye towards Afghan criers and continued to slaughter the poor Afghans.

We were very anxious for our father. The situation was very dangerous in Paktia. Civilians picked up guns to fight the US, NATO and Afghan national army and police. My father travelled by land from Kabul to Paktia and then back to Kabul once a month. The route was terribly dangerous. The Afghan Army and police were a good target for the Taliban. They were ill-equipped and poorly-trained and suffered the highest casualties, in contrast to the US, NATO and the Taliban. What could poor people do? If they did not join the army and police their families would starve to death, and if they did join, their lives were at great risk.

Poor Afghans gave their lives for no good reason. Some who fought against the US wanted to take revenge for relatives or friends who had been killed. Some just did not want the US and NATO in their country. Others fought for foreign governments and intelligences. Pashtuns were humiliated on a daily basis, as the war was in their villages, gardens and fields. Pashtuns were smashed by bombs, rockets, bullets, IEDs. Their houses, villages, gardens and fields were burned or destroyed. Their houses were raided at night. Their women and children were killed and men dragged to the US military prisons. The Afghan police were highly corrupt all over Afghanistan, but in particular in the warzone, which was mainly where the Pashtuns lived. Smoking heroin and cannabis was widespread amongst them. They stopped people in the bazaars, villages, fields, gardens, streets and roads and robbed them.

And so the Pashtuns went to the Taliban, picked up their ugly weapons and they fought against the government and NATO and US troops. And when they were killed, more people took up weapons to take revenge. NATO, US and Afghan police were not the only ones who oppressed them. They themselves oppressed each other. Still hostility prevailed amongst the Pashtuns. For instance, one hostile village, tribe or family went to the US or NATO troops' base and falsely accused their enemy of being Taliban or Al Qaeda, and then the US aircraft bombed without investigating. This happened several times.

We gave up hope on doctors and medicines because medical treatment did not work at all for my mother. So, we took my mother back to several Mullahs and other clergymen who issued *Tawiz*. The majority of Mullahs said genies had entered her body and she needed to come every evening until they forced them out. Going to a Mullah every evening meant paying each time we visited. Whatever Mullahs did they failed to heal my mother. We could not even think of the operation that the Pakistani doctor recommended, as we did not have $2,000. I often watched my mother suffer unbearable pain. My cousins came into our house and cried too, and blamed themselves for not looking after their own mother properly. My mother spent hours trying to assure them that they were not liable for the death of her sister. Najiba, Simaa Khala's last child, was now two years old and could talk. She spent most of her time in our house, playing with my siblings. Village women came to see how my cousins were doing without their mother. Each time village women came, they burst into tears. My cousins could not look after themselves properly and Merza Kaka was too busy working and saving money to remarry.

One day we were in the house when more terrifying news arrived. The information came from Jalalabad where my grandfather lived with my paternal uncles. Shukrya Amma, my father's youngest sister, who had married several years ago, lived tens of miles away from my grandfather's house. My uncles were too busy working in fields to feed their families. They failed to visit Shukrya Amma regularly and Grandfather was already over a hundred years old and unable to walk for miles. During these years of marriage Shukrya Amma had been horribly abused by her husband and his family. Most marriages in Afghanistan are fixed marriages and many marriages do not work out well. Either the husband doesn't like his wife or the wife doesn't like the husband. In both cases it's the women who suffer the most. If the husband does not like his wife he can easily marry not only one but two or three wives and it's perfectly acceptable in the society. But, if a poor woman doesn't like her husband she has no choice but to spend the rest of her bitter life with the man she doesn't love. Getting divorced is almost beyond impossible for women. Simaa Khala and Shukrya Amma were both amongst these unlucky women. Arranged marriage did not work for either of them. Shukrya Amma's husband did not love her from the very first day. He was poor and could not afford to remarry so he tortured her in a very beastly manner. He was not the only one; his parents and siblings also beat and abused her. Sometimes they beat her together, and then locked her in the cattle shed with their cows and sheep. There was nothing Shukrya Amma could do to stop them. They broke several of her bones. Her husband frequently threatened her with death. Sometimes he asked her to leave his house, but my poor aunt had nowhere but her father's house. How could a woman who spent her entire life inside a compound like a prisoner and never stepped outside find her father's house from such great distance? Shukrya Amma lived on under the tyranny and cruelty of her husband and his family for several years. Neighbours and villagers would hear her cries all the time. One time her husband stabbed her several times and smashed her face and head with a rock. And then he locked her in with the cattle to bleed to death. An elderly neighbour saw this tragedy, luckily felt sorry for her and decided to do something. He told my paternal uncles who took guns and hurried towards their sister's house. They found their sister badly wounded. She had been stabbed several times in the stomach, her entire face and body had turned dark and lumpy, and she was locked in the cattle shed to endure a slow death. My uncles beat her husband and took their sister to the Jalalabad hospital for treatment. Her wounds were so severe that the doctors told them to take her to a Kabul hospital. They did not have money to pay for the journey or for treatment, and so they borrowed from their friends. My father was on leave when Shukrya Amma entered our compound. Everyone was shaken when they saw her. Her face was covered with dark injuries. Her eyes were concealed with swollen wounds. She was covered with bandages and unable to walk. My father took his sister to several hospitals for treatment and she lived with us for a while. After some time her husband came, apologised, and promised he would not torture her again. But, he soon resumed, torturing her until this day, and there is no law to protect my Amma.

Shukrya Amma's story is just one of the many that happen every day all over Afghanistan. There are millions of unspeakable brutalities taking place against women. Women live under unimaginable cruelty all over the country. A decade has elapsed since George W. Bush, after the invasion of Afghanistan, said, 'The mothers and daughters of Afghanistan were captives in their homes… today women are free.' His assertion that his fatal invasion of Afghanistan brought freedom to Afghan women is as big a lie as his assertion that Iraq had weapons of mass destruction. A poll was conducted by TrustLaw, a Thomson Reuters Foundation Service, in 2011, which says Afghanistan is the world's most dangerous country for women.[38]

After twelve years of studying Tariq and, surprisingly, I graduated from school, but Arif failed and had to study the same grade again. Now it was time for Tariq and me to go to university, but before we did, we had to pass an entry exam. In 2006 over 80,000 students applied for the university in Kabul, but there was only one university and it could only enrol 20,000 students, and there was nowhere else for the other 60,000 students to study. The exam was quite tough, there were several papers filled with hard questions. If I did not go to university I would spend the rest of my life doing back-breaking labour for very little money. I failed to answer a single question. Tariq got a good result and was accepted in the construction engineering field but I failed. My parents were so happy when they found out that Tariq would become a future engineer, I did not dare tell them that I had failed and wouldn't be going to university. But I could not conceal it forever. Eventually my mother found out and it hurt her more than I imagined. She refused to talk to me for a long time. My parents had a dream for me to go to university and become a productive man.

By now I was certain about my future. I was going to work under the burning sun in the summer and in the brutally tough winters for the rest of my life. For a while, I worked as a labourer, sometimes carried rocks and bricks, sometimes worked as a brick-maker and sometimes people hired me to help bricklayers with construction. At weekends, I went to Kabul city to buy food for my family. The state of the people there was heartbreaking. As the war spread, poverty rose. Hunger forced more people into the streets of Kabul to beg. Sometimes there were more people begging in Kabul city than shopping and working.

As the war spread in the south, east and west, more people were killed, villages were destroyed, crops were burned and cattle were either bombed or killed in the crossfire. Therefore, many people were left with nothing. As the war intensified, people fled their homes. Villagers left their livelihoods behind. Some went to Pakistan and Iran, some took refuge in Kabul, which was safer than south of the country. Those who went to Kabul had no shelter or food. Many starved to death in the brutal winter. The president of the United States promised help. The state of ordinary Afghans was and still is heartbreaking and there is no one to take pity on them. Instead, they are devastated by US and NATO bombs and Taliban suicide attacks and IEDs.

Sometimes, Afghan media showed the true horror of the War on Terror. Afghans took the dead bodies of little children killed in US air strikes into the streets and burned the US flag. Hamid Karzay begged the US again and again to stop the killing, but the US and NATO forces accused even Afghan children and women of being insurgents and terrorists. People took the dead bodies of their relatives and villagers, put them in the middle of the road and cried for justice.

As the security situation worsened, my parents refused to let Tariq go to university, as it was too dangerous. Suicide bombers detonated themselves in every corner of Kabul and Afghanistan, and their victims were mostly civilians. Tariq had to travel through the crowded area to get to Kabul University where suicide bombers detonated themselves frequently. Sometimes US or NATO troops opened fire at civilians. It was painful for my parents not to allow Tariq to go university. Mother's dream was shattered; none of her sons would become doctors or engineers. What could she do? She was a poor woman with a heart filled with love for her children. Tariq insisted that he wanted to go and become an engineer. But our mother refused to let him.

Life became more fearful than it ever had before. Nobody knew which day would be their last. Afghans were surrounded with fear of war, poverty, disease, heroin, crime and all kinds of evils. During the Taliban regime at least we did not hear the frightening sounds of explosions, helicopters and aircrafts constantly; but now once again it was everywhere and frightened everyone, in particular hungry and unclothed children.

One day Tariq advised me to learn English so that I might get a job with one of the foreign organisations. I agreed and in the evenings attended his English class. I went for several months, but did not learn. I sometimes annoyed Tariq so much when I failed to learn that he refused to let me in class. Tariq told me that I was wasting his time, because my brain was rotten and I would never learn anything at all. I also wondered if there was something wrong with my brain and sometimes did not attempt to learn anything any more. But I was great in physical toil. I could do any sort of physical work available. In our village there were so many people desperate to find work and when there was an available job everyone wanted it, so labourers ended up fighting one another. Arif and I were too young to even argue with other workers. One time one labourer battered me in the face with a brick and broke my nose. I was in hospital for several days.

An angry US troop convoy became trapped in a Kabul traffic jam. Instead of waiting, they drove their armoured vehicle over civilian cars and injured several drivers. When civilians saw the soldiers' barbarity, they protested against US troops. Then the troops opened fire with machine-guns, killing several of them. Afghans already had so much anger in their hearts and on that day their anger burst. Throughout Kabul Afghans protested; they burned shops, buildings, government offices, set fire to the US flag and shouted, 'Death to Americans'. Almost all Kabul residents expressed their anger and hatred towards the US troops through violence. On that day, I was in the city to buy food. Amongst the protesters were people who came to riot. Shops and markets were looted and Kabul city was shattered. The poor Afghans were so angry at the Americans and their troops that they destroyed Kabul town. But their anger only hurt themselves and no one else. At the end of the day yet more Afghans had been killed and injured.

Winter arrived as usual, brutally cold. It was painfully hard watching rural Afghans who had fled the war to Kabul. Their children were dying every day, but slowly, one after another, from starvation and harsh weather. They had nothing to eat, no shelter to hide in and no clothes to wear, and were left exposed to the winter harshness. These refugees were interviewed. Every single one wanted something, not from humans because they had given up on humans, but from God – and that was death. One of those who escaped the US bombardments said, 'I asked God to grant me and my family death rather than this living.'

Another said, 'We will die here. We don't have any other choice. We can't go back because of the Americans and the bombardments.'

Another man said, 'My children are dying one after another in this freezing weather, so I decided to sell them each for 150,000 Afghani.' He grabbed a little girl by the arm who was not more than three years of age, she stood barefoot on the mud and snow, wore thin and ragged clothes and trembled in the freezing weather. 'She is my dearest daughter and I want to sell her,' said the man.[39]

Many of these people who were living in appalling conditions in Kabul camps had lost relatives during the bombardments. Where was that peace and freedom that the US president promised to the hungry Afghans? Birds frightened in the sky by the sound of their jet aircrafts and hungry and unclothed children, tormented women and helpless men in the ground. These horrible camps in Kabul that are filled with thousands of Afghans who have fled the bombs is a glimpse of western terrorism in Afghanistan. What is the difference between those people who flew aeroplanes into the New York skyscrapers and the US and NATO who behave many times more barbarically in   Afghanistan?

I Almost Fell out of the Tree of Life

For a while in 2007 I was desperate to find job. A man employed me to provide sand for him. Kabul River was not far from our house so I fetched sand from there. Arif came with me. We found a huge cave and a man warned me that the cave might collapse and bury me alive. He told me about an incident that took place a few days ago where twelve people had been buried alive in one of the caves while they were digging sand. The man left and I dug without taking his warning seriously. I worked in the cave for a few hours.

Suddenly I felt the cave moving. I crawled towards the exit very quickly and managed to get my head out of the cave, but not my body. Huge chunks of earth collapsed and crushed me against the ground. I felt like the whole planet was lying upon my back. I thought I would be out of this world in the next few moments. Arif screamed and thought I had perished. People ran from all corners to help me out. Chunks of earth piled on top of my body and were too heavy for people to move. The pain was unbearable and I thought my heart was going to burst any second. I could not breathe and I thought I was going to die. People who saw me were terrified. I felt that my eyes, face, heart, stomach, every part of my body might burst. I thought, these are my last moments, and I wanted to have a view of this world for one last time. I thought this time death was not playing with me, it had come to eat me.

The last thing I saw before I lost consciousness was men running with shovels and spades in their hands. They broke the gigantic chunks of earth, which lay on top of me. Some thought I had already died. Throughout my life death roared at me with its hungry stomach, but did not eat me, not even this time.

After some time I regained consciousness, looked around and saw people surrounding me. I tried to move my legs to stand, but there was a sharp pain in my back. Someone dragged me out and placed me in the wheelbarrow and Arif wheeled me home. The pain was so severe that I could not stay quiet for a moment. My mother was terrified seeing me in such a state. Tariq took me to *Wazir Akbar Khan* hospital. The doctors took an X-ray of my back and said there were several fractures. Doctors said they could not hospitalise me as there were countless people who were injured in the war who had come from a long distance and needed to be treated first. I was in excruciating pain and unable to stand or walk for several months. I knew how my mother felt now.

I was fed up with living; I was fed up with everything. Wherever I looked, there were problems and difficulties. Each day was as long as years of pain and anguish. The pain was so severe I could not even sleep. I worried I might never be able to work again. What else could I do? What future would I have if I was permanently disabled and couldn't walk ever again? These were the questions in my thoughts all the time.

I learned English from Tariq while I was injured. My brother was more than happy to teach me. He gave me a lot of work to do, which kept me busy in the daytime. He even brought several English grammar and conversation books to help me. During the day, I kept busy learning new words from the fat dictionary that Tariq had given me. I learned hundreds of words, but could not use them in sentences. Tariq really was a strange person. He was only a good friend of mine when I studied and bitterly hated me when I did not. Months elapsed, but my back pain did not fade away. My poor mother was anxious as well as my father and siblings for me that I might never recover. But, there was nothing they could do. I felt a burden to them as I was not able to walk on my own two feet, and they had to carry me around.

Life was already very hard and it became more difficult when I realised how bad our living conditions truly were. My mother's health deteriorated day after day. There was very little food. My siblings fought one another for a loaf of bread. Our family was very big, but there was only a single room for all of us. We ate, slept and sat in one room. In the darkness of midnight, if one of us woke up to drink water or use the toilet, they first stamped over several of us before getting out of the room. We were in dire need of a new room, but this was far beyond our imagination. We needed clothes, ours were worn out.

Eventually the fractures healed without treatment and I could walk again. As soon as I was able to stand on my feet, I took my wheelbarrow and went to help Arif carry bricks and rocks. I was not fully recovered, still my back was painful when I lifted heavy weights. But I had no choice but to carry on working. Arif helped me throughout and, after a while, I fully recovered. However, I did not stop learning English. Tariq introduced me to his own teacher. His teacher was very prominent in our area. I attended his class in the evening and asked Tariq to help me at night. I enjoyed learning and speaking English with my classmates.

It was almost winter when one morning I woke up and went out to find work. I stood in the *Sar Chawk* amongst hundreds of Afghans who wanted someone to hire them. It was extremely cold and windy. I stood for several hours until a man came and shouted, 'I need three (*Qawi*) strong guys to work for me for three days.' Everybody ran and surrounded him and begged him to pick them for the job. I too thrust myself into the crowd. I shook his arm to catch his attention. He looked at me and I asked him to give me the job. He laughed and said I was too young and weak to work for him. I stood for several more hours amongst the jobless, but nobody wanted me to work for them.

When I got home. I was very hungry. Mother cooked tomato and saved me a little with a piece of Naan. As I began to eat it, my three-year-old sister sat beside me. She took my Naan from my hand and began eating with me. I took my Naan back, but she helped herself to the tomato on my plate and ate it without the Naan.

'Are you very hungry?' I asked, once she finished eating my food.

She showed me her belly and said, 'Look, it's empty.'

A private American company employed people who could speak English as interpreters for the US force in Afghanistan. I didn't think I would pass their test as I could barely speak a few words; but I decided to try my luck. Surprisingly out of tens of young boys, I did pass. An American sat with me to take my details, but we failed to communicate with one another because I did not understand what he was saying. So, he called his interpreter to interpret for us. It was ironic, since I was about to become an English interpreter, but could not speak English! While the American gentleman asked me questions, I noticed his hands were delicate and smooth. It seemed as though he had never worked with them in his lifetime. His hands were not comparable with my tough thick, big, blistered and ragged hands. The man warned me through his interpreter that the job was highly dangerous and would put my family and my life at great peril, and if I was not willing to do it, I must not waste his time. What choice did a person in my position have? The man told me to wait until the US called their company for interpreters. On the way out, his interpreter warned me that I was not able to speak English well enough and should not attempt to work as an interpreter for the US.

In the late winter, I was assigned to work in Herat Province with the US. My mother cried and begged me not to leave the house. But nothing could stop me. Herat Province is situated in western Afghanistan and has a long border with Iran. Herat is a historical province and still one can see Alexander the Great's old town, which was erected around 300BC. Its inhabitants are mainly from the Tajik ethnicity and rather moderate and well-educated in comparison with the rest of Afghanistan. Herat's security state was far better than anywhere else in Afghanistan. Fewer suicide bombers detonated themselves and there were only a handful of Taliban with rarely any clashes with NATO or US troops and Afghan security forces. Nevertheless, I went far away from my mother and siblings to a new place. I was much happier for having a job and receiving a good monthly wage, and careless of the perils.

I was assigned to a US Army major. His job was to train Afghan national army and police officers. The major was a big gentleman and had quite an important job. But he did not like to train the Afghan Army and police, for he came to fight. I did not understand him at all when he spoke. Whatever he said or asked, all I could say in response was - yes. The first time he took me with him to a meeting was in a big hall, full of high-ranking Afghan Army officers. I had never spoken before so many people in my life. Soon, my whole body began to shudder. I stood beside the gigantic major and he began to speak to the officers. I was sure that the first day of my lucrative and comfortable job would also be my last. The major said one thing and I said something else to the Afghans. Neither the Afghan Army nor the US major understood what I was talking about. The major got mad at me on the very first day, as he had to repeat his sentences several times and I still could not get it. But he was a nice guy and let me keep my job. He hoped my English would improve as time went by.

My English did get better and I practised with the major. But I was far from being able to interpret what Afghan officers were saying to the major and what the major was saying to them. There was plenty of food for me to eat. I met other interpreters and made very good friends there. But my heart feared that I might lose my job. I was a young, inexperienced boy and usually annoyed the major when we worked. There was no love between the Afghan Army, the police and their US, Italian and Spanish mentors. They often quarrelled with each other. In fact, a short while before I started my job an Afghan soldier quarrelled with a US officer and he shot dead the US officer and injured his interpreter. The Afghan Army did not like to be bossed around by US or NATO troops. Most Afghan Army and police considered them as arrogant and rude people who looked down on them. And some Afghan Army and police soldiers considered them as invaders and hated them.

The major and the Afghans argued all the time, which put my job on the line, since the major expected me to interpret what the angry officers said to him and I was not able to do so. Once or twice a week we had to go to Herat city, to the police headquarters and work with them. The first time, when I boarded the heavily armoured vehicle and it drove towards the city, I was very nervous that a suicide bomber might blow us up. But nothing happened. I saw Herat city and it was far more beautiful than anywhere else in Afghanistan. It had not been destroyed too much in the decades of wars. Nevertheless, people were extremely poor.

Violence against women was much higher and so many of the helpless women burned themselves to death like Simaa Khala. Although Herat's inhabitants were much more moderate, women were in a terrible condition in the rural areas of Herat. Crime was another major problem there. Herat was packed with very dangerous gangs who harangued its inhabitants. Burglars kidnapped people regularly and demanded money from their relatives.

There were US, Spanish and Italian troops in Herat and they trained Afghan security forces. I was desperate to talk with all these foreigners. I wanted to know about these strange people, but it seemed as though they were not interested in speaking with Afghans.

In my spare time, I worked hard on my English, but failed to cling onto my lucrative job, and soon the end came. My badge expired and the company re-interviewed me, but I failed the second interview and lost my job. I had my job for only around three months and went back home filled with sadness. I was so sad that once again I took refuge in sleeping. I did not tell my mother that I had lost my job. She thought I had come home to visit her. Nevertheless, I did not want to carry rocks and bricks or be a brick-maker again. But I could not stay in the house.

Someone told me the British were in dire need of interpreters to work for them in Helmand Province. I sat before an Englishman and his Afghan colleague for an interview. At the end the Englishman told me that my English was not good enough. He told me to go home, study English and try again. So I spent day and night studying English. After a while I went back and sat at the interview table with another Englishman and his Afghan colleague. This time at the end of the interview the Englishman told me that I had managed to pass the interview but I was too tall to fit in their armoured vehicles. First they told me to learn English and I could do that, but I had no notion of how to shorten myself. But I soon realised that he was teasing me.

He put a paper before me and advised his Afghan colleague to tell me what was written on the paper. The Afghan gentleman told me that it said that I was fully aware of the dangers that existed in Helmand Province and I was willing to go there. After I signed it he asked me to provide him with a contact number in case I was killed or injured. What would happen to my shattered father who took food out of death's mouth for my siblings and me if he heard the news of my death? And what would happen to my tormented mother and hungry siblings if they found out that I was dead? I did not tell anyone in my family where I was going. My father and mother were well aware of what was happening in the southern part of Afghanistan and they would never let me go there even if we starved to death.

When it was time for me to go, I packed my stuff and spent some time with my family, and then I headed towards Helmand Province. I was not sure whether I would see them again. My poor family thought I was going back to Herat Province, to my comfortable job.

I got into a British military aeroplane and it flew high in the sky in the darkness of the night towards Helmand Province. As I disembarked, the heat hit me in the face. What a huge camp they had built in the desert there. The camp was called Bastion and belonged to the British forces, but US and other NATO troops were there too. I was frightened, just like everyone else who first arrived in Helmand Province. I remained in Camp Bastion for some days waiting to see where they would send me. There was no work to keep me busy in the British main camp. All day long I sat in a shadow and observed these peculiar people and their weird killing machines. They looked very charming, impressive and seductive, but they were designed to kill peace, beauty and love, and to deprive men, women and children of their lives. Journalist and author Chris Hedges called these charming, impressive and seductive machinese 'angels of death'.

If we use science and technology sanely in one place, we equally us them insanely in another place. Man's mind is too violent and destructive to use science and technology properly. With the sword of science and technology we had vanquished the brutality of the nature to a large degree, but then we turned the same sword against our fellow men and massacred each other in appalling ways. With science and technology human beings destroyed themselves in tens of millions in the twentieth century and built the most obnoxious weapons that could shatter everything in a glimpse. Science and technology helped us understand nature more, yet today we are more divorced from nature than ever before. With science and technology we kill nature. We have overpopulated the earth, and now we cut each other's throat for the limited resources of the world. Albert Enstein said, 'Technological progress is like an axe in the hands of a pathological criminal.' Governments are relentlessly hiring fellow scientists and technologists to invent terrible weapons for them so that they can kill and destroy defenceless humans around the world. Scientists and technologists have created nuclear, chemical and biological weapons and put them in the hands of these psychopaths who run our world. Humanity has been betrayed by some intellectuals. The scientists and technologists who invent these barbaric tools of butchering and destruction are as much responsible for the chaos and violence and exploitation in the world. When mankind takes one step towards true progress, he concurrently takes three steps backward towards barbarism.

Nevertheless, as I waited in Camp Bastion, I saw wounded British, American and Afghans arrive for treatment. Fierce fighting went on in every district of Helmand Province. I did not want to get injured and preferred death, since it seemed unfair to be poor and disabled. There was a missile launching pad near my accommodation; they called the missile GMLRS. The GMLRS frequently frightened me as it roared towards the sky with its long smoky tail. Each time they fired, my heart trembled and I remembered my past and all the horrors.

After twenty days in Camp Bastion, a British officer told me that I would be sent to the southern part of Helmand, to a district called Garmsir. Garmsir and the rest of Helmand Province was desert, there was a beautiful river and people inhabited both sides of the river. The British officer seemed to notice fear in my eyes. He told me not to be scared, that it was safe now because thousands of US marines had carried out a huge operation, which killed most of the Taliban, and they were there to help British troops. I spent my last night in Camp Bastion but could not sleep. I wondered if I would die or survive and see my family again. I don't know if I was born an adventurer, but my life was an endless adventure from the day I opened my eyes.

In the morning, I got my bag and walked alongside soldiers towards a Chinook helicopter as the hot weather burned my face and hands. The Chinook flew over the wild and endless desert. I was seated beside a tiny window with a good view of the spectacular desert. It seemed lifeless to me, but the *Kuchi* tribe of Afghanistan have been wandering about with their camels and other cattle and big, cruel dogs for centuries, bravely fighting the harshness of nature. As the Chinook flew higher in the sky, I had a more splendid view. The desert was split by a wonderful river and for one moment all the fear inside me disappeared. Nevertheless, the Chinook helicopter landed in a ruined compound and I disembarked along with others. This terribly ruined compound that the British and US troops were living in was once a Taliban *Madrasa,* and young boys had been gathered here in the past for radicalisation to fight for the Taliban against Mujahidin. The walls were covered with bullet and rocket holes. The British troops used the *Madrasa* as a Forward Operation Base, FOB Dehli it was called. Some time before my arrival Prince Harry lived there and in JTAC Hill, a few yards away from FOB Dehli.

Interpreters told me not to be scared. They said that the US marines had fought for several weeks with the Taliban and killed hundreds of them. They said FOB Dehli was filled with their dead bodies, and jet aircrafts had dropped huge bombs upon the Taliban that shook the entire Garmsir. However, the living conditions were tough in that dusty ruined compound. I was as much curious to see outside as I was frightened of it. My ears failed to pick up any noise of men, women and children who had lived in this dreadful warzone for so long.

'This is your weapon and listen to it carefully,' said a British commander one day. He handed me a device called I-com, which intercepted the Taliban while they conversed on radio. I dressed in a British military uniform, body armour and helmet to blend in with the British troops while on patrol, thus not becoming a target of the Taliban as they considered interpreters to be the eyes and ears of the foreign troops. Heavily armoured vehicles called Mastiffs dropped us in the middle of a main rough road. I had for the first time come across the true horrors of the War on Terror. Garmsir was a ghost town. No humans could be seen anywhere. Villages had been reduced to debris. Bombs gouged huge holes everywhere, and unexploded devices lay scattered all over.

We were surrounded by the poppy fields, which was a surprise for me. In fact everywhere was surrounded by poppy fields, even FOB Dehli itself. By now Afghanistan was once again the world's largest opium producer, despite the presence of large numbers of US and NATO troops. According to the economist and author F. William Engdahl:

> 'The US military is in Afghanistan for two reasons. First, to restore and control the world's largest supply of opium for the world heroin markets and to use the drugs as a geopolitical weapon against opponents, especially Russia. That control of the Afghan drug market is essential for the liquidity of the bankrupt and corrupt Wall Street financial mafia. And second, the aim of the US bases in Afghanistan is to target and be able to strike at the two nations which today represent the only combined threat in the world today to an American global imperium.'[40]

A soldier began searching the road with his mine detector and the rest followed him. We had to walk in each other's footprints otherwise one wrong step could have been a disaster for us. We walked through the poppy plants towards the ruined villages. The weather was boiling hot and soon exhausted us. We rested beside a bomb crater. Two soldiers walked down into the huge hole and took pictures. We passed through several lifeless villages. The patrol commander was looking for an Afghan to talk with. After some time an elderly man who had a spade on his shoulder appeared. The commander and other troops stood in his way.

The commander instructed me, 'Tell the man to lift his clothes up.' I did not understand what the commander meant. 'Tell the elderly man to lift his clothes up to make sure he is not a suicide bomber,' said the commander. He waited for me to ask and I was very embarrassed to ask a man who was older than my father to show his body.

Nonetheless, I greeted the elderly man first from afar and then asked him to do what the commander demanded. It looked like the elderly man had encountered British or US patrols before, because he knew what I was asking him. The helpless man was furious and cursed the British troops as he exposed his stomach and chest, then he turned and raised his clothes up to expose his back, and at last he exposed his legs.

Before we began to walk towards him, the commander said, 'Ask him to remove his turban from his head.' First, the elderly man refused, but he had no choice. Finally, he removed his turban and then we walked closer. I greeted the elderly man again. I apologised for what I had asked him to do. I could clearly see a pure and bitter hatred in the elderly man's eyes for the British troops. The commander asked questions such as, 'Where is the Taliban?', 'Where did they hide IEDs?' And several other similar questions.

But the answer to all the questions was the same, 'I don't know.'

I was sure even if the elderly Afghan knew about the Taliban and IEDs he would not tell the British troops after what they had done to him. He asked us to leave him alone; if the Taliban saw him talking with the foreign troops, they would accuse him of being a spy. In general people were pro-Taliban for Taliban did not harass or harm them as much as the US, NATO and Afghan police did. The Taliban lived amongst the local people, who now joined them to either take revenge or to force the foreign troops out of their villages.

We walked towards another village where some people still lived. On the way several men greeted us and I had to humiliate each one of them by asking them to expose their body for us. Before we entered the village, a man came in our way. He asked us not to enter the village, since their children and women were frightened of foreign troops. Nothing could stop us. The few children who were playing abruptly disappeared. Everyone refused to talk with us. The commander told the soldiers to rest and asked me to find the leader. He told me to ask the village leader if his village needed help.

'The only help we want from the foreign troops is for them to stop dropping bombs upon our villages. Two or three Taliban fire at the foreign troops, they hide themselves in our villages, and aircraft drop bombs and kill our men, women and children and we can do nothing; if we protest against them they accuse us of being Taliban,' said the village leader. I asked why most of the villages were lifeless. 'Weren't you here when thousands of *Amerikayan* stormed Garmsir and clashed with the Taliban?' the village leader asked me. 'There was a terrible war between the Taliban and the Americans and nobody could live in their villages so everyone fled to the desert where most are now living,' said the man.

Later another man brought three kids – two boys and a girl – who were injured. He said they had been injured when they were playing with explosives. The villager showed us many mortar rounds and other explosives that failed to explode during the war. Every day Afghans were killed by the old Soviet mines as well as US and NATO explosives and Taliban IEDs. For the time we stayed in the village, I was asked one question frequently: Why do the Americans keep bombing us? It was sad to see that they thought that only Americans invaded their country. Most did not know in Helmand that America brought tens of other countries to help dominate Afghanistan. For people in Helmand, all foreign troops were Americans. However, I had come to realise why those people fled to Kabul and chose to die by starvation and the cold weather. The war between the Taliban and the US and British troops had devastated everything there. Helpless people's villages were a battleground. The Taliban buried IEDs in the roads that Afghans used daily. The Taliban, US and British troops used villages for cover during fighting. Bombs were dropped on villages and helpless people were killed.

The US marines and British troops offered to pay compensation for the villages, houses and mosques they had bombed. But the Afghans needed to prove their houses had been destroyed first. They had to provide documents to prove that they owned the houses, provide several pictures of their houses, and bring a letter from the Garmsir governor to confirm the house belonged to them. What the British forces demanded was impossible for most. Cameras did not exist in Garmsir, in fact, few people knew what a camera was. Very few people had paper proof of their compounds and land, because they were not familiar with governmental systems and never had a decent central government in Helmand, and even when they had it in the past it was not popular amongst people. Providing a letter from the Garmsir governor was not possible, because the governor demanded bribe for writing the letter. However, the very few people who successfully provided all the documents that the British army needed received $300, $400 or sometimes $500, which was not enough money to build a house with. People argued that after all the destruction inflicted upon them, they were given an amount of money they couldn't even build a hut with.

The British officer always gave them one answer, 'We are not paying for the whole damage we have caused; we can give you a little money to help you with the re-building of your compound.'

People asked for compensation for relatives who had been killed either by the US or British troops. But the troops wanted proof and the only proof they had was fresh graves, and that was invalid for the US and the British. Hundreds of people sat under the burning sun from early in the morning until late afternoon in the hope of getting compensation for their ruined houses, to rebuild them, but most couldn't get anything.

Afghans' living state in Helmand Province was much worse than for the people in Kabul. Their life was completely ruined by the 'War on Terror'. The people who were being punished were extremely poor people whose lives had been destroyed in decades of war and had nothing to do with terrorism. For several years they lived with US and NATO bombs and yet did not know why

US and NATO troops came into their country in the first place. Poor villagers knew nothing about the rest of the world apart from their own small villages. They knew nothing about Osama Bin Laden, Al Qaeda and 9/11. An average Helmandi men barely travelled a few miles from his village at any stage in his whole life. The poor women barely walked a few yards from their own compound in their entire lifetime. Poor women were utterly unaware of the outside world.

The US, the British and the Taliban were not the only ones that turned the lives of poor Helmandis into hell; Afghan police and government officials were as much of a nightmare. A great number of police in Helmand were addicted to heroin and they robbed people in order to buy it for themselves. Police wages were very low. One day I went with the British to visit the police headquarters. It was alarming to see the state of the police. Most of the police soldiers were shrunken by the heroin they were taking. Most did not have a uniform and the few who had were very filthy. Their teeth were badly damaged and it seemed their AK-47s were too heavy for them to carry. Two types of people were joining the Afghan police. One, who was landless and jobless and could not feed his family; second were those who were heroin addicts. Both would rob helpless people everywhere. They broke into houses and stole whatever they found useful. They stopped the drivers and cyclists in the roads and robbed them. Anyone who tried to resist was tortured. Each time I went out on patrol poor Afghans cried out that the police force was turning their lives into hell. One of the reasons poor Afghans wanted the Taliban was to stop police coming into their villages. Afghan government officials were taking bribes too and became rich by exploiting helpless farmers. No government organisation provided service to the people without demanding a bribe.

A month elapsed but I witnessed no war. Everything seemed peaceful and Afghans who fled into the deserts during the US operation returned to war-torn villages and began to rebuild their bombed houses. I heard no bombs or rockets, but I did hear bullets. That was the British and US troops who fired at the Afghan drivers and cyclists who drove too close to the US and British vehicles. Regularly they fired at these people and sometimes they killed them.

Some months after my arrival, the British were tasked to go to the Nawa district of Helmand Province and clear the Taliban. It was the corn season and cornfields had given a good sanctuary for the Taliban. Strong British soldiers embarked in heavily armoured Mastiff vehicles at midnight and drove towards Nawa. It took several hours and all the soldiers were anxious, as they knew they would fight the Taliban. I was afraid and did not know what would happen to me. Would I get killed? Would my family receive my body? At last we reached Nawa district, early in the morning. Quickly we began our patrol in the cornfields and everybody was very vigilant, anticipating when the Taliban would start fighting. I listened to the I-com, picked up conversations and passed messages on to the patrol commander.

We walked for hours under the burning sun, but noticed no Taliban activity. It was midday when we walked into a garden; the poor gardener was asleep beneath the shadow of a pomegranate tree. The patrol commander told me to wake him. I tapped him and as he opened his eyes, he was shocked to see peculiar looking people standing above him with guns in their hands. I tried to assure him that we were not there to harm him, but the blood drained from his face anyway. We spent the rest of the day wandering in cornfields, but the Taliban did not fire at us. At the end of the day, we were all exhausted.

Early the next morning we went into the cornfields again and came across civilians who did not want to talk with us. Wherever we went civilians glared and refused to shake hands with me let alone the British. When the patrol commander asked them about the Taliban, they said they knew nothing. At midday we rested close to a village when I unexpectedly heard the frightful sound of RPG rockets and bullets. We came under Taliban fire from several directions. Throughout my life I had bombs, rockets, bullets, missiles and all other sorts of destructive weapons landing around me, but they were not fired at me. For the first time ever someone was firing at me and wanted to kill me. I wanted to provide bread for my siblings and parents, but I had become an enemy of the people who were anti-US and NATO.

British troops knew what to do while they were under fire, but I was neither a soldier nor had I been trained. I took refuge behind a wall while the British soldiers fired in different directions at the same time as retreating. Poor villagers were frightened and took refuge in their compounds. I did not know where to hide myself. My body shuddered like leaves in the wind and my mouth was as dry as the Helmand desert. I was frightened. I thought I was going to meet death at the very beginning of my perilous job. Bullets passed over my head one after another and I did not know which one would take my life. The Taliban stopped firing for a brief moment, so we escaped towards a village. We were walking beside a mud wall when out of the blue a Talib fighter on his motorcycle came face-to-face with us. The patrol commander shot him several times but, surprisingly, he escaped into the cornfields. The Talib's motorbike caught fire. The commander took his AK-47 and mobile phone and we all took cover while the motorbike burned before us. Soon we came under heavy fire again but this time I found nowhere to hide. I saw the fear in the eyes and faces of the soldiers. They were as frightened as I was. Soldiers fired from all around back at the Taliban with all the weapons they had with them. A soldier who held a machine-gun was crying as he looked for cover. Bullets buzzed above and around me and clouds of explosions rose up. Jet aircraft roared above our heads and its nasty sound hurt my ears. I was so regretful of coming into Helmand Province. I just wanted to have a job and help my miserable family. I wanted to desert Helmand if possible and never return. I did not want to die in Helmand. The rain of bullets did not stop buzzing around me. An aircraft came and tried to drop bombs upon the Taliban, but it failed, because it did not know where the Taliban were. A man with his son was caught in the crossfire. The man was frightful and his son was screaming. I called both of them to come and take refuge beside me. I tried to assure them not to be worried, but the man knew that I was far more frightened than him. I could hear children and women crying in their houses as the British and Taliban exchanged bullets and rockets. We retreated towards our base and, luckily, the Taliban did not dare to chase us. For several days I had earache. Sometimes I thought of leaving the job because I did not want to die or get injured, but there was no other job for me to do. I had to play with death in order to earn money.

One evening a US marine shot a driver who failed to notice the US convoy. The man was with his son, but luckily his son was not shot although the man was. They brought the man into the base for treatment and the next morning took him to Camp Bastion. But he died in hospital and the next day they brought his body back. The US marines gave his family 70,000 Afghani in compensation – 70,000 Afghani was $1,700. The life of an Afghan was worth $1,700! The way they dealt with the dead body of that poor man was shocking. It seemed they did not consider him as a human being. How would the poor man's family survive in this world without him? The US marines did not take the life of just one man, they also took the little food he earned for his hungry children and wife. What lives would those children and their mother have without the poor man the marine shot dead?

Soon after this tragedy another event shocked me. A few children found a Taliban IED somewhere in their village, which the Taliban buried for the US and British troops. The children found it and took it home with them. Their poor mother and her children gathered around the IED to see what had been found. As they tried to open the IED to see what was inside, it exploded. There was no hospital in Garmsir but a ruined one, which had no equipment. Villagers brought them into our base in the hope the British could save some of the badly wounded family. My heart cried watching the poor peasant weep over his torn up children and wife, begging the British to save his family. But it seemed like already a few of his children had left this world. The British sent the ones who were alive to Camp Bastion for treatment. I could not get those poor children and women out of my mind.

After a while the British had to go to Nawa district and drive the Taliban out of there yet again. Before I left I handed my salary to an interpreter to pass to my family in case I was killed this time. Again, at midnight we embarked in the armoured vehicles and drove towards Nawa. We drove through the wild deserts of Helmand Province for several hours. Everyone was filled with fear. The Taliban buried IEDs in the desert and drivers had to be careful where to drive. We first went to Lashkar Gah, centre of Helmand Province, and there we joined a battalion of the Afghan Army and their British advisers. I met the Afghan Army advisers' interpreter. We sat and made small talk. He said he would leave his job as it was very perilous, and look for a new one in Kabul. I wished him good luck. Our convoy left Lashkar Gah, and after some time we reached Nawa district. My I-com picked up a Taliban conversation, it seemed they had already set an ambush for us. I let the commander know what was happening. Soon we came under fire from the cornfields. The British and Afghan troops disembarked and returned fire. The bullets and RPGs came from all directions towards us. I did not know where to walk or where to hide myself, because the Taliban buried IEDs everywhere. What could I do but shudder while the bullets flew above my head?

After almost an hour of intense fighting, the commander asked everyone to climb into the armoured vehicles and take cover there. The British troops escaped the Taliban trap. The vehicles were heading towards the Nawa centre when someone told our commander on the radio that an interpreter had been shot. His body remained behind and he must go and pick the body up. We drove back into the Taliban trap and bullets came from all sides towards our armoured vehicle. The commander and a soldier went and collected the body of the interpreter. I grabbed the interpreter's leg and pulled him inside the vehicle. It was the man I had met in Lashkar Gah only a few hours before. He had been shot in the eye. The commander was a good guy and made sure I was not afraid of the dead body. He took some paper and covered the dead interpreter's blood-stained face. He was unaware that I had spent all my life seeing such tragedies. Anyway, the helicopter came and picked up the dead body as well as the injured Afghan and British troops and flew away. The next day we went to fight the Taliban again, but we spent most of our time trying to unearth their IEDs.

Every day seemed the last day of my life. I was frightful of IEDs and did not want to be torn apart because I knew how badly they destroyed the human body. I did not know when the wind of the dead would turn off the candlelight of my life. Each morning when I woke up, I first asked myself, 'Is this my last morning?'

This was my new job, wandering about in the IED and ambush fields of the Taliban all the time, observing Taliban bullets and RPGs buzzing above my head or landing around me. Watching soldiers being blown up by IEDs. Children and their small dreams die. Apache helicopters and aircrafts dropped bombs each time we came under fire and Afghan houses were reduced to ruins. I humiliated poor Afghans by forcing them to expose their bodies to make sure they were not suicide bombers. Not all of them were willing to expose their bodies to me. Some argued for several minutes and refused. Sometimes they diverted their routes in order to avoid us. Children were scared of the British and as we walked into their villages they screamed. Sometimes British troops kicked the already broken doors of poor Hilmandis and entered their houses, their women cried and begged me not to let the British harm them. I always assured them that nobody would harm them. Men begged me to teach the British troops our culture so that they would not abuse them constantly.

The British forces carried out innumerable large scale, perilous and destructive operations against the Taliban. However, most had no impact on them. During each operation the Taliban resisted as long as they could, and when they were unable to resist they merely abandoned the area and moved on to another village or district. Most of the operations were futile and did not weaken the Taliban momentum. The roots of the Taliban were in Pakistan. Their weapons and finance came from there and their leaders were hiding in Pakistan. So, it was pointless fighting them in ruined villages.

Wandering in the IED and Death Zones

After a while, the US marines left Garmsir district with, the British troops and went somewhere else to crush the Taliban, as well as devastate civilians and their livelihoods. The marines spent several months fighting the Taliban and kept them out of most parts of Garmsir. During this time some twenty or more young Americans and a large number of civilians lost their lives. As the US marines pulled out the Taliban moved in, and there were not enough British troops on the ground to stop them. All the killing, dying, destruction and the enormous amount of money that the US marines spent to oust the Taliban from Garmsir was futile, because they were back as soon as the US forces left. This was the case with the Soviet troops in Afghanistan for almost a decade. They had terrorised poor Afghans and killed large numbers of civilians, destroyed villages and farms in order to keep the Mujahidin out. They were as successful as NATO and the US troops were. They could keep the Mujahidin out of a village as long as they stayed in the village. During this time, either Mujahidin put their weapons down and became civilians or they fled and waited for an opportunity to strike at the Soviet troops. And if they failed to strike, they waited until the Soviets troops left the place, then they came back. Today, western politicians and their media boast to the world that they are defeating the Taliban, but in fact the reality is the reverse. Day after day the Taliban become stronger and their popularity amongst the rural Pashtun ethnicity is growing. Today the poor Pashtun peasant sees the Taliban era as a golden era.

After the US marines left Garmsir we fought the Taliban almost every day. My fear was fading and I was not as afraid of death as I was at first. The sound of bombs, bullets and rockets did not frighten me any more. In fact, I was more afraid of the sound of a bomb explosion when it only fell upon villages and houses. Half of my heart cheered alongside the British troops when bombs killed the people who fired at us, and half of my heart cried for the civilians who were crushed under the bombs. Soldiers came from the United

Kingdom, fought against the Taliban and became good friends of mine, but most of them impatiently waited to go back home and to never come into this brutal, harsh, burning warzone ever again. But I was different. War and dying zones were my home and I had never tasted life in a warless place. People of my age in Afghanistan did not know what peace really was. Only elderly people remembered peace, a long time ago.

Poor soldiers newly deployed to Helmand Province suffered in the beginning because they were unfamiliar with the tough climate and terrain. Large numbers of soldiers were my age and some even younger. At first they struggled, patrolling in the IED and ambush fields of the Taliban under the burning sun for hours. They were fearful at first, but later they would get used to it.

Most of the soldiers were very friendly and there was a strong bond of friendship between us. They treated me well and made me feel as though I was part of the team. We were together in the IED and ambush fields. When a soldier got killed or wounded we all felt the pain. Most commanders treated me with respect. They were very grateful of my work. Most of them used to say that 'without your contribution our task would have been impossible and without the information you give us many of us would have been dead or injured'.

Helmand weather was boiling in the summer and I was obliged to wander in the fields and villages alongside the British all day long and sometimes my legs refused to carry me. Walking in the rough fields and irrigation ditches was not an easy task. I did not mind all the hardships, but my heart hurt when I observed the oceans of bitter hatred in the eyes of Afghans for myself. When I walked in villages, roads, or streets most of the Afghans refused to shake hands or talk with me. I looked like a collaborator and traitor through their eyes. There was a local bazaar just outside FOB Dehli and each time I went out on patrol, shopkeepers and shoppers glared at me. Sometimes they cursed our patrol. Most refused to talk with us, unless they had to. There were a few questions that I came across most: Why do they bomb our villages? When will foreign troops leave Afghanistan? Why do you keep searching us this way? Why don't you guys stop police from robbing us?'

Most hungry, barefoot and tattered-clothed boys threw stones at our patrol. Their dogs would bark and attempt to bite us; when we walked into the villages, so many dogs were shot dead by the troops and the poor dog-owners sat in tears. Many British troops asked me, 'Why do the local people hate us so much?' I did not know the reason behind why they hated the NATO and US troops. But, today I do. It was because those children who threw curses and stones at the British saw America alongside her tens of allies invade their war-rugged country. Their fathers saw the Soviet Union invade their country and turn their world upside down. Their grandfathers saw the British Empire overrun their country. All these invaders brought nothing but death, destruction and misery.

After some time Ghurkha soldiers came. At first I did not know them, but soon I realised that they were from Nepal and had been fighting for the British Army for a very long time. They could speak Urdu and could interact with subjugated Afghans, as a lot of Afghans could speak Urdu. Most Afghans had learned Urdu in Pakistan while they were living in the refugee camps. Ghurkha soldiers were as much frightened at first when they came under attack, as I was. However, the Taliban regularly attacked patrol bases, so the 5scot regiment's A company commander decided to push the Taliban away. We left FOB Dehli at midnight and in the morning the operation began.

The Taliban were planning an ambush, I heard it on I-com so I let the commander know. We walked into the cornfields and everyone was vigilant. Poor Afghans fled their houses as soon as they saw us, since they knew that their villages would soon become a battleground. Some men begged me to tell the commander to go away from their village and from their houses so that they would not get obliterated during the battle. It was painful watching hungry children running after their mothers while they evacuated their homes. The sniper in our patrol spotted one or two Taliban and shot one of them. He thought he'd injured the Talib so we went to capture him. Capturing a man with a weapon in his hand was not an easy task. The patrol commander was a great man, I think his name was George. He always looked after me and made sure I did not panic. He told me to walk with him because should we come across the injured Talib he might need me. My whole body trembled. I knew there was a great chance that the Talib might fire at us instead of surrender. We walked into the irrigation ditches and were soaked in the water. As we reached the spot where the Talib was shot we found nothing but a blood trail that led to a knoll the British had built in the nineteenth century to defend themselves against local Afghans. When we reached the top of the knoll, the commander realised it was a trap. As we tried to find cover for ourselves, we came under fierce fire from several directions and bullets and RPGs flew above our heads, and there was nowhere for me to hide. There was a soldier beside me who was crying. Commander George sent someone to make sure I was OK. I had crouched and concealed my head between my legs, not wanting to get shot in the face. I remained like that and blocked my ears. For a while the British and the Taliban exchanged bullets and rockets and miraculously nobody was hurt on our side. The fierce fighting subsided, but the Taliban remained in position. The commander decided to stay in the knoll until the next morning and continue pushing the Taliban away from the area. So we remained there all night. Our clothes were soaked and as the temperature dropped we all began to shiver. I could not sleep while the bitter cold stung my body and my teeth chattered. I found a plastic bag and concealed my head inside it hoping it would save me from the dry chill of Helmand winter, but it did not work. I closed my eyes tight for a while and hoped the darkness would be gone when I opened them again, but still I was lying beneath the shiny stars. I stared at the moon for hours and remembered those hungry nights when my siblings and I demanded food from our mother with tearful eyes.

Soon, 5scot A Company was about to leave Helmand Province and were impatient. A soldier who was a good friend of mine asked me how long I would remain in the warzone. 'I don't know,' I said.

'Try to leave before you get killed,' said the soldier. The problem was that I did not know when I would be killed. I wanted to run away from that brutally harsh warzone, but did not know where to run since my whole world was a battlefield.

One evening a girl aged about thirteen came to our base, which was odd as females were not authorised to leave their homes. She said her parents were forcing her into marriage with someone against her will. British troops were entangled in a sensitive issue. The next day the tribal leaders came into our base for a (*Shura*) meeting. They took the girl back after they put up their land as guarantee that they would not harm her. But after some months the news came that they had killed her.

My life went by in one battlefield after another. One day I was deployed to a patrol base (PB) between the Taliban and the British troops. Local people were highly pro-Taliban, did not like the British, and bitterly hated the police. Before my arrival British troops and the Taliban clashed and the troops fired javelin missiles and heavy machine-guns and destroyed local people's livelihoods, but luckily no one was killed or injured. Village elders came to the base to protest against the destruction that had been inflicted upon them. A major who was a courteous man and just arrived in Afghanistan invited all the elderly men inside the base for a *Shura*. It was extraordinary to observe those elderly people quarrelling with one another in order to get an opportunity to express their anger before the others. Some said the British had killed their cattle, some said they had ruined their houses, and some said they nearly killed their children. At the end of the *Shura* they told the commander that they had been left with no alternative but to abandon their villages, houses, fields and farms and take refuge in Pakistan or Kabul or elsewhere. But the British assured them it would not happen again if they kept the Taliban out of their villages.

A poor elderly man said, 'We can't keep the Taliban out of our villages just like we cannot keep you, since you both have weapons.'

Inside the patrol base there were Afghan border police living with us. Almost all of them were opium addicts and would lift almost anything they considered useful. I had to keep an eye on my earnings at all times. I wandered in fields, ditches and villages from early in the morning until midday, and then after one or two hours I again left the base until the sun disappeared, every day. I could not keep my money with me because if I was shot there was a great chance that I would never see it again; besides that it would get wet as we usually walked in irrigation ditches to dodge IEDs. Leaving my wages at the base was very unsafe, since police regularly checked my belongings. I was always anxious for my earnings.

One time we were ambushed by the Taliban. I leapt to the ground and my left elbow crashed against a rock. It was very painful. I thought it will recover after a while. However, to this day it remains so.

Sometimes we would circle a village and go from house to house, frightening men, women and children as we unexpectedly entered their houses and made a mess of their clothes when we searched for weapons. The poor village elders quarrelled with me and blamed me for not stopping the British troops entering their houses. They told me, 'You are Afghan and you know about our pattern of life. You know that we don't want *Amerikayan* to break into our houses and see the faces of our women and make a mess. You tell them about our culture and customs and tell them we do not like it when they break our doors and search our houses.' Sometimes, poor people begged me to stop the troops from entering their compounds. Once when we ran into a compound rather abruptly to search, the women and children screamed at the top of their voices. I assured them that we would not harm them, but they were so afraid that they did not listen. I had sweets in my pocket and gave them to the children. I hated house searching; it hurt my heart each time we terrorised women and children.

The British troop commander would occasionally tell me to ask the elderly men who they supported: Taliban or current Afghan government and foreign forces. The answer everywhere was almost the same, 'We support no one and want none of you. We want you all to leave us alone. We are in peace without government, Taliban and *Amerikayan*. They all harm us.'

At midnight once when I was sleeping deeply, British troops unexpectedly fired mortars at the Taliban and the ugly sound frightened me out of my peaceful sleep. I had to wake early in the morning and accompany the troops and wander with them in the villages, fields and ditches all day long; sometimes we came under the Taliban fire and sometimes came across their IEDs. One day we had been out for several hours and we were shattered. The British troops rested in a village. Everyone leaned against the walls. I was exhausted.

A man whose clothes and turban were ragged who had a muddled beard and seemed strange approached us. The commander told me to ask him to expose his body before he came any closer. He first argued with the commander to leave the village, because he knew that it would be destroyed if fighting broke out between the Taliban and us. He kept telling me to tell the commander to leave, but we were weary so we ignored him. Then he walked towards a soldier and asked him to leave his village. The soldier told me, 'Tell this crazy man to go away.'

Another man shouted at the man who wanted us to leave, 'What is going on?'

'Again these crazies come for fighting and I am trying to tell them to leave but they are ignoring me,' said the odd man. We seemed crazy through the eyes of that man and he seemed crazy to us.

Winter arrived in Helmand Province and the Taliban's ambushes diminished. The Taliban could only fight US and NATO troops in the summer when the crops were high so that they could take refuge from aircraft. During the winter, the Taliban did not dare to ambush us, but their IEDs increased. They buried IEDs in the ditches, fields, villages, roads, streets, deserts and wherever they considered the foreigners might walk.

One night a bunch of Taliban were were burying their IEDs when the British spotted them. An aircraft came and dropped a huge bomb upon them. One survived, and according to the British troops, hid himself in a house. So the British grabbed me, took me with them and we went to catch the wounded Talib. As we reached the compound where the British troops believed he concealed himself, they kicked the old and broken door in and stormed in. They screamed and pointed their guns at women and children who were asleep. The children and women were all terrified. The troops forced everyone out of the rooms and made them sit in the cold weather outside. I took my helmet off and tried to reassure them that we were not there to harm them. The troops searched the house but the wounded Talib was nowhere to be found. The commander shouted at the females to tell him where the Talib had secreted himself. They swore to God that they had seen no man, their husbands were in the Afghan police and they were not pro-Taliban. The British failed to find the Talib, but they turned another entire village against them.

In midwinter, I had been sent to FOB Dwyer, which was situated in the desert in Garmsir and was a small base at the time, but later it became one of the largest US military bases in Helmand Province with its own airfield. My job was to accompany a mobile team of reconnaissance behind the enemy line. We drove in the wild deserts for several days. We rarely came across any human being. Sometimes, we drove right into the heartland of the Taliban, frightened them, occasionally clashed with them for brief moments, and then drove out again. Sometimes, we came across crowds of Afghans who were on a long journey from the north and central parts of Afghanistan and were attempting to enter Iran or Pakistan illegally in order to work there. My heart bled when I watched the state of those Afghans. They walked in the deserts for weeks with great difficulty. Their country was a warzone, there was no job for them and they had no choice but to start a journey full of suffering and menace in order to get out of their war-tattered country to find bread for their families. Each time I came across these tormented Afghans they had no food or water. I gave them my food and water and wish them a safe journey.

One night I was in FOB Dwyer watching TV. It was President Barack Obama's inauguration. I saw him speak before the crowds. I could barely pick up a few words from his inaugural speech. He seemed a good man. People around the world were happy that he would stop the madness that the US had started around the world under the George W. Bush administration. The top one percent of the United States population, the bankers and the corporations who rule the United States sent him with the 'Change' slogan, but he turned out to be even more aggressive than George W. Bush. Perhaps he is the only president in the face of the earth who has an assassination list and sends unmanned aircrafts around the world to assassinate human beings with a trial. The film director and historian Oliver Stone said, 'Under the disguise of a sheep's clothing he has been a wolf.' After becoming president he expanded the war in Afghanistan. He expanded the US military bases' web around the world, too. He increased the drone attacks in several countries and murdered large number of civilians in these attacks. And he is preparing for a war with Iran. His slogan was change, but he kept pursuing the George W Bush's foreign policy. He expanded the war in Afghanistan by sending 30,000 more US marines, which is perhaps the most destructive and aggressive force on the face of the earth. According to the UN body monitoring the rights of children in the last four years (since Obama came into power) US forces have killed hundreds of children in Afghanisan.[41] To the victims of imperial America's surprise Obama was awarded the Nobel Peace Prize for extending the war in Afghanistan, increasing drone attacks and expanding US military bases around the world.

An Afghan who stood over the dead bodies of twelve innocent people massacred by US Special Forces in a night raid on a single house said to Aljazeera news, 'Why are they giving Obama a peace medal? He claims to bring security for us, but he only brings death. Death to him.'

Another lady who lost everything when a US bomb fell on her village said, 'He doesn't deserve the award, he bombed us and he left us with nothing, not even a home.'[42]

I wandered with the British reconnaissance team in the tough deserts of Helmand Province and sometimes came under Taliban fire when we drove into their area of influence. Nobody was killed in the clashes, but one day one of the armoured vehicles drove over an IED somewhere in the desert and it killed, I think, one soldier instantly, and fatally wounded two others. I was scared of nothing as much as I was scared of IEDs. Those who were blown up by IEDs and died were the lucky ones. I did not want to get blown up by an IED, but I hoped that if I were, I would never open my eyes again.

I wanted to see my parents while I was OK. One night I flew back to Kabul, it was almost dawn when I arrived home. What a moment of joy and happiness it was. My family surrounded me and happy tears flowed from the eyes of my mother. My little brother and sister clung to my legs and asked me what I had brought for them. Our old house shone with happiness. My happiness was very brief, everything altered as soon as my youngest cousin, Najiba, stepped into our room. She had grown up without the love of her mother. By now, Merza Kaka had married a young rural girl who was under twenty years old.

Kabul had deteriorated much during the seven months I was in Helmand Province. It became the detonating ground for suicide bombers. There were more armed men in the streets and roads than there were civilians. Many private security companies operated in the city and all around Afghanistan outside any law, and some of these companies committed terrible crimes without being held responsible. By now the corrupt officials in the Afghan government and parliament had large amounts of money in numerous banks and they had several villas and gardens in several parts of the country. I walked into Kabul city with my father one day to buy food. Little children with tearful eyes as usual clung to people's clothes and begged. Women under the burqa surrounded by their children, cried out for a loaf of bread, and disabled men lay in the dirt and held their hands in the air in the hope someone would put money into them. Countless Afghans had been ejected from Iran, but their country was still burning in the fires of an unjust and immoral war. Some were starving to a slow death. Some had no choice but to sit in the streets and beg. One could see the pain of these endless wars in people's weary faces. All gateways of hope and optimism were closed before helpless Afghans who lived in the warzones for so long. A corrupt government eats their flesh and drinks their blood and NATO and US troops were slaughtering them for over a decade. And the Taliban was butchering them with their deadly suicide bombers and IEDs on a daily basis and filled the hearts of Afghans with fear and terror. Where could Afghans take refuge? Neighbouring countries were filled with refugees and they did not want any more.

My father wanted to know about my job. He said if it was perilous then I must not continue. But, I could tell him nothing but lie. 'If we have survived war, poverty, disease and other hardships of life so far then we might survive without you having to put your life at risk. And I might not forgive myself if you die in the struggle for providing food for your family,' he said. As I walked alongside him I noticed something very extraordinary: I had grown as tall as him. I was no longer a little boy. How did this happen that I failed to notice it? I still behaved like a child. I remembered every moment of my childhood, as if I was a child an hour ago.

I had brought a good deal of money from the IED-strewn death fields of Helmand Province. Enough for my mother's treatment, and to stop the hungry stomachs of my siblings. I spent twenty happy days with them all and then it was time for me to fly back to Helmand and play with death again. I was not certain whether I would see my family ever again since the state of security was deteriorating. So, I secretly let Tariq know where to collect my body if I was killed and begged him not to tell anyone in our family where I was working.

Struggling to Extinguish the Flames of War

Winter was over and it was fighting season once more. Again I was with the British troops in villages and fields, again poor Afghans glared and sometimes threw curses at us. Again we came across Taliban IEDs and ambushes. But I was experiencing something very wicked. I was enjoying war like some soldiers do. Each time we clashed with the Taliban I was thrilled and became rather indifferent towards the horrors and tragedies. The day we did not clash with the Taliban was a dull and boring day for me and for some soldiers. Now I had the courage to look death in the eyes.

Poppy harvest time came and it was exciting to walk in the poppy fields alongside the British troops and eat poppy seeds. It reminded me of my childhood, when I was in Khugyani. Some of the British were scared of poppy seeds and did not dare eat them; they thought it was opium. I encouraged them to eat poppy seeds, but most were too scared. Ghurkha soldiers loved them and ate them too, each time we went on patrol.

Eradication of Afghan opium was one of the main reasons for Britain to invade Afghanistan. In 2001 when Tony Blair was campaigning for the invasion and when opium production was at its lowest, he said,

> 'The arms the Taliban are buying today are paid for by the lives of young British people buying their drugs on British streets. This is another part of their regime we seek to destroy.'[43]

No effective measures have been put in place by the American, British or other countries to reduce opium production in Afghanistan. Sometimes they blame the Taliban for protecting opium and sometimes they say the reason they are not trying to eradicate opium is they don't want to alienate Afghan farmers. You alienate people when you occupy their countries and your soldiers walk with guns in their villages and streets and destroy their livelihoods. How can I believe in this ficticious and never ending War on Terror when they allow the real terror, Afghan opium, to thrive and ruin the lives of millions of human beings all over the world? The former deputy chief of the general staff of the armed forces of the Soviet Union says that drug trafficking in Afghanistan brings the US $50 billion a year, which fully covers the expenses of keeping their troops in Afghanistan.[44]

One day I was in FOB Delhi when the Afghan and British foreign ministers, along with the British ambassador and Afghan generals, paid a visit to Garmsir. I had been asked to stand beside the Afghan Army general and interpret while he briefed Doctor Rangin Spanta (Afghan foreign minister), David Miliband (British foreign minister) and other officials. I made loads of mistakes during the interpretation and was awfully embarrassed. I behaved very humbly before the foreign ministers. Both foreign ministers visited the Garmsir governor, but I realised Doctor Rangin Spanta was not happy with the progress of the British troops in Helmand Province. British ambassador Sir Sherard Cowper-Coles could speak one of the Afghan official languages, although I am not certain whether it was Dari or Pashtu; nevertheless, he seemed a nice guy and we had a chat inside the heavily armoured vehicle while we were on the way to the centre. After a brief conversation with the district governor and then lunch both foreign ministers visited the district bazaar and looked around before flying away again.

One day a tearful peasant was carrying his blood-covered son. As they entered FOB Dehli we could see he'd lost one of his legs. The child had stepped on an IED but, miraculously, was alive, though in a rather terrible state. The peasant was screaming. He begged me, the doctor and the medics to save his son. The doctor asked me to speak with the little boy in order to keep him conscious. I told the boy that everything would be fine soon because the British forces have got the best doctors and medical equipments. 'They will fix you overnight,' I said to him. The unfortunate boy stared at me and forced a smile. My war-weary eyes had not the power to contain my tears. I shed a tear for the wounded boy. I attempted to comfort the peasant who was screaming and begging us to save his son, but I did not have the nerve to look at this helpless father who was prepared to do anything to save his son. I began to lie to the peasant, telling him his son would be fine and even have his lost leg back. I told him the British forces have the equipment that would be able to fix his son's leg. When he heard that his son would have his leg back, he was so happy and thanked God, the British troops and me. The doctor asked me what I had told him that he suddenly became so happy. I told the doctor that I had lied to him that his son will have his lost leg back. , I thought my lie was helpful, but the doctor shouted at me to tell the truth that his son would never have his leg back and might not even survive.

I witnessed some of the most horrendous horrors of the War on Terror. It was wheat harvest time and the fighting between the British and the Taliban was fierce. Poor farmers worked under the burning sun all day long and even spent nights working. Sometimes they were bombed, because the troops thought they were burying IEDs. Nevertheless, farmers went through so much hardship for months and hoped one day they would reap a good harvest. But, in the warzones of Helmand Province after all the hardship and danger, farmers did not harvest their wheat crops. In the clash between the British and the Taliban, wheat fields caught fire and turned into ashes. It was heartbreaking to watch farmers rush towards their fields to stop the fire as bullets flew over their heads. Wheat crops were very dry and once fire reached them, it swallowed them in the blink of an eye and nothing could stop it. Hungry peasants watched helplessly as the fire destroyed their entire crop. After all that hard work under the burning sun and in the darkness of the night they would get nothing. They did not know what to do or who to hold responsible.

The words 'battlefield' and 'battleground' are very misleading terms. In the modern warfare, battlefield and battleground are where civilians live, work, eat and sleep. The modern battlefield is where innocent children play. The main victim of the modern warfare is the civilians.

When I saw people and their crops still devastated by war, I began to dislike war again. Indeed, I always abhorred war, because I knew from the day I was able to walk that war is that monster that devours men, women and children's lives. I knew that war was the God of destruction, violence, hatred, intolerance, ugliness, horror and poverty. But, this monster has a charming face: The more you get close to it the more you like it. Many young soldiers who spend a lot of time in the warzone become addicted to war. War intoxicated me with its charming face for a while, but the cries and the suffering of helpless human beings made me see the real face of war once again.

I wish those who observe or play war on the screen of their TV or hear on their radio, for one moment could see war through the eyes of the poor peasants of Afghanistan. If one really wants to know how ghastly war is, then one must see it through the eyes of those who are going through it. War is not what Hollywood movies portray and entertain people with. The reason that cunning and ignorant politicians in America and other western countries hide the true face of the war in Afghanistan and Iraq is that it is too ugly, and human beings would force them to end it. American journalist and author, Chris Hedges, who spent many years of his life in the warzones, said,

> 'We do not see war and images of war presented in films and novels nor the mythic narratives that the government and the press spins out for us. We never saw war in the televised images from Iraq, the war is always carefully packaged the way tobacco or liquor companies package their own poisons. The titillation is there but in doses we can digest. The reports give war a coherency and logic it never has in battle, we taste a bit of war's exhillirataion but are safe. War from Iraq is seen through the prism of US military and it comes complete with manufactured heroes and feel good stories about our own and an enemy that is always painted as barbaric and uncivilised. We can thrill the perversity of war even as we watch films or read books that are meant to denounce war. It's almost impossible to produce anti-war films and documentaries

that present images of battle: it's like trying to condemn pornography whilst showing erotic love scenes.'

Many farms were reduced to ashes at harvest time in the war between the Taliban and the British. The Taliban wanted the crops to burn, because that would turn more Afghans against the troops, although the British promised that they would pay compensation for the damage they had caused, if the peasants proved that their crops had been destroyed by British troops. Very few peasants received compensation. Most could not prove that their wheat crops had been destroyed. I would sit with a British officer and deal with those peasants whose crops had been burned. It was painful watching the weary faces in their ragged clothes and shoes walking for miles to our base to ask for compensation. It was more painful to watch those who did not receive any compensation.

30,000 fresh US marines arrived. Most had been deployed in the southern part of Afghanistan. Thousands of them were expected to come and take over Garmsir district from the British troops. So, the British troops conducted a few operations in north and south Garmsir to clear the Taliban before they handed Garmsir over. I walked besid the British day and night and sometimes came under heavy fire or across IEDs. Wherever we went villagers ran away and scattered in different directions to avoid the bombs, rockets and bullets. Aircraft sometimes dropped bombs upon the Taliban and sometimes flew low to scare them, but it terrorised women and children. I still vividly remember the tragedy of the last operation in north Garmsir. The British had the Afghan police with them searching houses. But police stole whatever they considered useful instead of searching. They broke the door of a house and stormed in. They pointed their guns at children and women and men, shot dead an unfortunate dog and shackled a man then dragged him out of his house. The poor elderly man who could barely walk followed the police and begged them to let go of his son, but the heartless police kicked him in the chest and the poor man fell to the ground, yet he stood again and begged the brutal drug addict police to leave his son alone. His children and grandchildren surrounded their dead dog and wept over it. I spent more than a year in Garmsir and wherever I went people cried out against the brutality of the police. The War on Terror did no good to any Afghan in the southern part of Afghanistan other than drug addicts and warlords. It was too easy for drug addicts to join the police and rob poor Afghans and torture them. What the western governments are doing to the Afghans is utterly inhumane. They have set a government over them which consists of people who committed terrible crimes against humanity, mafias, warlords, criminals and all sorts of incompetent and dangerous people and the sole reason they have hidden themselves in the shield of Afghan government is to fill their bags with money and build nice houses in Afghanistan, and invest their money in Dubai and elsewhere around the world at the expense of the suffering and misery of the Afghan nation. Yet, we see the western governments protecting them with their forces and taking billions of dollars out of the wealth of their nations and pouring it into the black-hole of Afghan government, and nobody knows where this money goes.

It was time for the British to evacuate Garmsir and go to a new district where there was no NATO or US presence, nor had there ever been. The district called Babaji was located in the heartland of Helmand Province and was one of the strongholds of the Taliban. I returned to Camp Bastion and waited for the British to prepare for the invasion of the Babaji district of Helmand Province. They were about to start a massive offensive against the Taliban, codenamed Operation Panther's Claw. I could see that this operation was not a simple one, since thousands of British, Afghan and Danish troops were organising themselves for it. I watched troops prepare for the operation and was excited by it. I was not sure whether this time death would play with me as it had been doing for all my life, or whether it would swallow the life out of me. After some days in Camp Bastion, it was time for me to leave with the British troops for the Babaji district. It was the height of the summer and the weather was scorching. The Taliban had already sown IEDs everywhere in the fields, villages and ditches for the British, Danish and Afghan. I did not have to walk in the fields and come under Taliban fire this time as I had been dispatched with a team whose job was to make sure no Taliban fled the Babaji district and no weapon reached the Taliban from outside. We set missiles and snipers on the edge of the desert and monitored the Babaji district from there. Thousands of troops stormed Babaji and aircraft hovered in the sky. Villagers were terrified and scattered in various directions. Soon the troops clashed with the Taliban, who showed strong resistance. I worked with a company of the Mercian regiment in Garmsir district and most of the soldiers were good friends of mine. Several of these soldiers with whom I worked in Garmsir were killed in Babaji in Operation Panther's Claw and I was extremely sad.

Poor civilians caught up in the war left everything behind, headed towards the desert and walked in the brutal heat under the burning sun with no water or food. We had to check them before we let them flee their villages to make sure the Taliban did not hide amongst them. It was heartbreaking, when the poor men begged us to give them water for their thirsty children. The commander could not give water away as he had just enough to keep his soldiers hydrated. Children with tearful eyes walked in the harsh deserts of Helmand Province with their shrunken stomachs and dry mouths. Seeing those children tailing their mothers reminded me of the day I was fleeing our village when I was only four years old. But, I did not walk under the burning sun and in the desert. Only lucky Afghans fled their villages. The unlucky ones were caught up in the fire and who knows how many of them were murdered. I had an I-com in my hand and sat alongside the British troops who monitored Babaji with their binoculars, and I watched the district all day, every day, being crushed.

Several young Afghan and British troops perished in the first week of the operation. Throughout that first week the fighting remained intense. I sat on the edge of the desert and watched the fighting, which started early in the morning and continued until evening. Dark clouds rose when bombs and rockets pounded Babaji. Fighting spread to almost every village and more people had to leave their homes. A woman and her family tried to flee her village and wanted to go somewhere through the desert. But, before she could get to the desert she had to cross the Helmand River. The poor woman drowned in the river in front of her husband and children. A few villagers came to bury her body a few yards from where we were stationed. Her husband came to tell us that he was burying his wife not an IED and that we should not bomb him. The commander felt sorry and expressed his condolences and said, 'If we knew that your wife was drowning, we would have come to save her.' Nevertheless, the intense war continued for several weeks. An interpreter who was a good friend of mine, who worked and lived with me for a year, had been drowned in the Helmand River while he was rinsing himself. The river swallowed his body for three days. The British troops thought that the Taliban might have captured him, but after three days his body re-appeared. Soon, another interpreter whom I met in FOB Price just a few days before the launch of Operation Panther's Claw stepped on an IED and was blown into pieces.

One night the British troops mortared everywhere and Apache helicopters hovered in the sky. For hours they bombed Babaji and I thought all the Taliban had perished. But when morning came it seemed like no Talib had been killed that night, even after all those widespread mortars. Several elderly men came to us and told us that the aircraft bombed fifty civilians to death while they were crossing the Helmand River to flee the war. They said several bodies of men, women and children had disappeared in the river. The commander knew nothing about the incident and told the men he would try to find out about it.

In the 07/07 appalling suicide attacks in London in 2005, fifty-two innocent humans perished at the hands of the UK's domestic terrorists. The British government until this day uses that to justify the immoral war thousands of miles away in a land that has been burning in the flames of the murderous empire's greed for the last three centuries. From the early nineteenth century until almost World War II the British Empire played a very negative role in Afghanistan. After World War II the British elites lost their empire, but not their imperialistic habits. In the 1980s the British government joined the United States and empowered religious fundamentalists in Afghanistan to fight against the Soviet troops. Ever since the Soviet Union's crash in Afghanistan they helped the US in their domination of Afghanistan and used every excuse to justify their aggression there, sending young boys to fight a war of domination of helpless people's land.

Operation Panther's claw dragged on for weeks, fighting remained intense until one morning I woke up and heard no bombs, bullets or rockets. The commander and a few other soldiers went searching for people who tried to flee their villages. But on that day nobody fled their village. A group of men told us that the Taliban had fled Babaji that night. It was extraordinary news. All the routes were blocked by the British during the operation and no ammunition could reach the Taliban, so they were left with no choice but to blend in amongst the civilians and leave the battleground. But that was not the end, the British, Afghan and Danish troops had to fight with their IEDs for several days to come. War-weary civilians returned to their ruined villages, houses and fields. They had to begin building their mud houses and mosques yet again.

Taliban fighters were playing a cat and mouse game with us. When the British and US troops defeated them in one village, they would simply move to another. If they were defeated there, they would move to the next one and would continue their fighting. Fighting the Taliban in the villages of Afghans is ineffective and makes no sense. Everybody knows that so long as the Taliban are being protected, given arms and money by the United States' ally, Pakistan, Taliban momentum cannot be destroyed.

Operation Panther's Claw came to an end and the British troops established several patrol bases to keep the Taliban out of the area. But soon the Taliban returned and to this day still fight the British in Babaji and so many people have perished. At the end of Operation Panther's Claw, I was shattered. I could no longer remain under the burning sun in the desert. I became ill, but luckily by drinking ten litres of water every day, and by taking a few pills that the medic had given me, I recovered. I stayed for so many months in Helmand Province and knew that my poor parents must have been deeply anxious for me. Yet again, I had survived the IEDs, bullets and RPGs of the Taliban, while some of my friends did not. Death yet again let me walk away. I had worked in the cruel warzones of Helmand for almost two years and I had survived.

The US and NATO presence only brought more destruction, pain and misery into the lives of long-tortured people. Their houses and villages and crops and they themselves were perpetually being shattered by the nasty and senseless war. By the passing of everyday anti-US and NATO sentiments increased amongst the people. More and more people took up weapons and fought the British and US troops in Helmand Province. The Taliban too stirred up the nationalistic and religious feelings of Afghans to fight the US and NATO troops. They reminded Afghans of their great-grandfathers and grandfathers who gallantly stood with empty hands against the powerful empires and forced them to march in the path of shameful defeat again and again. Afghans are exceptionally nationalistic and the Taliban are very aware of this fact. They consider their land as their mother and they are willing to sacrifice their lives to defend it.

Nevertheless, I have seen that this war never has been against any terrorism. If it was about terrorism then the real terrorism in Afghanistan is opium, which takes the lives of over 100,000 human beings each year across the globe, and the US and its allies have turned their blind eye towards this and allow it to flourish.

The Taliban are becoming powerful and gaining the support of local people in the Pashtun areas. They have been emboldened by the US and NATO withdrawl in 2014. The worst thing that can happen to the long-oppressed people of Afghanistan is to live under the cruel regime of the Taliban with their medieval ideology again, and I hope that time will never happen. One thing is very clear, luckily most Afghans don't want to live under their dark regime ever again. It is improbable for the Taliban to come back to power; however, it's very likely that they would increase instability in Afghanistan with the help of Pakistan for a very long time.

There are a few factors that make me pessimistic about the future of Afghanistan:

- The extreme unpopularity of the government, which is filled with mass-murderers amongst ordinary Afghans.
- Interference of neighbouring countries.
- Hostility amongst ethnic groups.
- Fragility of the Afghan security forces.
- Harbouring and supporting of the Taliban by the government of Pakistan and its intelligence service.
- The Taliban are becoming stronger and gaining the support of local people, namely the Pashtuns.
- The growing hatred for the US and NATO troops in Afghanistan, principally amongst Pashtuns.
- The fierce opposition of all neighbouring countries towards the long-term presence of the US military in Afghanistan.

Nevertheless, the end or cessation of the chaos and violence in Afghanistan is in the hands of the US and its allies; and they don't want it to end in the near future. The war in Afghanistan is like a tree whose branches are in Afghanistan but whose roots are in Pakistan. The United States and other western powers did not stop the Pakistani government and its secret service from supporting, funding and giving sanctuary to the Taliban and other terrorist groups. On the contrary, they have given it billions of dollars. So long as there is chaos and violence in Afghanistan, the US can justify its presence in Central Asia. The US and its allies have invested unimaginable amounts of money and resources in the last more than three decades in domination of the dreamland of the empires. The US has dominated this dreamland of the empires and it will not leave it any time soon. They will do everything they can to keep a foothold in Central Asia for an indefinite time. According to Russian historian Andrei Fursov, Central Asia is an important geopolitical zone from where China, India, Russia and Islamic world can be threatened, in this case those who control Central Asia can control the whole of Eurasia and possibly the world.

The United States president, Barack Obama said in his Cairo speech, 'Make no mistake, we do not want to keep our troops in Afghanistan. We seek no military bases there.' The ultimate objective of the US is a military base and a puppet regime in Afghansitan, not the destruction of the Taliban or Al Qaeda. Just recently Hamid Karzai announced that the United States wants to have nine military bases in Afghanistan after 2014.[45] In 2012, the US and its Afghan puppets signed a treaty called 'Enduring Strategic Partnership Agreement between the Islamic Republic of Afghanistan and the United States of America'. This treaty gives the right for the United States of America to have a presence in Afghanistan for another ten years. Recently the US declared Afghanistan as its major non-NATO ally. These US treaties with their Afghan puppets are nothing more than an attempt to hide the ugly face of its shameful domination of Afghanistan. The corrupt government in Afghanistan and its American and European masters tells us that the US permanent military bases are good for Afghanistan. They say that these bases will bring security into Afghanistan and put an end to the neighbouring interference in Afghanistan. Bringing security and prevent neighbouring countries' interference in Afghanistan is a fantasy. If they did not bring peace and stop neighbouring countries from destabilising Afghanistan in the last decade, how could they bring peace and stop the neighbouring intetrference in the future? The Pakistani government and its ISI have destabilised and taken countless lives in Afghanistan in the last twelve years, and the US and NATO have not stopped them.

The US permanent military bases are not in any way in the interest of oppressed Afghans; on the contrary it is against their interest. On the one hand the United States will do everything in its power to keep Afghanistan insecure, poor and dependant with a corrupt and oppressive Government in power, so as to justify its permanent military presence in Afghanistan. On the other hand extremists will use the US permanent military bases in Afghanistan as justification to continue their barbarity across Afghanistan for decades to come.

It has been over thirty years since the US first set fire to Afghanistan in 1979 and Afghans have been burning ever since. It turned Afghanistan into a trap and lured the Soviet Union into it. It empowered religious fundamentalists and handed the fate of helpless Afghans to them from the early 1990s to 2001. From 2001 until the present day helpless Afghans have lived under the bombs of the US in a state of constant terror. They have been killed, humiliated and terrorised ever since. For over thirty years the US and its allies have openly and covertly tormented, tyrannised and devastated helpless Afghans and no one knows when they will put an end to their barbarism and insanity and leave these helpless people alone. No nation on the face of the earth has been tormented and tortured and destroyed by the the United States for as much and for as long as the Afghans. May none of the imperialistic ambitions of the United States in Afghanistan be achieved.

Today Afghanistan remains a far-off and forgotten island of injustice and oppression. Today predatory imperialists have surrounded this forgotten island of injustice and oppression, playing their sadistic game of Imperialsm with its oppressed inhabitants. Many Asian, African, Latin American nations have torn away from the chains of Imperialism in the twentieth century and are breathing the air of freedom today, but helpless Afghans have remained shackled in the chains of imperialism in the twenty-first century.

To those who are locked in the cage of war and poverty in the forgotten island of injustice and oppression, I write 'don't despair'. To those who are caught in this macabre trap of sadist imperialists and without sin or felony are being killed, tortured and exploited, I write 'the morning of peace and justice will come one day'. To those hapless women who have become the main victims of this sadistic game, I write 'there is an end to this night of injustice and barbarity'. To those children whose playground has turned into an endless battleground, I write 'every evening the sun sets, it doen't mean it won't rise again'.

The End of My Tale

In late 2009, I fled Afghanistan for my life and I left my family behind in war-ragged Afghanistan. I have walked for months in perilous mountains, vallies, deserts and crossed seas and tried to reach Europe. I have been beaten and imprisoned by different human traffickers. I spent days and nights without food. I have almost drowned in stormy seas. Once I reached Europe, I soon realised that I was an illegal alien. I was homeless and lived on the streets of Europe for months in the freezing weather. In every country I went to, I was thrown away by the government. I was a fallen leaf from a tree that nobody cared for. Luckily, sometimes the police shackled me and threw me into a detention centre where I could have food and a warm bed for a while. When I was out of the detention centre, I spent the whole day, every day watching this new peculiar world and people. This new world was far different from the world I grew up in and these new people were far different from those around me throughout my life. For the first time I tasted peace. My eyes did not see any aggressive humans with weapons on them wandering in the streets and cities and causing trouble. Nobody stopped and asked them to expose their bodies. I saw no destructive aircraft bombarding people and scaring little children. My ears failed to pick up sounds of explosions. Streets and cities were not filled with humans who lost their legs, eyes, hands and other parts of their body in the way that war-torn Afghanistan was filled with disabled humans. Nobody detonated himself in the crowds. Women were as free as men. They walked alongside men and they worked alongside men, free of trouble. Cities were extraordinary, white, brown, yellow and black people, all were there. Watching and meeting humans with different colours, languages, customs and religions was the greatest thing that ever happened in my life. Sometimes, people suspected I was a troublemaker and tried to avoid me. Night was cold and the coldness stung me and did not allow me to take refuge in sleep. A few times, caring people picked me off the streets and let me sleep in their houses and allowed me to eat with them at their dining table.

Ordinary people in Europe were very kind and loving, and not as their leaders had portrayed when invading Afghanistan.

Nevertheless, I have come across thousands of helpless people from Afghanistan, Pakistan, Iraq and part of Middle East who fled their countries and living in appalling conditions in the streets of Europe. All these refugees I met in the streets talked about politics. Pakistani refugees criticised their incompetent politicians for the crisis in their country and accused them of being slaves and puppets of Western governments. Afghan and Iraqi refugees blamed the US and its allies for the destruction of their countries and their misery. We would spend days and nights in the streets of Europe complaining to each other about the dreadful living conditions in our countries. At night, I remained awake and shivered as snow buried me beneath it. Europe's snow reminded me of Afghanistan. I could still see the dark smoke of bombs, rockets, missiles, suicide bombers, IEDs rising towards the sky. I could still hear the cries of mournful mothers and fathers for their children who had been killed. I could still hear the cries of women for their husbands who lost their lives in this endless and appalling war. I could still see the dark clouds of war, violence, poverty, sorrow and misery over Afghanistan. I could still see oppressed Afghans sitting in the dark and neverending night of war, misery and poverty waiting for the morning of peace to come. It has been over three decades since peace forsook Afghanistan and yet it refuses to come back.

My war-weary heart cried for Afghanistan and wanted me to take it back there. We both already missed everything and did not know what to do in this highly complex and mechanical world. After months of hardship, sorrow and agony, I have settled down in the United Kingdom. I have reached a place in this journey of life where all excitement and adventure vanished. Life has become tasteless, empty, dull and boring.

I had known all sorts of pain but the pain of loneliness. In fact I did not even know what loneliness was. Now was the time to live with it. Spending every second of my life with loneliness melts my bones beneath my skin. It is so painful living with loneliness. There is nowhere to hide from it, wherever I go it is there with me like my shadow. Sometimes I try to take refuge in my memories, but it causes me pain. When I close my eyes my dreams take me back into the awful warzones of Helmand Province. Every time I breathe my heart secretly cries for me to escape from loneliness, but I am exhausted from escaping. Since the day I was born I have been on the run.

Where to run from these appalling wars, cruelties, exploitations, ideologies, murderous and hypocritical politicians – the nationalism, flags, racism, militaries, destructive weapons, divisions, media and its lies, corrupt education. I wonder why human beings are so indifferent towards these evils. Mankind is divided nationally, culturally, politically, religiously, economically, ideologically, and all these divisions breed terrible wars and catastrophes and yet human beings are so unconcerned with them. How much longer will human beings shed the blood of one another? For how much longer will powerful individuals, tribes, ethnicities, classes, countries and races exploit and suppress the other individuals, tribes, ethnicities, classes, countries and races? How much longer will the wealth of mankind be wasted on these ugly militaries and weapons? How much longer will humanity remain culturally, religiously, nationally, ideologically divided all across the globe? Why have humans not changed psychologically in these innumerable centuries and millennia? Humans have changed physically, but mentally they are almost at a standstill. We behave exactly the same as those people who behaved millennia ago. Why have all these untold books, ideas, systems, formulas, scholars, revolutions, leaders failed to free humans' minds? Why have human beings learned nothing from their history? Why don't they realise that the path they have been following takes them nowhere but to more appalling wars, exploitation, sorrow, misery. Throughout history human beings have been at war not only physically but culturally, ideologically, economically, politically, racially. It seems to me not only that human beings are not learning anything from their past, on the contrary they are clinging to their old and cruel cultures, ideas, dogma, superstitions, and habits. And still humans are solving their disputes and differences with war and violence. War and aggression have never solved any dispute and difference in human history, but humans don't understand this basic actuality.

THE END OF MY TALE

This earth belongs to no one, like air and sunshine. It is a temporary home for all human beings and other species, but man does not understand this simple fact. Man kills man in the name of country and flag endlessly. In the name of patriotism man commits appalling crimes. A lover cannot love only a part of his beloved but the whole of her. How can one love a patch of earth, but not this wonderful earth as a whole?

The world is becoming a more and more violent and barbaric place. Governments and men with power are more cunning and use new methods to take the mental freedom of human beings. Today giant corporations and banks rule the world. Economic inequality is creating a wider and wider gulf between the rich and the poor. The rich are becoming richer and the poor man is still where he was. Societies are becoming uglier and complex and exploit human beings in an exceptionally cruel manner throughout their lifetimes, and they make people behave like machines. Innumerable laws are being created to tell us how to think, how to live, work, sleep, and behave. These complex and mechanical societies with all their nonsense bring about tremendous amounts of unhappiness, anxiety, depression and sorrow in human beings' lives. Above all, these complex and competitive societies are splitting mankind from nature and the rest of the marvellous beings. One of the reasons that mankind is becoming more ruthless towards nature and other species is that we are no longer in contact with them. One harms the things that one does not know. Everywhere one looks one sees human beings confused, distressed, fed up, dissatisfied, fearful and distrustful of each other, in these complex societies.

Education is supposed to help a person know himself. Education is supposed to show humans the danger of ideologies. It is supposed to free humans' minds from the cages of nationalism and other ideologies and fear. It supposed to help humans to understand and tolerate each other. Societies do not need truly educated human beings, free humans, for they would shatter these immoral societies with all their terrible cruelties and their false promises. The existing education system only helps humans to know how to run these ugly and corrupt societies. The governments, the cruel men with the power, control education, they don't want troublemakers for themselves, they don't want human beings to question or challenge them, doubt their false promises. They want human beings to blindly conform, join the militaries and fight wars, continue their dull routine work, pay tax, be jingoistic. They don't want mentally free human beings, for they are dangerous and subversive. What does one have to do when the very systems, establishments, leaders, ideologies, that one thinks are helping him are on the contrary, enslaving him?

No revolution, system, leader, book or scholar can end the terrible wars, violence, exploitation, poverty, misery, chaos and all the other human crisis – and history is the witness, because history observed revolutions, systems, leaders and books, scholars' ideologies appeared and disappeared, but they failed to save humans from appalling wars, cruelties, exploitations, sorrow, misery, divisions. All revolutions, systems, formulas, books, ideologies, scholars have failed. They will never succeed in freeing mankind of these innumerable crises in the world. It is futile to fight, for they are the shadow of the inner crises. So long as a human is mentally enslaved and doesn't understand himself, nothing can be changed in the world. Over 99 per cent of human action is prompted by self-interest, but if one doesn't understand oneself than how can one understand what is in one's interest?

No one can free an individual's mind but an individual him/herself. The only path that leads an individual to psychological freedom is the path of observation of everything within and without him, questioning, probing, not blindly conforming, following and believing. Observation, questioning and probing are a storm that annihilates everything but truth. I am certain that the evil within man can only be conquered through self-understanding. There can be no peace in the world so long as there is no peace within man and peace within man comes through self-understanding.

THE END

INDEX

British troops established several
patrol bases, **321**

brotherhood's Islamic ideology, **8**

Bukhari (stove), **195**

Bullets buzzed, **298**

Burhanudin Rabani, **42, 87**

burying their IEDs, **309**

But-Hai-Bamyan (Bamyan Statues).,
211

butterflies, **98**

butterfly-mine, **98**

By mid 1985, there were
innumerable factions, **34**

C

cage of war and poverty, **325**

Camp Bastion, **289, 290, 299, 318**

Camunistanu (communists), **64**

cargos of rockets, **48**

cargos of weapons, **89, 101**

carpet factory, **151, 168, 170,
171, 172, 173, 176, 177, 187,
189, 192, 193, 200, 201, 210,
246**

carpet pattern, **170**

carpet weaving, **168, 170, 172,
193, 194, 210, 244, 245, 257**

cattle-herders, **118**

ceased fire, **54**

Central Asia, **191, 235**

Central Asian countries, **190**

Central Intelligence Agency (CIA),
18

Chaar-Aassyaa, **51**

Chadari (burqa), **80**

chains of Imperialism, **325**

chaos and violence in Afghanistan,
323

Charles Cogan the former director
of the CIA's operation in
Afghanistan, **26**

Charsade Bester, **97**

childhood freedom, **193**

children scavenging, **135**

Children were scared, **301**

Children with tearful, **319**

Chinook helicopter, **291**

CIA Afghan Task Force analyst
Michael Scheuer, **30**

clouds of bombs, **1, 221**

coalition government, **36, 124**

cold weather, **49, 53, 71, 95, 131,
141, 164, 174, 192, 195, 269,
294, 309**

Colin Powell, **218**

collaborator and traitor, **303**

coming invasion, **226**

Commander George, **305**

communism, **8, 15, 16, 17, 19, 23,
30, 42, 217**

US marines left Garmsir district, 302

Ustad Naqib and Ustad Halim, 168, 169, 170, 180, 189, 193

Uzbek, 3, 151, 195

V

vicious winter, 110

Villagers were terrified, 319

W

Warlords, 70

warlords, criminals, 318

war-ravaged village, 90

war-torn compounds, 121

war-torn country, 110

war-torn school, 94

Wazir Akbar Khan hospital, 284

We never saw Palang again, 58

wedding ceremony, 183, 184, 199

western Afghanistan, 286

western journalists, 51, 177

westerners, 178, 200, 222

wheelbarrow, 251, 267, 283, 285

whooping cough, 52, 53, 112, 122

William Blum, 23

William F. Engdahl, 192

Winter for the Afghans, 163

winter of 1995, 121

witch-doctors, 10

women were washing, 159

world history, 22, 38

World War II, 7, 27, 36, 221, 320

world's natural resources, 38, 220

wove silk carpets, 169

X

X-ray, 272, 284

Y

Yuri Andropov, the head of the KGB, 19

Z

Zardad's dog, 70, 72, 85

Zbigniew Brzezinski, 20, 192

Zinda Baad Taliba (long live the Taliban), 122, 231

Zulmay Kaka, 5, 6, 7

Notes

[1] Braithewaite, Rodric. 2011. Afgantsy: The Russians in Afghanistan 1979-89. pg 30.
Rodric Braithewaite (2011). *Afgantsy*. London: Profile Books LTD. 33.
[2] Ibid.
[3] Blum, Willian. *Chapter 53: Afghanistan - 1979-1992:America's Jihad.* Available: http://williamblum.org/chapters/killing-hope/afghanistan. Last accessed 05/02/2011.

[4] Ibid
[5] Ibid
[6] *National Security Archive.* Available: http://www.gwu.edu/~nsarchiv/. Last accessed 23/05/2012.

[7] Declassified, The Taliban. Full Documentary. Available: http://www.youtube.com/watch?v=wCTwXnDmUXE. Last accessed 25/06/2012.
[8] Blum, Willian. op cit.
[9] The Brzezinski Interview with Le Nouvel Observateur (1998). *The University of Arizona.* Available: http://dgibbs.faculty.arizona.edu/brzezinski_interview. accessed 03/11/2011.

[10] CNN, *Cold War, Soldiers of God ,Afghanistan.* Available. http://www.youtube.com/watch?v=IQBFXM1PIhM. Last accessed 19/09/2012.

[11] Chossudosky, Michel. The truth behind 9/11: who is Osama Bin Laden. *GlobalResearch.* [Online] 2005. [Cited: December 17/12/2012, 2012.] http://www.globalresearch.ca/the-truth-behind-9-11-who-is-osama-bin-laden/3198.

[12]Michel Chossudovsky . (2005). *The truth behind 9/11: Whose Osama Bin Laden.* Available: http://www.globalresearch.ca/the-truth-behind-9-11-who-is-osama-bin-laden/3198. Last accessed 08/11/2011.

[13] CNN, Cold War, Soldier of God , Afghanistan. Op cit.

[14] Inside the Taliban (National Geographics). Available : http://www.youtube.com/watch?v=f4cVVuSi2fI. Last accessed 29/07/2012.

[15] CBCnews.2004. Back to school in Afghanistan. available : http://www.cbc.ca/news/background/afghanistan/schools.html. Last accessed 23/032012.

[16] Back to school in Afghanistan. Video. Available: http://www.youtube.com/watch?v=0DMeq6lE5DA.

[17] CIA's clandestine War in Afghanistan. Available: http://www.youtube.com/watch?v=jIaPiB5c2-c. Last accessed 16/12/2011.

[18] Blum, William. op cit.

[19] Joya, Malalai. 2009. Raising My Voice. Pg 30.

[20] BA REWAYATE DIGAR,[2012, 22 July] TOLOnews. Available: ttp://www.youtube.com/watch?v=7GZpTHLvLrs. Last accessed 22/06/2012.

[21] US-funded Afghan militias 'beat, rob and kill with impunity'. *PressTV.* Tue Jun 21, 2011 2:57PM. Available: http://www.presstv.ir/usdetail/185669.html. Last accessed 02/10/2011.

[22] *Dr. Najibullah, the former president of Afghanistan.* 1989. available: http://www.youtube.com/watch?v=RWTYiOqKy7U.

[23] Fisk, Robert.2005. The Great War for Civilisation: The Conquest of the Middle East. pg 1048

[24] Rashid, Ahmad. Bamyan 1998-99: The Never Ending War. Pg.67-80. *Taliban.2000. I.B.Tauris & co ltd.*

[25] Geopolitics: A very short introduction. Pg.118. Oxford University Inc. New York.

[26] Engdahl, F. William. 2009. Full Spectrum Dominance:Totalitarian Democracy in the New World Order.

[27] Nehru, Jawaharlal. 1934. Glimpses of World History. Pg 43.

[28] Carl Kaysen, Robert S. McNamara and George W. Rathjens. *Nuclear Weapons After the Cold War.*

Available:http://www.foreignaffairs.com/articles/47143/carl-kaysen-robert-s-mcnamara-and-george-w-rathjens/nuclear-weapons-after-the-cold-war. Last accessed 05/ 02/ 2012.

[29] Thegaurdian. Washington gets explicit:It's 'War on Terror' is permanent. Available: http://www.guardian.co.uk/commentisfree/2013/may/17/endless-war-on-terror-obama. Last accessed 30.05/2013.

[30] Hays, Jeffery. (2008). *JAPANESE OCCUPATION OF CHINA.* available : http://factsanddetails.com/china.php?itemid=59. Last accessed 23/04/2012.

[31] David Ruppe. (2001). *U.S. Military Wanted to Provoke War With Cuba.* Available:http://abcnews.go.com/US/story?id=92662&page=1. Last accessed 03/12/2011.

[32] Jonathan Steele (2011). *Ghosts of Afghanistan: The Haunted BattleGround.* London: Portobello Books Ltd. 222.

[33] Frisk, Robert. 2005. Op cit

[34] Blum, William.concerning September 11,2001and the bombing of Afghanistan. available : http://killinghope.org/bblum6/sep11.htm. Last accessed 23/05/2012.

[35] BBC.2001. Al-Jazeera Kabul offices hit in US raid. Available: http://news.bbc.co.uk/1/hi/world/south_asia/1653887.stm. Last accessed 27/07/2012.

[36] CNN.2012.CNN report on eyewitnesses to Kandahar massacre. Available : http://valtinsblog.blogspot.co.uk/2012/04/cnn-report-on-eyewitnesses-to-kandahar.html. Last accessed 13/06/ 2012.

[37] GlobalResearch.Killings of Civilians in Afghanistan: US special forces covered up massacre. Available: http://www.globalresearch.ca/killings-of-civilians-in-afghanistan-us-special-forces-covered-up-massacre/18554. Last accessed 27/07/2012.

[38] TrustLaw, a Thamson Reuters Foundation Service.2011. TrustLaw Poll-Afghanistan is the most dangerous country for women. Available : http://www.trust.org/trustlaw/news/trustlaw-poll-afghanistan-is-most-dangerous-country-for-women/. last accessed 02/March/2012.

[39] Rethink Afghanistan. Afghan Refugees Describe the Horrors of War on Terror. Available : http://rethinkafghanistan.com/videos.php. Last accessed 15/ 09/ 2011.

[40] Global Research.2009. America's Phony War in Afghanistan. Available : http://www.globalresearch.ca/america-s-phoney-war-in-afghanistan/15761. Last accessed 02/08/2012.

[41] U.S. Violating Human Rights of Children, Says U.N. Committee. Available: http://dawn.com/2013/02/08/us-air-raids-kill-hundreds-of-afghan-children-un/. Last accessed 07/01/2013.

[42] Aljazeera.2009.Afghans' anger at Obama's Noble Peace Prize Win-10 December 09. Available: http://www.youtube.com/watch?v=OBHrnQTinGY. Last accessed 27/11/2010.

[43] Mailonline.2012. Afghan drug war debacle: Blair said smashing opium trade was a major reason to invade but 10 years on heroin production is up from 185 tons a year to 5,800. Available: http://www.dailymail.co.uk/news/article-2102158/Heroin-production-Afghanistan-RISEN-61.html. last accessed 14/04/2012.

[44] R.T.2009. Afghan drug trafficking brings US $50 billion a year. Available: http://www.youtube.com/watch?v=cRVZTMHen_E. last accessed 23/02/2011.

[45] thegaurdian. Afghanistan: Hamid Karzai reveals US will retain nine bases after withdrawl.Available: http://www.guardian.co.uk/world/2013/may/09/afghanistan-hamid-karzai-us-nine-bases-withdrawal. Last accessed 22/05/2013.